# Critical Perspectives on Wives

## Roles, Representations, Identities, and Work

Edited by Lynn O'Brien Hallstein
and Rebecca Jaremko Bromwich

**DEMETER**

**Critical Perspectives on Wives**
Roles, Representations, Identities, and Work

Edited by Lynn O'Brien Hallstein and Rebecca Jaremko Bromwich

Demeter Press
140 Holland Street West
P. O. Box 13022
Bradford, ON L3Z 2Y5
Tel: (905) 775-9089
Email: info@demeterpress.org
Website: www.demeterpress.org

Demeter Press logo based on the sculpture "Demeter" by Maria-Luise Bodirsky www.keramik-atelier.bodirsky.de

Printed and Bound in Canada

Front cover image: Shalene Valenzuela, Cinched In: Compounding, slipcast and altered cone 6 porcelain, 14"x14"x11", 2014.
Front cover artwork: Michelle Pirovich
Typesetting: Michelle Pirovich

Library and Archives Canada Cataloguing in Publication
Title: Critical perspectives on wives : roles, representations, identities, work Lynn O'Brien Hallstein and Rebecca Jaremko Bromwich, editors.
Names: Hallstein, Lynn O'Brien, editor. | Bromwich, Jaremko, Rebecca, editor.
Description: Includes bibliographical references.
Identifiers: Canadiana 20190094583 | ISBN 9781772581997 (softcover)
Subjects: LCSH: Married women. | LCSH: Wives. | LCSH: Married women—Social conditions. | LCSH: Wives—Social conditions. | LCSH: Wives-Motherhood.
Classification: LCC HQ759.C75 2019 | DDC 306.872/3—dc23

MIX
Paper from
responsible sources
FSC
www.fsc.org    FSC® C004071

For my husband, a true partner,
with whom I am working towards reclaiming
an emancipatory notion of wife.
—Rebecca Jaremko Bromwich


For my husband and two sons,
each of whom has helped me be a
bad wife but empowered mother.
—Lynn O'Brien Hallstein

# Contents

# Introduction

Lynn O'Brien Hallstein and
Rebecca Jaremko Bromwich

The 2017 film *The Wife*, which is set in the 1990s but also has flashbacks to the 1960s, explores the marital relationship between Joan (Glenn Close) and Joe (Jonathan Pryce) Castleman. *IMBD* describes the film in the following way: "A wife questions her life choices as she travels to Stockholm with her husband, where he is slated to receive the Nobel Prize for Literature." Released by Sony Pictures Classic in 2017, the official trailer for the film includes the following description: "And where Joe enjoys his very public role as Great American Novelist, Joan pours her considerable intellect, grace, charm, and diplomacy into the private role of Great Man's Wife." While the film is primarily set in the early 1990s, the flashbacks center on the early days of their relationship in the 1960s when Joan was one of Joe's writing students while he was a professor at Smith College. In one of those flashbacks, Joe and Joan went to hear a reading by an unnamed woman writer who is an alumnus of Smith. In an exchange between Joan and the woman writer, after the writer learns that Joan is an aspiring writer, the woman writer tells Joan, "Don't ever think you can get their approval." Joan asks, "Whose?" As the woman writer looks at a group of white men chatting behind Joan, she says, "The men's. The one's who get to decide who gets to be taken seriously." Joan replies, "A writer has to write." The woman writer replies, "A writer has to be read, honey." Through the flashbacks, then, the audience learns that both Joan and Joe were writers, but Joan seemingly gave up her writing and writing ambitions when she became Joe's wife and primary copy editor. Moreover, at a dinner after Joe receives his Noble Prize for Literature, Joan has the following conversation with the King of Sweden.

The King: Tell me about yourself. Do you have an occupation?

Joan: I do.

King: And, what is that?

Joan: I'm a king maker.

In this exchange with the King of Sweden, Joan clearly articulates her private-sphere role as the "Great Man's Wife." Thus, the film captures the complex relationship between a wife and husband and their roles within the private and public spheres; it also explores how a young, college-educated woman in the 1960s grappled with sexism and male dominance in relation to her own writing ambitions after she married and became the "Great Man's Wife."

The film is a beautifully acted representation of one wife's role, identity, and work in the private sphere, whereas her husband became a "king" in the public sphere through her support. Moreover, the flashbacks hint at the gender change that began to emerge in the 1960s but was in full force by the 1980s, and they accurately capture how a young, ambitious woman ultimately channels her own writing ambition in and through her husband as she retreats to the private sphere. Consequently, while set in both the 1960s and early 1990s, the film also captures just how much a so-called good wife needed to channel her ambitious in the private sphere so that her husband could realize his own ambitious in the public sphere. As such, the film also well represents a world of husbands and wives that many contemporary men and women believe we are now beyond. This book seeks to critically explore this assumption. The works in this volume explore historical situations where wives are involved as "king makers" for their husband and where this is socially mandatory work. As the film does, the contributions in this text also critically explore what happens when both a husband and wife have similar ambitious, how the roles and expectations between a husband and wife cultivate and impede those ambitions, and to what extent contemporary husband and wife roles have changed or not.

In *Critical Perspectives on Wives: Roles, Representations, Identities, and Work*, then, the contributors explore the ongoing tensions between the old and the new in the roles, representations, identities, and work of wives in our contemporary contexts. Indeed, as we write this in early

2019, it does seem that the lives of women and wives have continued to change or that wives have more options than Joan does in *The Wife*. Over the past two centuries, for instance, wives have gone, in law, from being under the doctrine of "coverture"—completely subsumed in the personhood of their husbands to the point of becoming the property of their husbands in common law jurisdictions—to being persons who retain rights (Canaday). Moreover, in the United States, Hillary Clinton, after being a presidential wife, became the first serious female candidate for president as the Democratic nominee in the 2016 presidential election. However, as some of the contributors here suggest and why *The Wife* may still resonate so much, contemporary wives' roles, expectations, and identities may not have changed as much as we think. Indeed, we believe that one of the reasons why the film is so resonant today is because it both captures and represents how much contemporary wifehood and husbands' and wives' roles, identities and work simultaneously have and have not changed. In fact, as we show next, one of the most significant reasons for the lack of change is because of how deeply tied the social understandings and material labour associated with wifehood are with discourses and tasks assumed to be associated with motherhood, even today. Thus, this text seeks to fill a gap in intellectual and academic knowledge about how contemporary wives are living their lives caught between the old and new.

## Studying Wives

This text also works to expand intellectual and scholarly conversations about wives because the very minute amount of intellectual and scholarly work done to date on wives is limited and focused primarily on the early post-1970s feminist changes in women's and wives' lives. For the most part, intellectuals and scholars have had little to say about wives, including feminist thinkers and scholars. One of the only exceptions was a feminist satire of wifehood from the 1970s. In one of the best-remembered pieces from the inaugural issue of *Ms.* Magazine, Judy Brady (then Judy Syfers) wrote a short (one-page) satirical feminist essay titled, "I Want a Wife." As Linda Napikoski, notes, "I Want a Wife" was a humorous piece that also made a serious point: "Women who played the role of 'wife' did many helpful things for husbands and usually children without anyone realizing" (par. 2). Brady opens the piece by writing, "I belong to that classification of people known as wives. I am a Wife. And, not altogether incidentally, I am mother" (par. 1). From the start, then, Brady notes that her role as a wife is intertwined with her role as a mother. For example, in the following paragraph, she writes: "I want a wife who will work and send me to school. And, while I am going to school I want a wife to take care of my children. I want a wife to keep track of the children's doctor and dentist appointments" (par. 2). Later, she also writes: "I want a wife who will take care of *my* physical needs. I want a wife who will keep my house clean" (emphasis in original par. 3). She ends the piece with the following: "My God, who *wouldn't* want a wife?" (par. 11). A question, we believe, that is also ultimately asked in *The Wife*. Brady's satire has had lasting fame, and as Napikoski suggests, "It is often used as an example of satire and humor in the feminist movement" (par. 8). Thus, while also implicitly intertwining motherhood and wifehood—rather than focus primarily on what Brady had to say about wives—her essay is used as an example of feminist satire and humor, probably, in part, to counter the anti-humor critique of second-wave feminisms.

Although Brady's short piece was written during the heyday of the 1970s feminist movements when activists were asking for and initiating change, the limited scholarly work (Hartog; Johnson; Yalom) on wives is situated within an early post-1970s context and changed landscape for wives and families. All of this work explores the impact of the large-scale cultural changes for wives living in the immediate aftermath of the 1970s: Miriam Johnson's book was published in 1988, Hendrick Hartog's book in 2000, and Marilyn Yalom's book in 2001. In other words, the limited scholarly work to date on wives emerged when women and wives began to live within the successes of 1970s feminisms. It explores how families generally, and wives and husbands specifically, changed as a result of the large-scale social, legal, and gender change brought about by 1970s feminisms while it also simultaneously recognizes how wifehood had not changed. These contradictions are also beautifully captured in *The Wife*. For another example, Yalom in *A History of the Wife* argues the following:

> The wife as a man's chattel, as dependent, as his means for acquiring legal offspring, as the caretaker of his children, as his cook and housekeeper are roles that many women now find

abhorrent; yet certain aspects of those antiquated obligations still linger on in the collective unconscious. Many men still expect their wives to provide some or all of these services, and many wives still intend to perform them. (1)

Moreover, both Johnson and Yalom note that women have changed expectations about what it means to be a wife. Even so, however, many women have continued to enact and practice more traditional roles and activities as wives. In other words, although Johnson and Yalom both recognize that 1970s feminisms changed the roles and expectations within families, they both also focus simultaneously on how some of the assumptions and expectations about family life and wives' activities and roles remained.

The post-1970s scholarly attention to wives also focuses on how contradictory expectations around economic support and work in the private sphere shaped wives' lives. As women began to take advantage of the educational and professional access women gained in the public sphere, more wives worked outside of the home, which also influenced how those women identified themselves and, importantly, how legal institutions understood women's new roles. As Hartog notes, by the mid-1970s, "Wives not only worked, but courts recognized that wives worked for wages. Identities as workers and mothers had become for many women more important, more salient, than their identities as wives" (309). Additionally, Yalom has argued that because of changed assumptions about women and work in the public sphere, "a wife cannot count on complete economic support within the marriage, nor on alimony if the marriage ends in divorce" (xv). Of course, one primary reason for this change in economic support is because women's identities as workers and mothers had become, for many women, more important, more salient, than their identities as wives, as Hartog suggests. Even so, however, as Yalom has also pointed out, "the wife is still expected to provide many of the same services she has always provided, such as childcare and housekeeping" (xvii). In other words, even though men and husbands are "expected to share some domestic responsibilities, and they are clearly doing more," husbands "have not yet become full partners as caretakers and homemakers, while most women are working as hard as the men in the workplace and slowly narrowing the gender gap in earning power" (xv).

## Wives and Mothers: Blurred Boundaries

As the above works suggests, demarcating the boundaries between "wife" and "mother" has continued to be difficult. In other words, part of the complexity of exploring the identities, roles, expectations, and work of wives within the early post-1970s context was that the boundaries and roles between "wife" and "mother" remained blurred, especially in the private sphere and despite the profoundly changed roles for (at least privileged) women in the public sphere. As Yalom has argued, "The 'wife' and the 'mother' share a fuzzy boundary. Their responsibilities often overlap and sometimes conflict" (xiv). To put it another way: wifehood and motherhood were often intertwined, and the boundaries between them blurred, especially in the private sphere, because both mother-work and wife-work were, and remain today, caregiving roles with caregiving work. As such, they continue to be seen as one in the same or deeply connected because they share similar activities, responsibilities, and work. Johnson, however, explores in detail how and why these boundaries have remained so fuzzy and argues that wifehood, rather than motherhood, is at the root of women's ongoing gender-based oppression in the private sphere.

In making this larger argument, Johnson contends that the boundaries between wifehood and motherhood are blurred because both are also deeply embedded in the private sphere and, most often, are seen as separate from the public sphere. Moreover, Johnson argues that both wifehood and motherhood became entrenched in the private sphere because of the ongoing post-industrialization public-private sphere divisions. More specifically, as Johnson has argued, by the nineteenth century, especially in the United States, as production was increasingly moved from the home, a new modern family began to emerge, in which the male worker went into the factories in the public sphere to work, and the female homemaker stayed home and managed the home and children. Following the Industrial Revolution, families and the private sphere became a refuge from the public world of work; a haven, in fact: "Husbands were to go out from the haven to work in the world and wives were to stay at home and cheerfully perfect it, to re-create the male worker. Wives were also to be mothers, cherishing children and preparing them spiritually and psychologically (though the word was not used then) to leave centered in the rising middle class, in time it came to affect all of the society" (Johnson 232). As a result, the public-private sphere split post industrialization created a "radical disjunction between home and work and the establishing of women in the former. This 'romantic' response eventually won out and was embodied in the doctrine of separate spheres" (Johnson 17). Thus, according to Johnson, by the mid-twentieth century, both the family and wives—especially for those with racial, economic, and educational privilege—were thoroughly privatized, and these privatized roles did not significantly change, even in the post-1970s feminist context.

Even though both are embedded in the private sphere, "wife" and "mother" must be kept analytically distinct:

> [By] separating the concept of mother from the concept of wife, it is possible to see that women are one thing when seen as wives and quite another when seen as mothers. The mother 'role' involves caring for and nurturing dependents, while the wife 'role,' if unmitigated by other status-giving relationships, involves being dependent on and in varying degrees subordinate to the husband. (Johnson 25-26)

In making a distinction between women as mothers and women as wives, however, Johnson also argues that "women's secondary status ultimately lies more in the structure of marriage than in mothering itself. I introduce the idea that women's mothering provides a basis for women's solidarity and power, but women's being 'wives' in the 'modern family' separates women from one another in the pursuit of husbands and isolates women from one another in nuclear families" (13). Finally, although she was writing in 1988, Johnson also makes what we would call now an intersectional analysis with the following conclusion: "Moreover, all males are not dominant over all females. Class and race privilege can overcome gender disadvantage in some instances, but heterosexual marriage is located in every class and race group. Perhaps this is another way of saying that marriage organizes gender relations in ways that are connected to but cannot be deduced from economic or political relations" (7).

Even though we concur with Johnson's argument that the two roles need to be analytically distinct, it has only been feminist maternal scholars (Green "Feminist Mothers"; O'Reilly; Horowitz) working on theorizing what Andrea O'Reilly first named *empowered mothering* who have taken up Johnson's suggestion most thoroughly in their focus on mothering. Yet little contemporary work has explored how wives' roles have continued to change (or not) in the 2000s. In this context, Fiona Green defines empowered mothering as a "counter narrative to the proscribed mainstream ideals and approaches to motherhood that are entrenched within Western contemporary society." She further says the following: "Andrea O'Reilly began using the term *empowered mothering* in the early 2000s to refer to the theory and practice of mothering that recognizes that women, children, and society at large, benefit when women live their lives as mothers from a position of agency, authority, authenticity, and autonomy" ("Empowered Mothering" 347). In other words, although feminist maternal scholars began the work of theorizing the potential for mothering to be empowering for both women and children when mothers can decide what constitutes good mothering outside institutionalized motherhood, those same feminist thinkers have rarely addressed wifehood, and feminist scholars continue to be primarily silent about wives and wifehood today. This volume works, then, to end that silence by continuing and updating intellectual and scholarly conversations about wives.

## Where We Are Now: The Contemporary Context

We believe that conversations about wives and wifehood must happen within a feminist paradigm that recognizes the still-changing contemporary context of family life and the roles within families. Today, there is no doubt that contemporary North American women continue to have different expectations and attitudes about marriage and family life and that wifehood and motherhood remain deeply intertwined in problematic ways. For example, a report titled "Trends in Attitudes about Marriage, Childbearing, and Sexual Behavior: United States, 2002, 2006–2010, and 2011–2013," published by the U.S. Department of Health in Human Services in 2016, details these changes:

> The composition of families in the United States has changed
> significantly over the past 50 years. These changes have resulted
> from a delay in the age of first marriage, a steep rise and then
> decline in the divorce rate, a lower fertility rate, an increase in
> cohabitation, a higher proportion of births occurring outside of

marriage and within cohabiting unions, and an increasing number of first births to older women. (Daugherty and Copen 1)

For American women today, one of the most significant effects of these changes is that they are marrying later. In fact, a 13 February, 2018 Pew report, titled, "8 Facts about Love and Marriage in America," suggests that according "to the U.S. Census Bureau, in 2017, the median age at first marriage had reached its highest point on record: 29.5 years for men and 27.4 years for women" (Geiger and Livingston 2). Moreover, most young women, especially middle-class, well-educated young women, continue to believe that becoming a wife is not central to their identities and future roles, and, instead, they centre their identities and roles on becoming well-educated professionals.

Contemporary wifehood is also shaped by changes to marriage more generally. The Pew Research Center report also begins by noting: "The landscape of relationships in America has shifted dramatically in recent decades. From cohabitation to same-sex marriage to interracial and interethnic marriage, here are eight facts about love and marriage in the United States" (1). Although the report focuses primarily on the changing landscape of marriage generally, it does have one significant finding in terms of contemporary husbands and wives. After noting that that only 28 percent of people marry for financial stability today and instead cite love for being the most important reason to marry (88 percent), "being a good financial provider was seen as particularly important for men to be a good husband or partner, according to a 2017 survey by the Center." The report continues: "About seven-in-ten adults (71%) said it was very important for a man to be able to support a family financially to be a good husband or partner, while just 32% said the same for a woman to be a good wife or partner" (1). Thus, attitudes towards marriage and wives and husbands remain caught between both new and old ideas, roles, and expectations.

Of course, another important and more contemporary layer of change to heterosexual relationship ideals and marital relationships was the legalization of same-sex marriage in the United States in June 2015. As with impact of the 1960s and 1970s social movements, the legalization of same-sex marriage has had contradictory effects. The legalization of same-sex marriage fundamentally challenged the heteronormativity of marriage, yet, at the same time, recent scholarship suggests that representations of gay marriages continue to employ heteronormativity. For example, in their analysis of televisual representations of gay families in *Modern Family, The New Normal, Sean Saves the World,* and *House Husbands,* each of which feature gay fathers, Clare Bartholomaeus and Damien Riggs contend that "the four television programs are united by homonormativity—they are premised on the heteronormative presumption of appropriate roles for fathers and mothers, men and women, and these are applied to the gay fathers with little interrogation" (169). This means that consistent with represent-ations of heterosexual couples in domestic television programs, series featuring gay male couples have worked to keep male characters in line with prevailing norms of masculinity and femininity, positioning one partner as the provider and authoritarian and the other within a feminine domestic and emotional frame. Thus, in North America, it is still true that "when one examines 21st expectations of wives, it is clear that the range of acceptable activities and behaviors has grown immensely, but in many ways the expectations in play today are every bit as unrealistic and restrictive ... the prevailing belief that women are now fully and obviously liberated from those restrictions needs to be questioned" (McKnight, this volume). Thus, *Critical Perspectives on Wives: Roles, Representations, Identities, and Work* enters this contemp-orary conversation about wives in order to update intellectual and scholarly feminist thinking about the roles, representations, identities, and work of wives today.

In doing so, first and foremost, this book hopes to fill the larger general scholarly gap about wives and to specifically end the silence about wives within contemporary matricentric feminist scholarship. We remain committed to initiating a contemporary conversation about wives with a matricentric-feminist focus in relation to wives because we share a political interest in feminist activism along with matricentric feminism—an academic theoretical orientation that integrates feminist scholarship, especially in relation to matricentric feminist thinking that is matrifocal in its perspective and emphasis (O'Reilly). Moreover, we are also committed to the idea of employing and integrating our own intellectual interests about wives and our personal experiences as wives. Moreover, although we concur with Johnson's early argument that wife-work and mother-work ultimately should be analytically separate, the work here reveals not only how much wife-work and mother-work remain enmeshed but also how entrenched the roles, representations, identities, and work of wives continues to be premised on the contradictory and conflicting gender assumptions continuing to shape women's lives today—all of which make it difficult to separate wife-work and mother-work fully. Additionally, given that the previous work on wives was centred in a North American context, this volume also hopes to enlarge the discussion of wife-work and mother-work by exploring both in different cultural contexts. Finally, by offering contemporary critical perspectives on wives, this book also hopes to offer insights about how women, but most especially wives, may resist and change their roles and lives.

## Chapter Overviews

To investigate contemporary critical perspectives on wives, this book has three sections. The tension between the separate and distinct roles of mother and wife and the ways these roles are enmeshed is a theme flowing throughout this volume, but it is most prominent in Part 1: Wife-Work and Mother-Work Today. Part II of the book, Wife-Work in Different Cultural Contexts, explores wives' lives in different cultural contexts, and Part III, Resisting and Changing Wives' Roles and Lives, explores how wives have resisted their roles and expectations of wives and how these can be changed or should be changed in order to tease out wife-work from mothering.

In Part I, Natalie McKnight, in her chapter "No Time Off for Good Behavior: The Persistence of Victorian Expectations of Wives," discusses historical Victorian expectations of wifely labour and self-abnegation, and critically explores the extent to which contemporary cultural expectations of the role of wives depart from, but continue to reinforce, their selflessness. McKnight contends that the sexual revolution notwithstanding, mainstream Western cultures still expect that women put their families before themselves, and women who cannot successfully juggle these myriad tasks end up feeling like failures. McKnight further explores how contemporary wives diverge from their Victorian, middle-class predecessors in that they can have careers, several in fact: one at work and at least one at home. Yet she contends that if they want the approval of friends, family and society at large, wives can never seem more invested in their professional careers than they are in the home-front, nor should they complain much about the burdens of their position—all of which continues Victorian expectations of wives.

Next, Leanne Letourneau's chapter, "Invisible Wives: Analyzing the Consequence of Sameness," analyzes Quebec's marriage policy and action plan on domestic violence and argues that policies contending that heterosexual couples and sexual minorities are the same fail to examine the complexities of sexual minorities, not only at the personal level but also at the structural. Her chapter examines the ways in which reliance on the concept of sameness results in the invisibility of sexual minority wives and their relationship to marriage and domestic violence. Letourneau contends that focusing on sameness results in the perpetuation of gender norms and fails to acknowledge how sexual orientation, gender, race, socioeconomic status, age, etc. intersect and, therefore, create experiences for sexual minority wives that may be different from heterosexual ones. To understand the relationships of sexual minority wives, an intersectional approach must be used.

Jane Marcellus, in her chapter "'Office Wife,' 'Two-Job Wife,' 'Work Wife': The Marriage Metaphor in Popular Culture Represent-ations of Women's Paid Labour," interrogates the enduring use of the term "wife" in relation to women's paid labour. Marcellus argues that although the term "office wife" was originally used to rhetorically split women from one another, "two-job wife" was used to split women individually by deeming them selfish for wanting both home and career (like "superwoman" later). After a close reading of The Office Wife (book and film), Marcellus uses semiotics and discourse analysis to examine representations in news media, magazines, and television shows. She critically explores whether "wife" can be a term of feminist unity or whether it inevitably reinforces female subordination.

In "Abused Wives and Divorce Mediation in Ontario: The Perspectives of Thunder Bay's Mediators," Robyn Pepin focuses on the perspectives of seven mediators in Thunder Bay, Ontario, Canada to explore what happens to abused women if a mandatory mediation information program is practically implemented into the divorce process in Northwestern Ontario. The chapter speculates on the potential effects of mediation on children's educational achievement. Utilizing a qualitative and feminist methodology, the chapter reports on a study that reveals Ontario family law rules are not universally implemented because attendance at the new mandatory information session is not legally required in Thunder Bay. This research is important for common-law women and wives who are mothers, as it indicates that there are mediators who do not consider the long-term consequences of their professional actions on women's and children's well-being and safety during mediation procedures and post-mediation.

In "Birthing a 'Jewbilly' Identity through Wife-Work and Mothering: The Lineage of Family Narrative from Appalachia to Suburbia," Hinda Mandell uses narrative inquiry to explore the stories told in her family about her New York toddler and her Appalachian antics. In a broader sense, the goal of the chapter is to understand how a family uses narrative as a sense-making tool, especially when a wife marries into a family with a lineage different from her own. In addition, the chapter critically explores the identity implications for the young daughter to inherit such a narrative and details how a wife journeys to learn about her husband's roots and her daughter's story.

Part II begins with Ariadne A. Gonzales's chapter, "*Mujeres Trabajadoras*: Examining the Role of Mexican Immigrant and Transnational Wives," which describes the situation of transnational, undocumented, and immigrant Mexican domestic workers. These workers make up a portion of the border employment sector in the United States, yet little is known about their occupational lives and experiences while working in the U.S. and maintaining ties to Mexico. This chapter studies the actual work practices rather than abstract representations of work by centering on the working immigrant wife, mother, and daughter. In doing so, Gonzales also explores the meaning of work that is created and negotiated along with the variability of domestic work that is juxtaposed with issues of immigration, work, and life on the border between South Texas and Mexico.

Next, Suzanne Kamata, in her chapter, "Behind the Screens: Mary Elkinton Nitobe and Mary Dardis Noguchi," critically explores the contributions and erasure of two American wives of Japanese luminaries. Kamata looks at how Hideyo Noguchi, the renowned bacteriologist whose image appears on the Japanese 1,000 yen note, and revered statesman, author, and agriculturist Inazo Nitobe, the former face of the 5,000 yen bill, were both married to American women named Mary. She explores how these cosmopolitan, interracial marriages were anomalous in a country that has traditionally valued racial purity and where marriages between Western women and Japanese men remain rare to this day. Kamata looks into how the reputations of these husbands have remained secure and have perhaps even expanded, whereas their wives have faded into obscurity. This chapter explores how, ignored or not, these American wives played a part in the successes of their Japanese husbands. Kamata illuminates the contributions of these women, argues for their acknowledgment, and posits possible reasons for their erasure.

In "The Socialization of Fulani Young Girls as Good Wives: A Persisting Pedagogical Ideal in the Context of Social Change," Ester Botta Somparé examines the role of wives among the minority Fulani cultural group living in the coastal region of Guinea. Somparé critically explores how, in this society, marriage is considered to be the most important event of a woman's life, and she looks at how the education of young girls is focused on preparing them for marital life—one that requires pastoral and domestic skills as well as becoming submissive and obedient to the husband and the family-in-law. Somparé's interviews, conducted with women of three generations, show that girls' training to become good wives has changed in some ways and in other ways has remained consistent over seventy years. The author also enquires into how education has changed in the context of social transformations in the region.

The chapter by Rebecca Jaremko Bromwich and her mother, Beverley Smith, titled "Considering Family Law in Counting Wife-Work apart from Mother-Work," opens Part III. The chapter explores how doctrines about spousal support under Canadian family law may be a fruitful source of possibilities to contemplate about how to better account for, and value, the unpaid labour—including emotional labour—that is traditionally understood to be wife-work. It explores the nuanced distinction between the overlapping roles of mother and wife. The chapter first discusses the history of accounting for unpaid labour in Canada and documents how little statistical tracking of it there is. The authors argue that unpaid labour should be reinstated in the annual long form census. Then, this chapter suggests mechanisms that could serve to ameliorate the precarious economic positions of women tasked with doing disproportionate amounts of unpaid labour relative to men, particularly those large numbers of women still in traditional, heterosexual marriages with higher-income male spouses.

In her chapter "What Is a Wife? Partnering and Mothering in Freeform's *The Fosters*," Holly Willson Holladay explores the first season of *The Fosters*. Holladay explores how Stef and Lena reflect partnering and parenting vis-à-vis the changing nature of the "ordinary" family. Holladay argues that *The Fosters* pushes against the historical representation of same-sex couples as simultaneously heteronormative and desexualized through its explicit focus on lesbian sexuality and the unique challenges presented to lesbian wives. Moreover, she maintains that the series' focus on lesbian wives disrupts the traditional masculine/feminine gendered expectations that guide both representations of heterosexual couples and same-sex husbands. Finally, Holladay contends that *The Fosters* politicizes lesbian relationships by addressing the legal and cultural frameworks that same-sex couples face as they seek legitimization of their relationship. As such, *The Fosters* offers a compelling representation of lesbian wives that complicates and redefines what it means to be a wife and mother in the twenty-first century.

Jo Scott-Coe's chapter, "More than 'the Sniper's Wife': Kathy Leissner Whitman and the *Mad Men* Mystique," critically explores the intensely intimate portrait of marriage revealed by correspondence authored by Kathy Leissner Whitman before her murder by her husband Charles Whitman, who also killed his mother. The chapter explores how in 1966, as now, erasure of women's stories was the secondary result of public terrorism. In 1966, the night before Charles Whitman climbed the tower at University of Texas at Austin to commit what was then the most deadly rampage shooting in American history, he murdered two women in the privacy of their bedrooms. He killed his mother, Margaret, who was a devout Catholic seeking divorce from her husband after twenty-five years of marital abuse, as well as his twenty-three-year-old wife, Kathy, who had completed her degree and just finished her first year teaching high school science, despite four years of marital turmoil. Scott-Coe argues that, "on a cultural scale, Whitman's private brutality can be read as a flashpoint of confused and entitled white misogyny at the cusp of second-wave feminism"— the attacks happened two years following passage of the Civil Rights Act and three years after publication of *The Feminine Mystique*. With machismo vocabularies of "law and order and safety" still dominating our discourse of violent spectacle, women's perspectives must be preserved and engaged. Finally, Elisavietta Ritchie contributes five poems about the aspects of wifehood to close the book.

We conclude by returning to the film *The Wife*. As we noted earlier, we believe that the now award-winning film resonates with so many because the film explores the complexities of a wife's old roles and expectations in relation to a husband with similar ambitions at a time when women's roles and expectations were changing. As such, the film also explores to what extent contemporary husband and wife roles have and have not changed. Our ambitions in curating this anthology overlap with the evident interests as the makers of the film; however, it is also our hope that this text nuances and intellectualizes the conversations begun by the film. Indeed, by investigating critical perspectives on wives in different cultural contexts and examining how wives have resisted their roles, *Critical Perspectives on Wives: Roles, Representations, Identities, and Work* is a first step in expanding our understanding of the roles, representations, identities, and work of wives in contemporary contexts. Moreover, this text also begins to fill a gap in intellectual and academic knowledge about how contemporary wives are also living their lives caught between the old and new. Thus, we also hope that this book resonates for all who believe, as we do, that it is now time to unpack the ongoing complexities of wives' roles, representations, identities, and work in ways that allow wives to continue to move beyond being kingmakers to being makers of their own lives.

## Works Cited

Bartholomaeus, Clare, and Damien W. Riggs. "Homonormativity in Representations of Gay Fathers on Television: Reproductive Citizenship, Gender and Intimacy." *We Need To Talk About Family: Essays on Neoliberalism, the Family and Popular Culture*, edited by Roberta Garrett, et al., Cambridge Scholars Publishing, 2016, pp. 157-76.

Brady, Judy (Syfers). "'I Want a Wife,' the Timeless '70s Feminist Manifesto." November 11, 2017, www.thecut.com/2017/11 /i-want-a-wife-by-judy-brady-syfers-new-york-mag-1971.html. Accessed 20 May 2019.

Canaday, Margot. "Heterosexuality as a Legal Regime." *The Cambridge History of Law in America*, edited by Michael Grossberg and Christopher Tomlins, Cambridge: Cambridge University Press, 2008, pp. 442-71. doi:10.1017/CHOL9780521803076.014

Daugherty, Jill, and Casey Copen. "Trends in Attitudes about Marriage, Childbearing, and Sexual Behavior: United States, 2002, 2006–2010, and 2011–2013," *National Health Statistics Reports*, vol. 92, 2016, pp. 1-11.

Geiger, Abigail, and Gretchen Livingston. "8 Facts about Love and Marriage in America." *Pew Research Center*, 2018, www.pewresearch. org/fact-tank/2018/02/13/8-facts-about-love-and-marriage/. Accessed 20 May 2019.

Green, Fiona. "Empowered Mothering." *Encyclopedia of Motherhood*, edited by Andrea O'Reilly, Sage Publications, 2010, pp. 347-48.

Green, Fiona J. "Feminist Mothers: Successfully Negotiating the Tension between Motherhood as 'Institution' and 'Experience.'" *Mother Outlaws: Theories and Practices of Empowered Mothering,* edited by Andrea O'Reilly, Canada: Women's Press, 2004, 125-36.

Hartog, Hendrick. *Man and Wife in America: A History.* Harvard University Press, 2000.

Horowitz, Erika. "Resistance as a Site of Empowerment: The Journey away from Maternal Sacrifice" in *Mother Outlaws: Theories and Practices of Empowered Mothering*, edited by Andrea O'Reilly, Women's Press, 2004, 43-58.

Johnson, Miriam. *Strong Mothers, Weak Wives.* Berkeley: University of California Press, 1988.

Napikoski, Linda. "I Want a Wife: Judy Brady's Legendary Feminist Satire." *ThoughtCo*, 2018, www.thoughtco.com/i-want-a-wife-3529064. Accessed 20 May 2019.

O'Reilly, Andrea, editor. *Mother Outlaws: Theories and Practices of Empowered Mothering, Toronto, Canada: Women's Press, 2004.*

Yalom, Marilyn. *A History of the Wife.* HarperCollins Publishers, 2001.

# Part I

## Wife-Work and Mother-Work Today

Chapter One

# No Time Off for Good Behaviour: The Persistence of Victorian Expectations of Wives

Natalie McKnight

In the Victorian age, wives were expected to conduct themselves as martyrs to their families. Non-saints need not apply. Victorian conduct books for women advised a kind of self-abnegation that makes contemporary wifehood seem almost idyllic in comparison, or so one may think at first glance. Certainly, most twenty-first century wives would bristle at the dictates set out by the leading guides to wifehood, which I will highlight throughout this chapter. And it was not just the conduct books that dictated unrealistic expectations — domestic novels, poetry, and periodical essays and short stories all contributed to norms that left married women with a limited range of acceptable activities and behaviours. Sarah Ellis, one of the most popular Victorian conduct book authors, writes in *Wives of England* (1843) that women should approach marriage with "an habitual subjection of self to the interests and happiness of others" (55). In *Woman's Mission* (1840), another influential conduct book, Sarah Lewis similarly argues that women were meant "to live for others" (51, 46). Isabella Beeton echoes the same sentiments in her extremely popular *Mrs. Beeton's Household Management*, which was published in installments in 1859 and 1860 but reprinted many times in the nineteenth century and is still in print today. Although Beeton focuses more on the nuts and bolts of household management, as her title suggests, the assumptions she makes about women's role echo the earlier ideas of Ellis and Lewis. In contrast, when one examines twenty-first century expectations of wives, it is clear that the range of acceptable activities and behaviours has grown immensely, but in many ways, the expectations in play today are every bit as unrealistic and restrictive, as I will show below.

Let us begin by further examining nineteenth-century norms for wives. The proscriptions for women from Ellis, Lewis, Beeton, and other authors of nineteenth-century nonfiction and fiction related to domesticity are not only relentless in their call to abandon self-interest but regularly contradict themselves. Lewis warns women not to become too boring because if they do, they will fail to sustain their influence over their husbands and children; somehow, women are supposed to be simultaneously selfless and have an interesting enough self to captivate their fellow family members. Exactly how one is to pull this off is left to the imagination. And although Ellis tells wives to quash their own interests for the sake of the interests of others, she also advises that "none should give up more than they are prepared to resign without grudging, whether noticed and appreciated or not" (33). The entire gauge of a woman's worth is based on her serving the needs of others pleasantly and productively; even developing interests is something a woman should do not for herself but for the sake of increasing her entertainment value for her husband and children. But Ellis fails to address how one can constantly place others first without resenting the situation, particularly when the sacrifice is unappreciated.

In another conduct book, *The Women of England: Their Social Duties and Domestic Habits*, published in 1843, Ellis specifies the appropriate daily emphasis of dutiful Victorian women. Women should not ask themselves what they should do to please themselves or "to be admired," or even ask what they can do "to vary the tenor of [their] existence." Instead they should ask themselves the following: "How shall I endeavor through this day to turn the time, the health, and the means permitted me to enjoy, to the best account?—Is anyone sick? I must visit their chamber ... Is anyone about to set off on a journey? I must see that the early meal is spread ... Did I fail in what was kind or considerate to any of the family yesterday?" (9). And if that litany was not clear enough, Ellis summarizes her chief point several pages later, when she writes that a dutiful woman must "lay aside all her natural caprice, her love of self-indulgence, her vanity, her indolence—in short, her very *self*—and assuming a new nature ... spend her mental and moral capabilities in devising means for promoting the happiness of others, while her own derives a remote and secondary existence from theirs" (15). Clearly, in her eyes, women are unapologetically and unambiguously the second sex; their happiness is completely subordinated to the happiness of others.

Coventry Patmore's long poem *The Angel in the House* (1854) established one of the most famous Victorian images of the ideal wife. In fact, the phrase "angel in the house" has come to be used as shorthand for the dutiful nineteenth-century woman. In Book I, Canto IX, Patmore writes the following:

> Man must be pleased; but him to please
>
> Is woman's pleasure; down the gulf
>
> Of his condoled necessities
>
> She casts her best, she flings herself:
>
> How often flings for naught (lines 1-5)

Here again, the tone is unapologetic: women should serve men selflessly, whether or not they are appreciated or even effective in their efforts. The message to Victorian women was the same whether they turned to conduct books, poetry, or the host of domestic angels that Charles Dickens and other nineteenth-century novelists portrayed. Their role was to make the home a harmonious haven by focusing on the needs of everyone around them, never themselves.

Compared to such sentiments, twenty-first century expectations of wives seem far less constraining. Women can work outside their home in any profession; they can choose to marry or not marry without being stigmatized as "old maids"; they can explore their interests and passions beyond the domestic sphere and solely for their own pleasure; they can have children or elect not to have children without being considered failures; they can marry each other. It would be difficult to argue that the role of wife has not evolved for the better. Yet our contemporary expectations of wives insidiously perpetuate damaging aspects of the Victorian norms, including some of the contradictions that make the ideal impossible to live up to. Although women have far more choices than ever, both in terms of professions and domestic arrangements, more is expected of them than ever. And although they are encouraged to pursue a range of professions, working or not working is not really a choice for many women: most need to work to contribute financially to their families. In "Women Have Made the Difference for Family Economic Security," an article published by the Washington Center for Equitable Growth, Heather Boushey and Kavya Vaghul summarize the findings from the recent Current Population Survey, which shows that "across all three income groups [low-income, middle-class, and professional families] women significantly helped family incomes ... and saved low-income and middle-class families from steep drops in their income" that would have occurred because average salaries have not kept pace with the rate of inflation. The costs of healthcare and education have particularly outpaced salary increases. Boushey and Vaghul also note that due to the "increasing instability and stagnant growth in family incomes, families have had to find ways to cope—including a growing reliance on the earnings of women. The role of women in the United States has transformed from predominantly being a wife or mother to being all of these things *and* a breadwinner."

Despite women sharing in the breadwinning, the expectations of women's commitment to the domestic front are not much less demanding than they were for nineteenth-century wives who did not work outside the home. Women are still expected, implicitly and explicitly, to manage the household—a phrase that includes everything from cooking and cleaning, to doing laundry and paying bills, coordinating the children's complex schedules, scheduling medical appointments, etc. Although men contribute more around the house than they have in the past, the underlying assumption, not always articulated but often felt, is that the woman is mainly responsible and the man is just "helping out," a phrase that assumes a secondary role. Women are not talked about as "helping out" around the household. Even though I have been writing about Victorian and contemporary domestic issues for two decades and therefore should know better, when I started looking for the most recent statistics on the division of household responsibilities, that's precisely the phrase I used when I queried "how much do contemporary men help out around the house?" Knowing better does not keep even educated women from perpetuating old assumptions about divisions of labour, even when women realize they are harmed by these assumptions. In fact, it turns out that women tend to do a greater portion of domestic duties the higher their pay is and the higher the status of their jobs, which is the opposite of what one may expect. The theory is that women overcompensate for their level of income and responsibility by trying to be even more domestic than they would be if they had less professional responsibility and pay—perhaps as a way of minimizing their threat to male partners (Thompson 5). Women typically do about eighteen hours of housework a week compared to ten for men (Thompson 2). In fact, husbands create seven additional hours of housework for their wives, according to one study (Reaney). The additional labour at home is not just a burden on women's time and energy—it also negatively affects their pay. A recent *Boston Globe* article points out the connection between unequal distribution of household work and lower pay for women: "The big reason that having children, and even marrying in the first place, hurts women's pay relative to men's is that the division of labor at home is still unequal, even when both spouses work full time. That's especially true for college-educated women in high-earning occupations: Children are particularly damaging to their careers" (Miller A13). Women now face the triple bind of believing that they should have good careers but also feeling guilty about their own success and then assuaging the guilt by piling more work on themselves at home. And because they perceive themselves as having a greater responsibility at home, they have a tendency to avoid challenges and responsibilities at work that could lead to promotions and higher pay. It's no wonder that stress-related autoimmune diseases are on the rise for women. According to a recent *Huffington Post* article, autoimmune diseases "are plaguing a rapidly growing number of Americans, especially women. (According to the National Institute of Allergy and Infectious Diseases, almost 80 percent of people with autoimmune disorders are female)," and stress appears to be one of the leading causes of the diseases (Magner; see also Nakazawa).

Today, in addition to working outside the home, women have to do many of the household chores without the range of help (in most cases) that would have been typical in many middle- to upper-class homes in the nineteenth century. Victorian ladies were not supposed to do housework at all; as Daniel Pool points out, "that was, after all, the whole point of being a lady—you didn't have to do anything, except tell the servants what to do" (219). He goes on to say that "manual labor of any kind would have cast serious doubts on your eligibility to be received in polite society" (219). Even a small household with a very modest income would have a "maid-of-all work, a girl who cooked, cleaned, scrubbed, mended, [and] looked after the children" (219)—a girl, in short, would do the bulk of what most full-time working mothers now manage. A family with a professional man as head of the household (such as a doctor or banker) would probably have "a cook, a housemaid, and a nurse" (220). Similarly, Susan Lasdun in *Victorians at Home* states that an unassuming middle-class home would typically have two to three servants (23). Granted, the Victorians had far fewer labour-saving devices than today, so cooking, cleaning and laundry would all have taken far more time than they do today. But it's still disconcerting to think that most middle-class Victorian women had servants to do most of the housework even though they themselves were not working outside the home, whereas the majority of middle-class women in the U.S. today are working and doing the bulk of the household chores.

It is particularly strange that an even division of labour still seems so elusive when one considers that historically the sharing of breadwinning and domestic responsibilities has more often been the norm than the model in which the husband leaves home for work and the wife oversees the house, which is a recent model that has only really dominated from the beginning of the Industrial Revolution until the 1960s—a relatively brief blip in human history—and a trend that has really only affected the middle classes. Before that brief blip, men and women divided the breadwinning and childrearing labour: from hunter-gatherer societies to agrarian communities, each gender had its role in providing for the family and both pitched in to raise and train the offspring. Men hunted, women gathered, and both taught their offspring to do the same. On farms, men tended to do the heavier chores, whereas women tended the garden and helped with the animals, and both men and women taught their children to do the same. In villages, tradespeople tended to live where they worked with all members of the family pitching in, so breadwinning and childrearing went hand in hand. Only with the Industrial Revolution did work shift outside the home for large sectors of the population, leaving middle-class women to dominate the home front and the childrearing (Broughton and Rogers 6-7). Yet the Industrial Revolution model is the one still clung to. For some reason, the sexual revolution notwithstanding, women are still expected to put their homes and families before themselves, and women who cannot successfully juggle the myriad tasks described above while building a successful career end up feeling like failures. And even when they can juggle these responsibilities successfully, they may still feel like failures because they are too exhausted and harried to perform any of them as well as they would like. So yes, wives can have careers—several of them at the same time, it turns out—one at work and at least one at home. And if they want the approval of friends, family, and society at large, they should never seem more invested in their professional careers than they are in the home front, nor should they complain much about the burdens of their position. That would make them unpleasant, and women are still expected to be pleasing—that much has not really changed.

Nor does significant change seem likely to occur anytime fast. As Emily Bobrow points out in a recent article in *The Economist*, "men, too, are struggling with a similarly burdensome bundle" of work/ home conflicts. They still feel the pressure to be the main wage earner, but they also feel the pressure to contribute equitably at home, something that is difficult to do when they have taken the kinds of high-pressure jobs many feel they are expected to hold. As Bobrow summarizes, "when mothers pull back from work for child-care reasons, they may earn less money, but they are still seen as good women. When fathers do the same, they are often seen as lesser men" (89). Men are in a bind that will make equalizing the division of home labour difficult to resolve; women are still more validated for being domestic and putting family first than men are. And until those expectations change, substantial changes in the unequal division of labour will probably not happen.

Changing unrealistic expectations of wives and mothers will be particularly difficult, as women themselves inforce them as much or more than anyone else, even while suffering from them. Women are often their own worst task master. In *Discipline and Punish*, Foucault famously writes about the spread of disciplinary mechanisms from the nineteenth century to today. He analyzes a trajectory of discipline that moves ever inward, starting with extreme physical and public torture at the beginning of the modern age and moving to disciplines that are more subtle and insidious and are internalized by the disciplinary subject:

> "Discipline" may be identified neither with an institution or with an apparatus; it is a type of power, a modality for its exercise, comprising a whole set of instruments, techniques, procedures, levels of application, targets ... And it may be taken over either by "specialized" institutions (the penitentiaries of "houses of correction" of the nineteenth century), or by institutions that use it as an essential instrument for a particular end (schools, hospitals), or by pre-existing authorities that find in it a means of reinforcing or reorganizing their internal mechanisms of power. (215)

Foucault goes on to suggest that the family is the ultimate disciplinary mechanism, "the privileged locus of emergence of the disciplinary question of the normal and the abnormal" (216). The family is, after all, the main source of our understandings of gender roles as well as marital and parental norms; family structures shape individuals and replicate themselves more powerfully and pervasively than more official agencies of the state or church (the traditional and more obvious sources of discipline). Foucault sums up the trajectory from external to internalized discipline when he writes that "one can speak of the formation of a disciplinary society in this movement that stretches from the enclosed disciplines, a sort of social 'quarantine', to an indefinitely generalizable mechanism of 'panopticism,'" where generalized surveillance is what keeps the subject in check (209). In comparing our current condition to that of a victim of public torture in the eighteenth century, Foucault claims that "we are neither in the amphitheater, nor on the stage, but in the panoptic machine, invested by its effects of power, *which we bring to ourselves since we are part of the mechanism*" (my emphasis, 217). We police ourselves, in other words; we are our own jailers.

This is particularly true of women because historically they have had a subservient position in society, and, therefore, they have had more restraints to internalize. Among the disciplinary mechanisms

Foucault analyzes is the intense scheduling that comes with modern life (6-7, 11). Instead of controlling subjects through the punitive physical practices of past centuries, such as public whippings or throwing people in the stocks, modern societies are regulated by relentless schedules and regimens. "The body," Foucault writes, "is caught up in a system of constraints and privations, obligations and prohibitions" (11). Although Foucault is specifically addressing changes in the carceral system, he is ultimately addressing all disciplinary subjects—in short, everyone. And what he describes about the relentlessly scheduled inmates of the "house of young prisoners in Paris" in the nineteenth century—with every half hour allotted to specific activities from the time they wake up to the time they go to bed (6-7)—seems comparable to the schedules of contemporary overworked wives and mothers: lengthy work hours on the job, time-consuming commutes, child care commitments, domestic chores, and fitness programs, an element of physical discipline relatively alien to the Victorian women. We no longer wear corsets—we have internalized our corsets with our emphasis on tight abs. We are our own corsets. And even though exercise clearly seems healthier than wearing confining whale bone, think a moment about the number of people who have been in physical therapy for strained muscles and tendons from weight lifting, stress fractures from marathon training, plantar fasciitis from jogging, or torn knees and broken bones from skiing and other sports. Even yoga, one of the least damaging of all exercise activities, has a track record of causing compression fractures. Clearly, there is a degree of self-inflicted physical punishment in our exercise routines. Even with no injuries, our aerobics and Pilates and weight lifting sessions clearly crowd our already overcrowded schedules. Walking, the most benign exercise and one that requires the least amount of scheduling, has succumbed to this drive to measure and control now that many of us count our steps with our FitBits and other health apps and participate in team step challenges. I cannot walk to the water cooler down the hall without carrying my phone because I do not want a step to go uncounted. This obsessive focus on measuring and recording our physical activity seems like the logical progression of the disciplinary mechanisms Foucault describes. Our lives are scheduled within an inch of our lives. Our packed schedules and our emphasis on achieving and measuring physical fitness create a good condition for maintaining docile political subjects, as Foucault points out throughout *Discipline and Punish*. If the aim is to create a society full of people who will maintain the status quo and submit to authority because they are already controlling themselves so severely and are too busy to pay much attention to what is being done by those in power, then the aim has been achieved. According to Foucault, that is one of the main insidious purposes of schedules and regimens; it is all about control, keeping power in the hands of the already powerful. To keep the populace obedient, we do not have to flay people alive in public any more, as the opening of *Discipline and Punish* so brutally describes. All we have to do is keep them ruthlessly busy, so they are content to spend their down time binge watching the latest, most popular cable offerings. In terms of gender politics, the scheduling and regimens and self-monitoring result in a situation that is obviously unequal, but that is widely tolerated, as many women flatly reject the notion that they are the victims of injustice and that the concerns of feminists are their concerns.

Foucault's analysis of the "carceral archipelago" (297) carries over into his analysis of gender roles in *History of Sexuality*. In this book, Foucault discusses how the family and the expectations of the "social body" discipline women's bodies so they are "qualified and disqualified" to conform to a sociosexual norm (104). Contemporary mothers may no longer have to go out into public chaperoned to assure both their safety and decorous behaviour, but who needs a chaperone when every waking moment of one's day is scheduled, like the days of the Mettray inmates Foucault describes in *Discipline and Punish*? (293- 95). Who needs strict admonishments to be selfless when there is simply no time to be selfish in the first place? And who needs a corset or girdle when we are monitoring our weight, BMIs, miles run, steps taken, and calories eaten? No one could place us under as much relentless scheduling, physical restrictions, observation, and recording as we do ourselves. Victorian norms evolved in part to control women, as norms since the beginning of civilization have attempted to control women and thereby control lineage and the continuation of property ownership in the male blood line (see Engels 26-30). Contemporary norms function similarly.

The restrictions that horrify us when we look at nineteenth-century regulations of women's lives and bodies seem somewhat less horrifying when placed in context of the day-to-day realities of contemporary wives and mothers. I'm not suggesting that twenty-first century wives face as many restrictions as their Victorian counterparts, but I am suggesting that the prevailing belief that women are now fully and obviously liberated from those restrictions needs to be questioned. How liberated is anyone who has no time to herself? How liberated are we when we relentlessly monitor our diet and exercise? We have earned the right to vote, to be educated, and to pursue any career. These are not small victories. But is the current quality of life for the average full-time working wife really the ideal we should be shooting for? Just because progress has been made, does not mean we should not try to carve out a less confining and more equitable existence.

## Works Cited

Beeton, Isabella. *Mrs. Beeton's Household Management*. 1861. Rev. ed. London: Ward, Lock & Co., 1949.

Bobrow, Emily. "The Trap." *The Economist*, June/July 2017, pp. 86-91.

Boushey, Heather, and Kavya Vaghul. "Women have made the difference for family economic security." Washington Center for Equitable Growth, 2006, www.equitablegrowth.org/research-analysis/women-have-made-the-difference-for-family-economic-security//. Accessed 21 May 2019.

Broughton, Trev Lynn, and Helen Rogers. *Gender and Fatherhood in the Nineteenth Century*. Palgrave MacMillan, 2007.

Ellis, Sarah. *The Mothers of England: Their Influence and Responsibility*. D. Appleton & Co., 1844.

Ellis, Sarah. *The Wives of England: Their Relative Duties, Domestic Influence and Social Obligations*. Langley, 1843.

Ellis, Sarah. *The Women of England: Their Social Duties and Domestic Habits*. J. & H. G. Langley, 1843.

Engels, Friedrich. *The Origins of Family, Private Property and the State* (1884). Translated by Alick West, 1942, Marx/Engels Internet Archive. www.marxists.org/archive/marx/works/download/pdf/origin_family.pdf. Accessed 21 May 2019.

Foucault, Michel. *Discipline and Punish: The Birth of the Prison*. Translated by Alan Sheridan. Vintage, 1977.

Foucault, Michel. *The History of Sexuality.* Translated by Robert Hurly. Pantheon, 1978.

Lasdun, Susan. *Victorians at Home.* Viking, 1981.

Lewis, Sarah. *Woman's Mission.* William Crosby & Co., 1840.

Magner, Erin. "The On-the-Rise Autoimmune Diseases That Every Woman Needs to Know About." *Huffington Post,* 13 Oct. 2016, www.huffpost.com/entry/the-on-the-rise-autoimmun_n_12460244. Accessed 21 May 2019.

Miller, Claire Cain. "Studies show motherhood, housework linked to pay gap." *Boston Sunday Globe,* 14 May 2017, p. A13.

Nakazawa, Donna Jackson. "The Autoimmune Epidemic: Bodies Gone Haywire in a World Out of Balance." Exc. from *The Autoimmune Epidemic: Bodies Gone Haywire in a World Out of Balance* (Touchstone/Schuster). *Alternet. Personal Health,* 18 Mar. 2008, www.alternet.org/story/80129/the_autoimmune_epidemic%3A_bodics_gone_Haywire_in_a_world_out_of_balance. Accessed 21 May 2019.

Patmore, Coventry. *The Angel in the House.* Cassell & Co., 1891.

Pool, Daniel. *What Jane Austen Ate and Charles Dickens Knew: From Fox Hunting to Whist—the Facts of Daily Life in 19th Century England.* Touchstone, 1993.

Reaney, Patricia. "Husbands Create 7 Hours of Extra Housework for Their Wives." *The Huffington Post,* 19 Feb. 2016, www.huffingtonpost.com/entry/husbands-create-7-hours-of-extra-housework-for-their-wives_us_56c72146e4b0ec6725e23e2c. Accessed 21 May 2019.

Thompson, Derek. "Yes, Men Should Do More Housework." *The Atlantic,* 10 Dec. 2013, theatlantic.com/business/archive/2013/12/yes-men-should-do-more-hosework/282165. Accessed 28 May 2019.

Chapter Two

# Invisible Wives: Analyzing the Consequences of Sameness

Leanne Letourneau

## Introduction

Jean Carabine contends that all women are measured against an ideal woman who is white, heterosexual, able bodied, and if a mother aged eighteen to forty (63). This construction of an ideal woman may be extended to include cisgender women. Patricia Hill Collins illustrates that the image of a wife implies a heterosexual wife/mother with biological children in a racially homogeneous nuclear family (47). Neither of these conceptions of a woman or a wife applies universally. For example, women of colour and lesbian feminists emphasize that these constructions conceal racial and sexual differences (Collins 175; Richardson, "Locating Sexualities" 71). Therefore, when contending that sexually diverse wives (self-identified women who are physically and/or romantically attracted to other women) and heterosexual wives are the same, sexually diverse wives are simply compared to a normative ideal. As a result, claiming sameness is insufficient to validate policy issues because the specificities of sexually diverse wives are not acknowledged.

For example, equal rights framing employs the sameness claim to justify legalizing same-sex marriage; however, as this chapter will illustrate, differences exist not only between sexually diverse and heterosexual wives but also among sexually diverse wives. Further-more, this critique of sameness applies in relationship problems. Domestic violence, for example, is depicted as men inflicting violence on women because of gender inequality (MOJ 2). This depiction does not necessarily reflect the reality of domestic violence among sexually diverse wives.

Therefore, in this chapter, I will first exemplify how asserting sameness for marriage equality in Canada perpetuates gender-norm stereotypes, including the construction of a wife and mother; and fails to question how intersecting forms of oppression, such as racism, classicism, ageism, and heterosexism affect sexually diverse wives. Next, I will analyze Quebec's action plan on domestic violence to highlight how the heteronormative framework renders invisible sexually diverse wives' experiences. Acknowledging different experiences in both situations is important; otherwise, an implied universal understanding of what constitutes a wife predominates in public policy—an understanding that devalues those who do not meet the required expectations. Since an intersectional lens is crucial for comprehending sexually diverse wives' experiences and for highlighting that a definition of a wife can differ culturally, historically and geographically, I will conclude by suggesting ways of incorporating intersectionality in policy.

## Marriage Equality

In Canada, marriage is regulated both federally and provincially. The federal government is primarily responsible for determining most laws regarding marriage, including who can marry, and the provincial governments are responsible for determining the rules surrounding solemnization (Hogg 714-15). However, despite the federal government's jurisdiction in defining marriage, in May 2003, British Columbia's Court of Appeal expanded the definition of marriage to allow sexually diverse couples to marry (Larocque 100), followed by Ontario in June 2003 (117) and Quebec in 2004 (189). The federal government decided not to appeal these decisions (142), and in 2005, the definition of marriage was changed federally in what became the Civil Marriage Act.

The majority of litigation leading up to the Civil Marriage Act was based on the equality section (section 15) of Canada's Charter of Rights and Freedoms (Smith, "Framing Same-Sex" 13). Consequently, equal rights framing was used to contend that sexually diverse and heterosexual couples were the same and should have the right to marry (Mulé 79; Warner 225). However, since declaring that sameness obscures the differences between these groups, critically questioning the implications of the sameness argument is essential.

## Implications of Claiming Sameness

### Marriage as a Heteronormative Institution

Comparing sexually diverse women and heterosexual couples to justify the formers' right to marry depicts them as "good citizens" seeking inclusion into the institution of marriage (Gaucher 65; Richardson, "Claiming Citizenship?" 392). This type of inclusion is a form of assimilation in which sexually diverse wives are expected to conform to the heterosexual wife role. In other words, it incorporates sexually diverse wives into an already established institution where the rules and standards have already been set (Young 164). Therefore, instead of providing equality, legalizing same-sex marriage has perpetuated and legitimized a privileged heteronormative institution.

Heteronormativity is a norm that marginalizes those who do not conform. It presumes heterosexuality in our daily interactions in which the male-female dichotomy plays a central role (Rosenfeld 632); it is embodied in the ways people talk, dress, act, and engage with others (Jackson 153), and it is institutionalized through laws and policies, such as marriage, that are based on a heterosexual model (Smith, "Queering Public Policy" 100). Therefore, heteronormativity regulates what is normal in terms of sexuality and gender. Despite the assertion that same-sex marriage would challenge the normativity of family and de-gender marriage (Boyd 268), heteronormativity continues to prevail.

As a result, marriage continues to be perceived as a site for raising children in a legitimate relationship (Young and Boyd 218)—a site where girls are still socialized into believing they will marry a man and have children (Boyd 266) as well as a site where the construction of women as caregivers continues to exist (Boyd 276). In other words, marriage continues to be a place where women are expected to have a wife/mother role and to be socialized into it. These types of gender-norm stereotypes reinforce the ideal of what constitutes a normative wife, which is an ideal that all wives are expected to achieve, not just sexually diverse ones. What is significant in this context is that the ideal of a normative wife does not leave room to question how the concepts of wife and mother are defined and experienced in relationships with two women.

For example, if sexually diverse wives choose to be mothers, they need to search for ways to achieve this status outside of their relationship as well as to question how motherhood and family are defined (Dozier 129). Not only does this disrupt the implication of a women's dual role as a wife/mother, but it illustrates that sexually diverse wives may negotiate what it means to be a mother as well as a family. In this way, sexually diverse women exemplify that the roles of wife and mother are distinct. Jacqui Gabb, for example, contends that the way that lesbians (which I include under the concept of sexually diverse wives) are different from heterosexual wives challenges the concept of motherhood:

> To some extent it is precisely because of our 'unnatural' status-our disruption of the reproductive narrative-that lesbians pose such a threat to heterosexual society. We signify the performativity of all motherhood, and analogously by our evident (homo) sexuality, we sexualise all parenting (Gabb 127-28).

Therefore, if sexually diverse wives signify the performativity of motherhood, then they also signify that the roles of wife and mother differ.

However, although sexually diverse wives may disrupt the reproductive narrative, this same narrative prevents some sexually diverse wives from being recognized as mothers, such as nonbiological co-mothers. For example, the heterosexual conception of women in a wife/mother role also implies a biological connection between mother and child (Reed 46). When sexually diverse wives choose to become mothers, claiming this role for both wives may not always be possible (Gabb 125). Consequently, nonbiological co-mothers are rendered invisible when their role as a mother is not validated, including by family and friends (Comeau 160) and in some cases, by the biological co-mother (Park 5). This invisibility stems from the heterosexual conception of motherhood (Reed 40), which, therefore, exemplifies the need to define and negotiate the concepts of mother, family, and wife instead of promoting sameness.

## Intersectional Considerations

Additionally, focusing on the idea that sexually diverse and heterosexual wives are the same constructs sexually diverse wives as a homogeneous group with the same needs and realities. This universal construction simply normalizes the experiences of the dominant members of the group (white, middle class, young, able and bodied) while marginalizing the experiences of everyone else (Bernstein and Reimann 5; Dick 155). Presenting sexually diverse wives as a homogeneous group, for example, does not recognize that some sexually diverse wives cannot have a public relationship. Disclosing one's sexual orientation or gender identity (being out) is necessary for a public relationship; however, it is also a privileged choice (Bernstein and Reimann 6) that not all sexually diverse women have. In this way, those who cannot disclose their sexual orientation or gender identity confront barriers in establishing a public relationship, which may limit their choices regarding marriage and/or having children.

Furthermore, "being out" may be more difficult for sexually diverse wives who rely on their communities for social support. For example, sexually diverse women of colour may depend on family and friends for support against a racist society (Bernstein and Reimann 6). As a result, they may need to choose between their relationships and their families. Additionally, those who are dependent on the healthcare system or social services must decide on whether to present themselves as a couple or as friends. This is a concern especially for those who are institutionalized, such as older sexually diverse wives (Walsh et al. 22).

Therefore, using sameness to justify legalizing same-sex marriage simply perpetuates gender-norm stereotypes while neglecting to consider the different ways that women experience being a wife. Even though I refer to sexually diverse wives, heterosexual wives are not homogeneous either and require an intersectional lens in order to move beyond the normative conception of a wife/mother—a conception that affects all wives. Critiques regarding the use of sameness in describing sexually diverse and heterosexual wives can also be applied to relationship problems, such as domestic violence.

## Sexually Diverse Wives and Domestic Violence

In this section, I focus solely on the conception of sexually diverse women in their role as wives. A primary reason for this approach is the lack of literature surrounding sexually diverse wives/mothers in the context of domestic violence. For example, a study on lesbian mothers and intimate partner violence by Jennifer Hardesty et al. in 2008 indicates that previously, there was no literature or studies on this topic. They argue that a possible reason for this gap is to maintain a positive image of gender and sexually diverse communities, especially in the face of ongoing struggles for equality rights ("Lesbian Mothering" 192). Another possible reason for this gap may be due to custody concerns. According to Hardesty et al., a primary concern for mothers was losing custody of their children ("Lesbian Mothering" 200) either because they did not have legal rights to their children ("Lesbian/Bisexual Mothers" 30) or fear of losing custody to the children's father ("Lesbian/Bisexual Mothers" 42). Therefore, due to a lack of information regarding sexually diverse mothers and domestic violence, only the wife role will be analyzed in this section.

## Framing of Domestic Violence as Heterosexual

Domestic violence is an example of how heteronormative expectations render invisible the experiences of sexually diverse wives. For example, Janice Ristock states that "when we acknowledge lesbian abuse, we keep our focus primarily on the victims and plug lesbian abuse into the theories we have developed to explain heterosexual abuse" (4). Consequently, most of the existing information concerning sexually diverse wives and domestic violence is often based on a heterosexual framework. A contributing factor to this framework is studying domestic violence in sexually diverse couples using methods designed for heterosexual couples (Badenes-Ribera et al. 48; Hassouneh and Glass 311). As a result, studies may not adequately reflect the experiences of sexually diverse wives. One of the ways to counter this invisibility is by challenging the gender-norm stereotypes that inform understandings of domestic violence.

There are various ways that gender-norm stereotypes construct how domestic violence is understood. For example, women are expected to be dependent, nurturing, and passive, whereas men are expected to be more assertive, autonomous, and less caring—therefore, creating the victim-perpetrator dichotomy, also known as the "public story" of domestic violence (Donovan and Hester 161). This type of narrative is supported by the myth of lesbian relationships, which is a myth depicting lesbian relationships as a type of utopia where women are in loving, egalitarian, and nonviolent relationships (Brown 251; Hassouneh and Glass 319). Even though the myth was created in the 1970s by radical lesbian feminists to validate their relationships and say that women were not violent like men (Hassouneh and Glass 312; Walters 251), it reinforced gender-norm stereotypes (Hassouneh and Glass 319). Therefore, domestic violence among sexually diverse women has been invisible because the conception of women as nurturing contradicts the idea that women can be abusive. Furthermore, the predominance of the "public story" informs not only the general understanding of domestic violence but also policy.

For example, domestic violence policy is a site where gender (often cisgender women) is depicted as the primary axis of oppression. This understanding of domestic violence renders invisible the experiences of sexually diverse wives (Dempsey 390) because it fails to consider that every relationship does not have a male-female dichotomy. If the two parties involved are both women, then the argument for gender oppression is limited and fails to consider the power and relationship dynamics of sexually diverse wives. Therefore, understanding how domestic violence among sexually diverse wives differs from hetero-sexual wives' experiences is essential for creating policy reflecting these differences. Finding prevalence rates to justify the need for research and funding is an important step (Ristock 13).

Some authors, according to Ristock, contend that domestic violence among sexually diverse wives occurs as frequently or possibly more than heterosexual wives (10). In this way, rather than claiming that sexually diverse and heterosexual wives are the same and should have the same rights, the claim is that they experience the same amount of violence in their relationships, which needs recognition and solutions. However, as Katie Edwards et al. highlight in their literature review, estimates of prevalence rates range from 1 percent to more than 97 percent (113), which suggests that a prevalence rate has not been determined. In Canada, a study by Betty Jo Barrett and Melissa St. Pierre obtained a prevalence rate of 36 percent among gay, lesbian, and bisexual individuals (16). However, due to lack of information in

Canada, it is difficult to compare these results for accuracy. Regardless of whether a prevalence rate is found, it is important to question what percentage is enough to justify that domestic violence among sexually diverse wives is a policy problem and/or is it only justified if the numbers are comparable to heterosexual women. Next, I analyze Quebec's action plan on domestic violence to illustrate some of the ways a heteronormative framework is used.

## Quebec's Domestic Violence Action Plan

Quebec's domestic violence action plan was chosen for two reasons. First, Quebec has a history of including gender and sexually diverse communities in its policies. For example, it was the first Canadian province to include sexual orientation as a prohibited ground of discrimination in its human rights legislation in 1977 (Hurley 4). The second reason is the recognition in Quebec's 1995 domestic violence policy that lesbians' experiences of domestic violence were hidden by a heterosexist and homophobic society (Quebec 48), which is significant because it illustrates that domestic violence among sexually diverse couples was acknowledged by the Quebec government prior to legalizing relationship recognition. Despite the recognition of lesbian domestic violence in the 1995 policy, there was very little visibility in the action plans and discourse that followed. It was not until the 2012–2017 action plan that sexually diverse women were listed again as a vulnerable population. However, the action plan continues to use a heterosexual framework.

As mentioned previously, most of the 2012–2017 action plan is based on an implicit understanding that women are the victim and men the perpetrator. For example, the action plan states that "gender equality is the primary condition for the elimination of domestic violence" (2) and that "the safety and protection of women *victims* and children are the priority when it comes to intervention strategies" (my emphasis, 2). Furthermore, one of the objectives of the action plan is to "promote the establishment of egalitarian relationships between women and men as well as between girls and boys" (5). Each of these suggests that domestic violence occurs because of inequality between men and women, which follows the normative conception of domestic violence.

## Vulnerable Categories

Depicting domestic violence as an issue of gender inequality constructs the experiences of heterosexual wives as normative. This type of construction is most evident when the action plan lists anyone, such as sexually diverse women, who do not conform to the dominant image of a white, middle-class, young, able-bodied, cisgender, and heterosexual woman. For example, the populations that are named as vulnerable include, in addition to Indigenous populations: elderly women, women with a disability, immigrant women, women from cultural communities, members from lesbian, gay, bisexual, transsexual, and transgender communities as well as male victims of domestic violence (MOJ 111). Regarding this list, the term "cultural communities" is used in the action plan but not defined. There is an implication that the concept refers to communities in which higher amounts of domestic violence are expected, and it is often used in connection with immigrant communities.

Despite the attempt to include individuals considered vulnerable to domestic violence, such as sexually diverse women, simply naming them is a tokenistic way of inclusion and a weak form of visibility (Strid et al. 559). This type of inclusion fails to acknowledge the multiple ways these groups may intersect and how those intersections may impact their experiences of domestic violence. For example, there can be a sexually diverse woman who is an immigrant and has a disability. The ways these factors intersect will affect how these individuals experience domestic violence, and the experience may be different from a sexually diverse woman of colour or a heterosexual woman of colour.

Additionally, few measures in the action plan suggest ways of understanding domestic violence in vulnerable populations. Instead, there are measures to provide awareness raising tools to vulnerable populations, including those directly related to immigrants, "cultural communities," and the LGBTQ community (6). Some of these awareness raising tools include a video addressed towards "immigrants and people from cultural communities" (6) as well as information leaflets on domestic violence to immigrants (8). These measures may inform vulnerable populations about domestic violence, but the action plan does not indicate whether these awareness campaigns are imposing a normative Western view of domestic violence or whether they are based on the known experiences of these populations.

The action plan also mentions adapting intervention tools for vulnerable populations (11); however, adapting intervention tools designed for heterosexual couples may not be effective for sexually diverse wives. Intervention tools should be developed based on the realities of domestic violence among sexually diverse women. The action plan does indicate that it will support research on "domestic violence issues in vulnerable populations" (18); however, it supports research and prioritizes research on vulnerable populations with different levels of commitment. Without the knowledge base to understand the realities of domestic violence, interventions will continue to be adapted and will be primarily informed by a hetero-normative framework. Therefore, what is needed is an intersectional framework to understand not only domestic violence but all relationship issues concerning sexually diverse women.

## Conclusion: Intersectionality in Policy

Comparing the sameness of sexually diverse and heterosexual wives is significant because as long as sexually diverse wives are compared in relation to what is normal, they will be integrated with dominant heteronormative society in which the wife/mother role predominates. They may challenge these conceptions; however, this may still require the validation of their relationship. Alternatively, they may be marginalized when they deviate from normative standards. Since examining these problems from an intersectional lens reveals that comparing sexually diverse and heterosexual wives maintains a superficial view of the former, moving beyond this depiction requires an intersectional approach. Otherwise, policy solutions will not be based on the needs and realties of sexually diverse wives but adapted from the already existing heteronormative framework.

Including intersectionality in policy requires incorporating the voices of sexually diverse wives. For example, if the policy issue concerns domestic violence, then including voices of sexually diverse wives who have experienced it will answer various questions. Including voices will reveal how domestic violence is perceived as a problem; it will reveal how intersecting factors—such as race, age, immigration status, gender identity, and ability—influence and/or contribute to domestic violence; it will reveal whether current policy measures are effective as well as what is needed; it will highlight the types of power dynamics existing within their relationships and the role these dynamics have in domestic violence; and it will contribute to the knowledge gap regarding sexually diverse mothers and domestic violence. All of these factors are important because policy is not experienced in the same way by all individuals (Hankivsky and Cormier 8), and until the voices of those affected are heard, policy will be unable to effectively address relevant issues. This leads to the question of how to include the voices of sexually diverse wives in policy.

Tiffany Manuel states that improving policy requires research that "can serve as an intellectual basis for more thoughtful deliberation" (196). Therefore, including the voices of sexually diverse wives in research is a step towards policy inclusion. This type of solution requires resources and funding for researching the needs and realities of sexually diverse wives, including areas such as immigration, poverty, racism, transphobia, and access to healthcare. Each of these issues requires an intersectional lens to understand how sexually diverse wives experience these issues differently. Next, is the question of how to include the voices of sexually diverse wives in research.

One of the ways of including voices of sexually diverse wives in research is to encourage individuals who are involved in both academics and activism, as they will not only have greater opportunities of engaging with individuals at the grassroots level, but also be able to push for this research to inform public policy and bring these voices into other areas of academia. Therefore, rather than having heterosexual-based knowledge inform policy, the specificities of different communities, including sexually diverse wives, can be included.

Finally, LGBTQ activist organizations can advocate for policy inclusion while ensuring that they are inclusive in their representation. In the case of sexually diverse wives, this type of inclusive representation could entail creating spaces where all sexually diverse women are given opportunities to have a voice and be heard. Therefore, activist organizations will be in a better position to frame policy issues that reflect the needs of their constituents.

Sexually diverse wives can be found in every social group and occupation; they are from various educational backgrounds and social classes. However, they are rarely seen or heard. Historically, their voices were silenced in the women's movement due to homophobia

(Warner 78) and in gay men's organizations because of sexism (Warner 80). Therefore, it is important that sexually diverse wives are visible and have a voice so that their experiences can be understood and that policy solutions will reflect those experiences. Whether or not sexually diverse wives are the same as heterosexual wives should not be a determining factor for policy inclusion. There is not a universal way of being a wife. The mainstream conception of a wife is a social construction that is based on a heteronormative understanding of what is expected—a conception based on an ideal normative woman. Therefore, what constitutes a wife needs to be redefined by women in a way that will empower all women, not in a way that creates a hierarchy of acceptability.

**Works Cited**

Badenes-Ribera, Laura, et al. "Intimate Partner Violence in Self-Identified Lesbians: Meta Analysis of its Prevalence." *Sexuality Research and Social Policy,* vol. 12, no. 1, 2015, pp. 47-59.

Barrett, Betty Jo, and Melissa St. Pierre. "Intimate Partner Violence Reported by Lesbian-, Gay-, and Bisexual-Identified Individuals Living in Canada: An Exploration of Within-Group Variations." *Journal of Gay and Lesbian Social Services,* vol. 25, no. 1, 2013, pp. 1-23.

Bernstein, Mary, and Renate Reimann. "Queer Families and the Politics of Visibility." *Queer Families, Queer Politics: Challenging Culture and the State,* edited by Mary Bernstein and Renate Reimann, Columbia University Press, 2001, pp. 1-17.

Boyd, Susan B. "'Marriage Is More Than Just a Piece of Paper': Feminist Critiques of Same Sex Marriage." *National Taiwan University Law Review,* vol. 8, no. 2, 2013, pp. 263-98.

Brown, Carrie. "Gender-Role Implications on Same-Sex Intimate Partner Violence." *Journal of Family Violence,* vol. 23, no. 6, 2008, pp. 457-62.

Carabine, Jean. "Heterosexuality and Social Policy." *Theorising Sexuality,* edited by Diane Richardson, Open University Press, 1996, pp. 55-74.

Collins, Patricia Hill. *Black Feminist Thought: Knowledge, Consciousness, and the Politics of Empowerment,* 2nd ed. Routledge, 2000.

Comeau, Dawn. "Lesbian Nonbiological Mothering: Negotiating an (Un)familiar Existence". *Mother Outlaws: Theories and Practices of Empowered Mothering,* edited by Andrea O'Reilly, 2004, pp. 155-67.

Dempsey, Brian. "Gender Neutral Laws and Heterocentric Policies: 'Domestic Abuse as Gender-Based Abuse' and Same-Sex Couples." *The Edinburgh Law Review,* vol. 15, no. 3, 2011, pp. 381-45.

Dick, Caroline. *The Perils of Identity: Group Rights and Intragroup Difference,* UBC Press, 2011.

Donovan, Catherine, and Marianne Hester. *Domestic Violence and Sexuality: What's Love Got to Do with It?* Policy Press, 2014.

Dozier, Raine. "Guy-Mums Unite! Mothering Outside the Box." *Queering Motherhood: Narrative and Theoretical Perspectives,* edited by Margaret F. Gibson, Demeter Press, 2014, pp. 127-39.

Edwards, Katie M., et al. "Intimate Partner Violence Among Sexual Minority Populations: Critical Review of the Literature and Agenda for Future Research." *American Psychological Association,* vol. 5, no. 2, 2015, pp. 112-21.

Gabb, Jacqui. "Imag(in)ing the Queer Lesbian Family." *Mother Outlaws: Theories and Practices of Empowered Mothering,* edited by Andrea O'Reilly, Women's Press, 2004, pp. 123-30.

Gaucher, Megan. "One Step Forward, Two Steps Back? Relationship Recognition in Canadian Law Post-Same-Sex Marriage." *Atlantis,* vol. 36, no. 2, 2014, pp. 61-72.

Gouvernement du Québec. *Politique d'Intervention en Matière de Violence Conjugale: Prévenir, Dépister, Contrer La Violence Conjugal,* Gouvernement du Québec, 1995, www.scf.gouv.qc.ca/fileadmin/publications/Violence/Prevenir_depister_contrer_Politique_VC.pdf. Accessed 22 May 2019.

Hankivsky, Olena, and Renee Cormier. "Intersectionality and Public Policy: Some Lessons from Existing Models." *Political Research Quarterly,* vol. 64, no. 1, 2011, pp. 217-29.

Hardesty, Jennifer, L., et al. "Lesbian Mothers in the Context of Intimate Partner Violence." *Journal of Lesbian Studies,* vol. 12, no. 2-3, 2008, pp. 191-210.

Hardesty, Jennifer L., et al. "Lesbian/Bisexual Mothers and Intimate Partner Violence: Help Seeking in the Context of Social and Legal Vulnerability." *Violence against Women,* vol. 17, no. 1, 2011, pp. 28-46.

Hassouneh, Dena, and Nancy Glass. "The Influence of Gender Role Stereotyping on Women's Experiences of Female Same-Sex Intimate Partner Violence." *Violence against Women,* vol. 14, no. 3, 2008, pp. 310-25.

Hogg, Peter W. "Canada: The Constitution and Same-Sex Marriage." *International Journal of Constitutional Law,* vol. 4, no. 3, 2005, pp. 712-21.

Hurley, Mary C. "Sexual Orientation and Legal Rights: A Chronological Overview." PRB 04-13E. Parliamentary Information and Research Services, Library of Parliament, 2005, www.lop.parl.gc.ca/content/lop/researchpublications/prb0413-e.htm. Accessed 22 May 2019.

Jackson, Stevie. "Sexuality, Heterosexuality, and Gender Hierarchy: Getting our Priorities Straight." *Sex, Gender & Sexuality: The Basics,* edited by Abby L. Ferber, et al., Oxford University Press, 2009, pp. 142-56.

Larocque, Sylvain. *Gay Marriage: The Story of a Canadian Social Revolution.* Translated by Robert Chodos, et al. James Lorimer and Company Ltd, 2009.

Lenon, Suzanne J. "Marrying Citizens! Raced Subjects? Re-thinking the Terrain of Equal Marriage Discourse." *Canadian Journal of Women and the Law,* vol. 17, no. 2, 2005, 405-21.

Manuel, Tiffany. "Envisioning the Possibilities for a Good Life: Exploring the Public Policy Implications of Intersectionality Theory." *Journal of Women, Politics, & Policy,* vol. 28, no. 3, 2006, pp. 173-203.

Ministère de la Justice (MOJ). *2012-2017 Government Action Plan on Domestic Violence,* Gouvernement du Québec, 2012. Revised November, 2015, www.scf.gouv.qc.ca/fileadmin/Documents/Violences/Plan-action-2012-2017-EN.pdf. Accessed 22 May 2019.

Mulé, Nick J. "Same-Sex Marriage and Canadian Relationship Recognition-One Step Forward, Two Steps Back: Critical Liberationist Perspective." *Journal of Gay and Lesbian Social Service,* vol. 22, no. 1-2, 2012, 74-90.

Park, Shelley. *Mothering Queerly, Queering Motherhood: Resisting Monomaternalism in Adoptive, Lesbian, Blended and Polygamous Families,* State University of New York Press, 2013.

Reed, Elizabeth. "Lesbian, Bisexual and Queer Motherhood: Crafting Radical Narratives and Representing Social Change through Cultural Representations." *Women: A Cultural Review,* vol. 29, no. 1, 2018, pp. 39-58.

Richardson, Diane. "Locating Sexualities: From Here to Normality." *Sexualities,* vol. 7, no. 4, 2004, pp. 391-411.

Richardson, Diane. "Claiming Citizenship? Sexuality, Citizenship, and Lesbian Feminist Theory." *Thinking Straight: The Power, the Promise, and the Paradox of Heterosexuality,* edited by Chrys Ingraham, Routledge, 2005, pp. 63-84.

Ristock, Janice. *No More Secrets: Violence in Lesbian Relationships,* Routledge, 2002.

Rosenfeld, Dana. "Heteronormativity and Homonormativity as Practical and Moral Resources." *Gender and Society,* vol. 23, no. 5, 2009, pp. 617-38.

Smith, Miriam. "Queering public policy: A Canadian perspective." *Critical Policy Studies,* edited by Michael Orsini and Miriam Smith, UBC Press, 2007, pp. 91-110.

Smith, Miriam. "Framing Same-Sex Marriage in Canada and the United States: Goodridge, Halpern and the National Boundaries of Political Discourse." *Social and Legal Studies,* vol. 16, no. 1, 2007, pp. 5-26.

Strid, Sofia, et al. "Intersectionality and Multiple Inequalities: Invisibility in British Policy on Violence against Women." *Social Politics: International Studies in Gender, State and Society,* vol. 20, no. 4, 2013, pp. 558-581.

Walsh, Christine A., et al. "Elder Abuse and Oppression: Voices of Marginalised Elders." *Journal of Elder Abuse and Neglect,* vol. 23, no. 1, 2011, pp. 17-42.

Walters, Mikel, L. "Straighten Up and Act like a Lady: A Qualitative Study of Lesbian Survivors of Intimate Partner Violence." *Journal of Gay and Lesbian Social Services,* vol. 23, no. 2, 2011, pp. 250-70.

Warner, Tom. *Never Going Back: History of Queer Activism in Canada*, University of Toronto Press, 2002.

Young, Iris Marion. *Justice and the Politics of Difference.* Princeton University Press, 1990.

Young, Claire, and Susan Boyd. "Losing the Feminist Voice? Debates on the Legal Recognition of Same Sex Partnership in Canada." *Feminist Legal Studies,* vol. 14, no. 2, 2006, pp. 213-40.

Chapter Three

# "Office Wife," "Two-Job Wife," and "Work Wife": The Marriage Metaphor in Popular Culture Representations of Women's Paid Labour

Jane Marcellus

In a November 2015 *New York Magazine* article, Liz Krieger argues that everyone needs a "work wife"—someone to "dissect cryptic e-mails," offer support in meetings, and enjoy "a kinship and shared history" at work that is "special and intimate." The relationship is not romantic, she notes. "You need only pledge to love and honor in an office setting."

Although Krieger's assertion that "your perfect work wife can be of any gender or sexual preference" suggests twenty-first-century gender-role fluidity, mainstream media since the year 2000—including *CBS News* (Lipton), the *Wall Street Journal* (Shellenbarger), as well as social media memes ("Work Spouse Memes")—have depicted these relationships as male-female. In a *Slate* article from 2004, Timothy Noah traces the office marriage concept to Mary Richards and Murray Slaughter from *The Mary Tyler Moore Show*, which premiered in 1970, but he says the terms "work wife," "work husband," and "work marriage" entered the lexicon in a 1987 *Atlantic Monthly* article. In that article, David Owen describes "a particular Platonic intimacy that frequently arises between male and female employees working in close proximity" (22).

The related term "office wife," however, is much older. Common in the 1920s and 1930s, it appears in magazines, novels and film as a humorous yet mildly pejorative term for a man's secretary. In early representations, the "office wife" competes with the "home wife" for their shared "husband's'" affections, raising the spectre of adultery. The iconic example is Faith Baldwin's 1929 novel, *The Office Wife*, about a secretary who falls in love with her married boss. A film version was released by Warner Brothers in 1930. The adultery theme is common in recent depictions, which treat affairs as an ever-present danger when men and women work together. Both older representations and more recent ones treat office marriage as a social phenomenon that is periodically discovered and reported rather than a media construction.

Building on my previous work on media representation of employed women, this chapter interrogates the enduring use of wife in depictions of workplace relationships. After discussing early-twentieth-century representation, including Faith Baldwin's *The Office Wife* (both book and film), I turn to later examples, and ask why the marriage metaphor continues to be used and, more specifically, why the word "wife" endures to describe employed women. Has the meaning of "office wife" (and its variants such as "work wife" and "office spouse") changed over time? Drawing on Stuart Hall's assertion that media and culture are "co-constituted" (1-3), I argue that the workplace marriage is less an actual social phenomenon than a recurring media construction that serves to marginalize women in the workplace, where, as work wives, they are always potentially and dangerously "other women."

## The Office Wife Emerges

The term "office wife" is rooted in the history of women as clerical workers. Until the late nineteenth century, most business clerks were young men who copied documents by hand (Davies 5). Women began to fill in for male clerks during the Civil War; their numbers grew with the post-war business expansion and the invention of office machines, notably the typewriter, patented in 1874 (Kessler-Harris 76). By the 1890s, feminists such as Charlotte Perkins Gilman and Frances Willard were urging women to liberate themselves from economic dependence on men through paid employment, and jobs experts, such as Mrs. M. L. Rayne, recommended typing as an easily acquired skill that allowed a woman to support herself. Accepted as low-cost machine operators, as they had been in the textile mills, women themselves were known as "typewriters." Although the term conflated woman and machine, typing and its companion skill, Gregg shorthand, offered financial independence to millions of women who entered office work "out of ambition, economic hardship, or the pure desire for emancipation" (Kittler 194). The image caught on in popular culture. In the 1897 novel *The Type-Writer Girl*, protagonist Juliet Appleton, twenty-two and unmarried, sets out to make her living in London. A bicycle-riding "new woman," she finds adventure with her typewriter, including one job working for anarchists. Although this Juliet eventually meets her "Romeo," she gives him up voluntarily when she realizes he is engaged to another woman. Loyal to her own sex and cherishing her independence, she remains, in the end, a "type-writer girl" (Rayner).

After the turn of the twentieth century, a backlash against women holding paid jobs, combined with moral panic about women spending time alone in offices with male bosses, laid the groundwork for the family discourse in office relationships. Although the first use of the term "office wife" cited in the *Oxford English Dictionary* is Baldwin's novel (*Office Wife*), the term had begun to appear in newspapers and magazines before that. "Office wife? Well, what of it? Every modern girl laughs at that," one secretary told a Nebraska newspaper in 1923 (Marcellus 87). By the 1930s, when the economic Depression intensified prejudice against employed women (Kessler-Harris 251), the term was commonplace in business magazines aimed at men, such as *Forbes* and *Fortune*, as well as women's magazines, such as *Ladies Home Journal*. In a variation, secretaries were office debutantes, who used clerical jobs to find husbands. Although "accomplished and valuable," these women supposedly saw business as a "passing career" and would inevitably "leave the office for new interests in homes of their own" (Royal 103).

Whether office debutantes or office wives, women were constructed according to a domestic discourse that saw them in wife-like roles and marginalized their professional desires, focusing instead on men's needs. *Fortune* argued in 1935 that what a man wanted at work was:

something as much like the vanished wife of his father's generation as could be arranged—someone to balance his checkbook, buy his railroad tickets, check his baggage, get him seats in the fourth row, take his daughter to the dentist, listen to his side of the story, give him a courageous look when things were bleakest, and generally know all, understand all. ("Women in Business II" 55)

Similarly, the *Saturday Evening Post* noted the following:

A man chooses his secretary much as he chooses his wife, and for much the same reasons. She looks good to him. He sees a slim, engaging young woman with a frank smile and a readiness to approve of him…. The alliance—may we say business love at first sight—works about as most marriages do. (Ragan 11)

Meanwhile, women who worked in offices were instructed to see themselves in wife-like roles. One secretarial manual compared the office wife to the home wife or "housekeeper," noting the similarity of their respective tasks. For example, whereas the home wife was required to "know how to use odds and ends of food," the office wife should "know how to use odds and ends of supplies." Both had to "be willing to carry through minor duties, especially the monotonous ones," "buy supplies economically," and "be patient with interruption." The home wife had to "make food attractive," whereas the office wife had to "put through neat, well-arranged work." And whereas a home wife had to please her family, an office wife had to please her boss (Faunce and Nichols 10). As the 1935 *Fortune* article makes clear, secretaries were expected to take on domestic chores such as his personal shopping ("Women in Business II" 55).

Already her boss's helpmeet, the office wife could hope, if the boss were unmarried, to become his actual wife. "How fast can a good secretary become a good wife? *I'll show you*," an ad for Pillsbury flour proclaims. *Literary Digest* ran "Making Miss Office Wife into Mrs. Home Wife," humorously urging young men to choose a secretary before choosing a wife, with the plan of ultimately marrying her. Competition for the "husband's" attention was common, with magazines often alluding to adultery. Noting that a secretary was privy to "important business secrets of which even his wife must often remain ignorant," one article advises enlisting the wife's "understanding cooperation" to avoid suspicion (Harrington 57). *Ladies' Home Journal* asked in a 1938 opinion poll, "Do you think an attractive secretary is a threat to her husband's married happiness?" Fifty-nine percent of respondents said no, whereas forty-one said yes ("What Do the Women of America Think" 40).

## Faith Baldwin's *The Office Wife*

Although the office wife appeared in various forms of popular media, notably magazines, Faith Baldwin's 1929 novel, along with the film made a year later, stands out as the iconic early representation. Baldwin (1893–1978) was a popular novelist who wrote more than eighty-five books, mostly romance novels, intended for "the housewife and working girl" ("Faith Baldwin"). Enormously popular in her heyday, she earned over $300,000 in 1936—the equivalent of over $5 million today, even though it was the height of the Great Depression—thanks to publication of five new novels and four earlier ones being made into movies that year. According to her *New York Times* obituary, "She always wrote about people who had money, good breeding, and high morals" ("Faith Baldwin, Author").

The book *The Office Wife* centres on a young secretary, Anne Murdock, who works for a publishing company headed by Larry Fellowes. When Larry's regular secretary— in love with him but hopelessly over the hill at forty—becomes ill, Anne fills in, impressing him with her skill and charm: "Somehow the whole room seemed to settle into a becoming and suitable background for the small girl with red-gold hair and the pointed, ardent face, whose crossed legs and short skirt revealed silken delightful knees" (20). When he asks her to work with him that evening, Anne is thrilled: "To work with The Chief ... and to work with him through the quiet evening hours, the office hum silent, the lamplight shining on the big desk, shut in with beauty, beauty reflected in the panel walls, beauty in the drawn draperies and the opening roses—" (21).

Although Anne has been dating an underling, Ted O'Hara, she begins to see him as dull and immature compared to Larry. Discussing the future, Anne and Ted argue:

"If you'd marry me—I swear, Anne, with you beside me I'd get to the top."

"But—I want to get to the top—myself!" (38).

Scoffing at this remark, he says she'll "get no further," as a woman: "Anne—you were made for love—for marriage—for your own man—a home—for babies. You weren't made to waste yourself in an office.... Marry me, and be a woman and not a machine" (39). As the voice of convention, Ted cannot believe that a woman would turn down a marriage proposal to pursue her own goals—the two being mutually exclusive. Anne, meanwhile, is a modern young woman who sees her future differently, particularly once she is hired as Larry's permanent secretary.

Of course, Larry is married, and he assumes she will marry Ted. Despite growing attraction, the two remain chaste, but when Larry invites Anne to join him and his wife, Linda, at a resort where they are vacationing—ostensibly to take dictation and type letters—Anne learns Linda is involved with another man. Loyal to her boss, Anne's first reaction is shock: "What on earth could Linda see in this man? Linda, who is married to Lawrence Fellowes?" (126-127). Reluctantly, Anne agrees to marry Ted, vowing to be a "good wife" (238). Then Linda confesses and asks Larry for a divorce. When Linda learns that Anne has broken her engagement, she urges Larry to pursue her. The book ends happily, with Anne and Larry engaged to be married.

The film version closely follows the book, but introduces a minor character—an author named Kate who proposes a book on the phenomenon of the office wife. Dressed in a suit, bowtie, and fedora and smoking a cigar, Kate toggles between male and female perspectives, wisely able to understand both. "The modern business-man's secretary is closer than his wife, yet not his wife," she tells an incredulous Larry early in the film. Later, the camera moves close enough to show a page from her manuscript: "Give her six months at the side of any absorbed businessman and the office wife's efficient sympathy has reduced the influence of the wife at home to that of a mere maker of beds and pancakes."

What sets *The Office Wife* (both book and film) apart from contemporary representations is its acceptance of office romance, even when it leads to divorce—then legally complicated and often scandalous—rather than reinforcing conventional moral choices. In her foreword, Baldwin writes that "this business of the office wife is a distinctly modern problem," which came about when work outside the home made women worldlier than previous generations. Unlike their grandmothers—content "to sit waiting for some man to come along and, in return for certain approved services, support them for life"— and their mothers, happy to find an "eligible" man, modern girls "measure the men they meet by the yardstick of the man who has already arrived"—their bosses. "And the unfortunate part," Baldwin continues, "is that men who are already successful and powerful are generally men who have married in their youth." Discontented, "the young business woman of today" is a "misfit" who becomes "for good or for evil, 'the office wife'" (x-xi).

Baldwin's work stands out in the frankness with which it negotiates the supposed tension between romantic love and work, and the way it views divorce and even adultery. Had the film been made later, the ending might have been changed. The Hays Code—ratified by the Board of Directors of Motion Picture Producers and Distributors of America in March 1930 but not fully enforced for several years—was aimed at maintaining "social and community values" ("Motion Picture" 1). It singled out adultery as "sometimes necessary plot material" that should not be "justified or presented attractively" ("Motion Picture" 3). Although Anne and Larry do not have sex, their relationship is forged through the veiled adultery of her office wife role. Moreover, they could not have gotten together without Linda's affair liberating them. In this way, adultery—both veiled and actual— and divorce lead to a happy ending for all characters. Nevertheless, both the book and movie reinforce the notion that paid employment and marriage were mutually exclusive for a woman. When Anne assumes that she will continue as Larry's secretary after their honeymoon, he forbids it. Despite her earlier declaration to Ted that she wants to "get to the top" herself, she accepts Larry's decision. Baldwin's work, in the end, reinforces the assumption of the era that a woman should quit her job when she marries.

Overall, early-twentieth-century media representations that construct secretaries as office wives reinforce traditional gender roles by putting women into a domestic discourse. During the period when increasing numbers of women were entering the workforce, this served to allay anxieties over women's paid employment. Moreover, at a time when unmarried couples living together was unthinkable, the office wife trope made the long hours that a woman often spent alone with her male boss morally legitimate in the public imaginary. Yet the office wife also constructed women with jobs as "other women"—a threat to the home wife. The only way out of the conundrum was to quit her job and let a husband support her.

## The Office Wife at Mid-Century

The 1920s and 1930s were the heyday for the "office wife." However, the trope lingered in magazines, which continued to run occasional stories about the supposed phenomenon, sometimes subverting it. "Office Baby," a short story from *Ladies' Home Journal* in 1940, teases readers into thinking the protagonist is giving birth to her married boss's child. It turns out that she is a wife whose income is needed at home. The plot takes an unexpected feminist turn when the boss's wife threatens to leave him if he goes through with plans to fire her for being pregnant—upending the assumption that wives are jealous of secretaries (Farrar 43). *American Magazine*'s "My Office Wife" from 1946 offers a twist, too. "Unlike most husbands, I don't have to tell the little woman what a hard day I've had at the office. She knows. She is my secretary," begins this piece by Alvin E. O'Konski, U.S. representative from Wisconsin (49). Having his wife serve as his secretary, O'Konski believes "has made us successful as partners in marriage" (49). Moreover, no one suspects adultery. As a constituent tells him, "we know that if you're holding a girl on your lap in that fine office in Washington, the girl is your wife" (88).

However, other stories from the 1940s still treat office wives as a threat to marriage. In 1949, *Coronet* ran "My Husband Had an Office Wife" by an anonymous wife jealous of her husband's secretary. "Ellen" is not the "glamourous, contriving female" found in film but a "well-meaning, conscientious secretary who, deprived of a home and husband of her own, transfers her affections, energies, and allegiance to her employer" (118). Yet when Ellen helps him choose fabric for a new suit, the wife confronts her over lunch. Recognizing that Ellen has "a shrewd mind" and "because survival in business in difficult is for a woman, she had used every means to secure economic security"

(119), she deems herself superior because she is younger, prettier, and able to cook and make her own clothes. She tries to set Ellen up with a bachelor friend, but Ellen has no interest in him. Eventually, she forces the secretary to resign and move to a new city. Later, she is happy to learn that Ellen, though "a tired, pinched woman of middle age," has married. Although she never suspects an affair, she warns that office wives are not just found in Hollywood scripts but are "a live and dangerous reality" (122). The story reinforces multiple assumptions about gender roles, privileging marriage as the proper sphere for women and deeming unmarried office wives—even innocent ones—as "the other woman."

In addition to magazines, the office wife appeared on radio. Catherine Martin argues that like Margo Lane of the 1930s radio drama *The Shadow*, post-World War II characters such as Effie Perine of *The Adventures of Sam Spade* and Claire Brooks of *Let George Do It* provided "a model of femininity that downplays the transgressive nature of her employment" (17). Office wives were acceptable radio characters because, like their magazine counterparts, they "straddled the line between professionalism and domesticity" while making it "clear that wedded bliss—preferably with their employer—was their ultimate goal" (17).

Martin says the term "office wife" fell into disuse on radio by the 1950s (16). The few examples that appear in magazines during this decade suggest the term had become outdated—even a joke. In 1951, the *Saturday Evening Post*—the same magazine that had claimed twenty years earlier that a man "chooses his secretary much as he chooses his wife, and for much the same reasons" (Ragan 11)—ran "Does Ex-Office Wife Share Man's Woes, or Just Laugh?" In the brief editorial, the *Post* notes columnist Dorothy Dix's response to a reader who asked if working before marriage makes a woman a better wife. Dix, then ninety but still publishing columns (Allured and Gentry 211), said office work helped a woman understand "how terrific is the strain of life upon men, how killing is the pressure under which they work" ("Does Ex-Office Wife"). *Post* editors asked a secretary to comment. She "laughed for twenty minutes" at the old-fashioned idea ("Does Ex-Office Wife"). The office wife had apparently become, by 1951, a cliché.

By 1959, Baldwin also saw that the old office wife trope had changed. Her story, "Office Wife, Jr.," from *Good Housekeeping*, tells of

"Amy," a young stenographer for a "big firm." The daughter of a former "office wife," Amy knows to wear an "attractive, but not revealing dark-hued workaday dress," "no perfume, but a faint whiff of toilet water," to "pay attention to posture" and that good secretaries "keep their voices low" (Baldwin, "Office Wife, Jr." 270). Determined to marry her boss, she also knows what to do: "You pick your man, you grow to know him as you know your own hand, you discover his strength and his weakness, and you make yourself indispensable" (273). But unlike Anne Murdock, Amy is crushed when her boss marries a debutante. Remembering that her mother married not the vice president she worked for but her father, a warehouse worker who went on to manage it, she determines to stay at her desk and do her job for its own sake, hoping a man comes in an "unseen future" (274).

By the 1960s, the term "office wife" seems to have gone into remission, although the concept never fully disappeared from media representation. Della Street on the *Perry Mason* television series can be seen as an office wife—unsurprising since the show was based on novels written by Erle Stanley Gardner in the 1930s. In a 1971 episode of *The Beverly Hillbillies* titled "Elly the Working Girl," Granny—who remembers seeing Baldwin's *The Office Wife* in the theater as a young woman—dresses Elly in 1920s "flapper" clothes and teaches her to "wiggle walk" so she will "catch a fella" in her new job as a secretary. But like the 1951 *Saturday Evening Post* critique of Dorothy Dix, the joke is on Granny's outdated idea. Media interest in the office wife as a man's secretary seems to have come to an end.

### *The Mary Tyler Moore Show* and Beyond

Premiering in the wake of the women's liberation movement of the late 1960s and 1970s, *The Mary Tyler Moore Show* occupies a critical position in its representation of paid labour and marriage. As Bonnie Dow notes, it was "not the first working-woman sitcom" but "the first to assert that work was not just a prelude to marriage" (24). No "office debutante," protagonist Mary Richards rejects marriage to pursue an independent life in TV news. Yet as Dow says, the show situates Mary in a family discourse. Noting that she is at times a mother, wife, and daughter not only to her boss, Lou Grant, but to others in the office, she says "these roles are not always distinct" (40). Todd Gitlin sees her as more of a daughter to Lou, who acts as a "gruff, sentimental father" (215). Although Susan Douglas notes that Mary calls Lou "Mr. Grant" and is often seen typing (205), there is no sexual tension between them. Nevertheless, the family trope parallels earlier representations, for just as the media construction of secretary as "office wife" served to alleviate fears about women's employment earlier, so does Mary's "family" role in the 1970s. As Dow writes, "The sitcom's reliance on a family paradigm ... is a comforting vision of *adjustment* without *change*" (44). By "slotting" a career woman into the familiar structure of a family, "the feminist challenge posed by Mary Richards is contained and made less threatening"; her "niceness" is a contrast to news media representation of feminists as "angry, militant, and aggressive" (45). The role has shifted, but it has not gone away.

Noah's contention that the office marriage on *The Mary Tyler Moore Show* was between Mary and Murray Slaughter is intriguing. As her equal rather than her boss, Murray is unlike office husbands such as Larry Fellowes in *The Office Wife*, in which patriarchal power and female submission are sexualized. In contrast, Murray sits beside Mary, where they often confide as equals. And unlike the serious Larry Fellowes or even the gruff Lou Grant, Murray is affable. That Noah would see Mary and Murray as an office couple may signal a shift in thinking about the nature of office relationships in the 1970s—bridging the old office wife representations about male bosses and secretaries with ones in which men and women have relatively more job equality. Although secretarial work is still female dominated, it is not secretaries who are the work wives of later media representations, nor is the goal actual marriage.

Noah draws on Owen's 1987 *Atlantic Monthly* article, which has a provocative tone similar to "Making Miss Office Wife into Mrs. Home Wife" from 1930. Like both earlier and later representations, it purports to analyze office marriage as a recently discovered social phenomenon. Like articles in *Fortune* ("Women in Business II") and *Saturday Evening Post* (Ragan) from the 1930s, it is male centred: "Work marriage is a relationship that exists between certain people of the opposite sex who work at the same place. For example, let's suppose that you, like me, are a man" (Owen 22). Continuing with a list that resembles the duties common to both the office wife and home wife from the 1939 secretarial manual (Faunce and Nichols), Owen asserts that the reader's work wife is the woman in the office who "(a) as you walk past her desk on your way to a big meeting, tells you that you have dried shaving cream behind your ear; (b) has lunch with you pretty often; (c) returns stuff she borrows from your desk; (d) tells you things about her other (home) husband that he wouldn't want you to know." The list continues with items such as "complains to you without embarrassment about an uncomfortable undergarment" and "doesn't comment on how much you eat, drink, and smoke" (22). Owen says work marriage is "better than home marriage" because a work wife would never "grab hold of your stomach and ask, 'What's this? Blubber?'" (22). As described here, the workplace environment is one where men and women appear to have more structural equality than they did in the earlier era—a shift that makes sense, since the women's movement brought more varied job opportunities to women. Yet with its focus on male needs, it reinforces notions of workplace hierarchy, making women once again the wives in a male-centred family trope.

Women's magazines also ran stories on office marriage. In 1991, *Mademoiselle* ran "Everything But Sex" by *New York Times* columnist Maureen Dowd. "Once it was a meeting of bodies, now it's a meeting of minds," the teaser claims. Citing a University of Michigan study claiming that "nonsexual love relationships" in the office were "common," with 22 percent of managers claiming involvement in one, Dowd claims that "not all relationships between men and women end up in bed" but are "friendships with intense feelings of loyalty and trust," enhancing performance by "couples" (121).

Dowd's story ran with a sidebar, "My Life as an Office Wife," by a woman who claims that her "office boyfriend" made Monday morning exciting (Farbar 123). Although "he had a succession of girlfriends and I had a similar parade of men march through my life," nothing equaled the chemistry between them (123). Even after leaving the job, he is still the one she turned to for reassurance that she is a "talented, terrific woman" (181). What is intriguing about this story is that although Farbar does not use the term "office wife" or any of its variations in the story, *Mademoiselle* editors use it in the headline.

"The Other Woman in His Life," from *Redbook's* December 1998 issue, is a first-person account by a wife who is jealous of her physician husband's office wife (Davis). In what seems an updated version of the

1949 *Coronet* story, this wife views the work relationship as a threat, although there is no hint of sex when "Michelle" calls their house on a Sunday to discuss a medical case. She interviews a psychologist, Dr. Bringle, who advises her that the women in the office are "more a part of your husband's life than you are" and that she needs to communicate her needs (78). The rest of the story recounts other wives with similar stories, advising readers on how to "get him back" and "edge her out" (82). The focus is on women's looks, calling one "perky" (81), with little mention of career aspirations—either the wife's or the office wife's.

## Return of the Office Marriage

Articles about the office marriage returned in force after the turn of the twenty-first century. Like those from the 1930s and Owen's 1987 article, several emphasize a social phenomenon that is presented as brand new. What seems to have set off this revival is then-National Security Adviser Condoleezza Rice's apparent slip in 2004, in which she referred to President George W. Bush as "my husb..." at a Washington D.C. dinner party (Kipnis; Harris). Although she never publicly explained the remark, gossip followed about Bush and Rice, and the phenomenon of workplace marriage began to be reported more frequently.

In 2005, Dowd—author of the *Mademoiselle* spread from fourteen years earlier—wrote that she hoped Bush "doesn't have any more work wives tucked away in the White House." The president, she said, was in the habit of giving jobs to "supremely powerful" women "not qualified to get them." Although the latest was Supreme Court nominee Harriet Miers, a "stolid Texan called 'Harry'" and a "bachelorette," Dowd listed others, including Rice, whom she also called a "bachelorette," and speechwriter Karen Hughes, a "cheerleader." Such women, Dowd claims, were "self-sacrificing, buttoned-up nannies serving as adoring work wives, catering to W.'s every political, legal and ego-affirming need." Speculating that Bush's need for powerful women was rooted in his relationship with his mother, Dowd writes that "W. loves being surrounded by tough women who steadfastly devote their entire lives to doting on him, like the vestal virgins guarding the sacred fire, serving as custodians for his values and watchdogs for his reputation" (Dowd, "All the President's Women").

Chock-full of sexist stereotypes, Dowd's column dismisses women's qualifications, including that of Rice, a former Stanford University professor who became the first Black woman to serve as secretary of state (Condoleezza Rice). Instead, she focuses on sex, although rather than speculating on adultery, she desexualizes them as "buttoned-up nannies."

That same year, *Gentleman's Quarterly* advised all men to get a work wife. Using the term interchangeably with office wives, Tom Prince claims in his article to have three—distinguishing them from love interests but joking about adultery. He writes the following: "For the record, let's stipulate that the other women in a man's life are great. His wife is great, his girlfriend is great, and—if he has one of each— well, they're both great." A work wife is different, he says— "a fellow corporate soldier to share the smirks, the laughs, the deep, plaintive groans of incredulity, and the rare moments of self-awareness." She is "the other woman your wife might just let you keep" because she is "nonthreatening in age, looks, or ass size." Alluding to Rice's "my husb..." remark, she is not a threat because she is "like Marcie to George W.'s Peppermint Patty." Making degrading remarks about other women in the Bush White House, he notes that given her looks, Hughes would "never be mistaken" for Monica Lewinsky.

In a similar tone, John Intini begins his 2006 article from *MacLean's* with innuendo:

> It starts innocently enough. Usually with coffee. Then the occasional lunch, during which you share a few laughs and a bit of gossip. Before you know it, you're shooting cellphone text messages back and forth to one another during meetings and childishly mocking the grease stain on the back of the company hotshot's pants in a secret code only the two of you understand. Sound familiar? Then you probably have an "office wife."

Once the term for "old-fashioned secretaries," Intini writes, "office wife" now has "a new far richer meaning" since the "office wife (or 'work husband')" is "an equal." He quotes "Dave," who wants to remain anonymous, as saying, "It's a professional affair without the sex. ... Does it have to be with someone of the opposite sex? I think so. Is it sexual? I don't know."

Although Intini's language is gender neutral in that he uses "work husband" and "work spouse" interchangeably with "office wife," he interviews only men, emphasizing benefits to men with one or more wives. And like the articles from a century before, Intini alludes to the potential for adultery, as he interviews a marriage counsellor who advises making the relationship a "threesome" by including the real spouse socially. Costs or benefits to women, both real and imagined, are not discussed, and women's perspectives are never included. Just as Noah credits Owen with being the first to notice this social phenomenon, Intini credits Prince.

In a rare article centring on men and women both, Sue Shellenbarger asks whether office spouses should get a Valentine. Her light feature lacks the degrading remarks about women found in Dowd's and the male-centered perspective found in Owen's, Prince's, and Intini's. Yet she uses veiled allusions to adultery to make the article provocative: "For Valentine's Day on Monday, Amy McMahon will be celebrating twice. She's preparing a romantic candlelight dinner for her longtime boyfriend and giving him a gift card from his favorite fitness website. That same day, Ms. McMahon will be giving her 'work husband' some small heart-shaped cakes and a sentimental card." Defining "office spouse" as "a term for co-workers with close relationships," Shellenbarger says it is "uncharted territory" for Valentine's Day but one that those like McMahon celebrate "to acknowledge their bond." In her interviews, Shellenbarger focuses on "spouse-like" activities, such as shopping for work clothes—apparently no longer the problem it was for the wife writing in *Coronet* in the 1940s. To inoculate against the adultery threat, she interviews an associate professor of psychiatry at Harvard Medical School, who cautions that a Valentine could be "taken the wrong way" by a real spouse, as well as the founder of a California group, Beyond Affairs Network, who cautions against "emotional affairs" that have not "yet" become sexual. Neither acknowledges that "office marriage" is a real phenomenon. Having raised the issue of adultery, she deflects it and emphasizes that if the work spouse relationships are open, regular partners do not mind. One husband interviewed said he "appreciates" his wife's work husband for the support he gives her in the office.

Mental health professionals interviewed often reinforce gender roles. In a *Today Show* segment from 2006, NBC's Matt Lauer asks a psychologist why men and women form couples at work—beginning with the assumption that they do. The answer in this short interview is a gender stereotype—because women are "emotional" and men want "nothing to do with emotion" ("Do You Have"). Some stories even advise cutting off relationships without discussing the effect this might have on women's ability to network or the work itself. In 2011, *CBS New Moneywatch* ran "Office Wife? Time to End the Workplace Relationship" (Lipton), warning that much harm can come from male-female friendships at work. Although the show acknowledges that "a light-hearted workplace union" can be beneficial, arguments between members of the "couple" could be disruptive and "a whiff of an affair"—even when there is not one—could ruin reputations.

Similarly, the popular medical advice website *WebMD* offers a cautionary article, advising readers how to keep work relationships from developing into affairs (Hatfield). Defining "office spouse" as "the new relationship phenomenon that's developed as Americans work longer, harder, and in closer proximity with colleagues of the opposite sex," the article warns that "you do work closely with someone of the opposite sex all day long, Monday through Friday, in many cases upwards of 60, 70, or even 80 hours a week" (Hatfield). Focusing on the ever-present danger of an affair, the psychologist interviewed notes, "I'm not opposed to males and females working together.... But it's a thin line between an office spouse and an affair." To avoid an affair, men and women should not share personal information, carpool, have lunch, or drink together (Hatfield). This solution—embraced by U.S. Vice President Mike Pence—damages women's professional networking opportunities (Khazan), an economic burden that *WebMD* does not mention.

Despite the warnings, some magazines have continued to run stories on the benefits of a work wife, particularly for men. In 2013, *Gentleman's Quarterly* ran "How to Score an Office Wife" (Stephenson). "My first office marriage came naturally, almost effortlessly. There was never any formal proposal. No exchange of rings. But at a certain point, it became clear I had a work wife," Seth Stephenson begins (120). When that ended, "I surveyed my options: the high-powered execs, the lowly assistants, the randos who sit over by the printer station whose jobs are still not entirely clear to me," even considering a male "work wife"— "the hulking mailroom guy with the forearm tattoos and graying ponytail" (120). He advises men wanting a work wife that one partner should be married in real life, for "remember that the prime directive of the work marriage is to bolster stability and comfort in the workplace. Not to introduce chaos" (120). The other should be "actively single," since dating is fun to talk about. Finally, he advises "never marry down (on the org chart)" because power relations make it hard to "bitch" honestly—"A work marriage is most likely to thrive when it is a partnership of equals" (12). Stephenson's quip about the "hulking mailroom guy" is a rare reference to homosexual "work marriages." Krieger's 2015 article acknowledges the possibility, as does a brief 2016 story in *Glamour* describing two female friends who started a successful e-mail newsletter together. Yet it's not clear whether they call themselves work wives or if that's writer Wendy Naugle's spin on their partnership.

## Social Phenomenon or Media Construction?

It is difficult to know if the marriage metaphor would exist as a way to discuss workplace relationships if it had not been a recurring staple of media representation for almost a century. As Hall says, media representation does not simply mirror an event. Rather, it constructs it, making the relationship between media and culture co-constitutive (1-3). Although some people claim to have an office wife or work marriage, would marriage as a metaphor for work relationships occur to anyone if it were not periodically being rediscovered as a new trend and "reported" in the media? What if the question were about male-female colleagues, friendships, or, in a variation on the family trope, office siblings? Whatever the answer, the trope is known primarily through media, which present it in various eras as an endlessly new social phenomenon.

Like office wife depictions from the past, early twenty-first century representations focus on the wife, positioning first secretaries and then professional women as subservient to men. No magazine stories focus on how a woman can find a work husband or what one would do. In stories aimed at men, women are to be "scored" (Stephenson 120) and are objectified as "nonthreatening" in "ass size" (Prince). Although actual adultery is not the focus, almost all allude to it so that it seems like an actual threat.

The underlying message in these portrayals is that all women in the workplace are potentially "other women" even if no actual affair occurs. As Laura A. Rosenbury contends in the *Harvard Journal of Law and Gender,* the persistence of the work wife trope has real legal and economic implications for women, since "the marriage metaphor ... keeps gender front and center at work despite legal changes designed to cleanse the workplace of oppressive gender roles" (348). Moreover, the tenacity of traditional gender roles is important: "Some portrayals of work wives may continue to reinforce gender hierarchy by portraying women providing traditionally gendered care from positions of subordination" (404). Although she claims that others "may ultimately permit more individuals to reimagine the roles of both men and women within families and workplaces" (404), the work wife, like the earlier office wife, may be a new misfit, reinforcing traditional family roles.

Yet change is possible. Although the impact of *Obergefell v. Hodges,* the legalization of gay marriage in the U.S., and the #MeToo and #TimesUp movements remain to be seen, at least one magazine writer offered hope in 2018. "In the #MeToo era, when the power of women-led whisper networks roars to life, female work relationships feel more important than ever," writes Julia Carpenter, suggesting the work wife and its synonyms are a thing of the past.

Time will tell.

## Works Cited

Allured, Janet and Judith F. Gentry, editors. *Louisiana Women: Their Lives and Times/Dorothy Dix.* University of Georgia Press, 2009.

Baldwin, Faith. *The Office Wife.* Triangle Books, 1929.

Baldwin, Faith. "Office Wife, Jr." *Good Housekeeping* October 1959, pp. 80-81 and 270-275.

Carpenter, Julia. "The Evolution of the Office 'Work Wife." *CNN* 8 Mar. 2018, www.money.cnn.com/2018/03/08/pf/women-work-wives/index.html. Accessed 22 May 2019.

"Condoleezza Rice." *Biography,* 2019, www.biography.com/people/condoleezza-rice-9456857. Accessed 22 May 2019.

Davies, Margery. *Woman's Place is at the Typewriter.* Temple University Press, 1982.

Davis, Miranda. "The Other Woman in His Life." *Redbook*, December 1998, pp. 78 and 81-82. Print. "Do You Have an Office Spouse?" *Today*, NBC-TV. 23 June 2006.

"Does Ex-Office Wife Share Man's Woes, or Just Laugh?" *Saturday Evening Post*, 14 July 1951, pp. 10 and 12.

Douglas, Susan J. *Where the Girls Are: Growing Up Female with the Mass Media*. Three Rivers Press, 1994.

Dow, Bonnie. *Prime-Time Feminism: Television, Media Culture, and the Women's Movement Since 1970*. University of Pennsylvania Press, 1996.

Dowd, Maureen. "All the President's Women." *New York Times*. 5 Oct. 2005, query.nytimes.com/gst/fullpage.html?res=990CE6D81130 F936A35753C1A9639C8B63. Accessed 22 May 2019.

Dowd, Maureen. "Everything But Sex." *Mademoiselle*, Feb.1991, pp. 121-23.

"Faith Baldwin." *Encyclopedia Britannica*, 2019, www.britannica.com/ biography/Faith-Baldwin. Accessed 22 May 2019.

"Faith Baldwin, Author of 85 Books and Many Stories, Is Dead at 84." *New York Times*. 19 March 1978, p. 38.

Farbar, Jennifer. "My Life as an Office Wife." *Mademoiselle,* February 1991, 123 and 181.

Farrar, Rowena. "Office Baby." *Ladies' Home Journal,* September 1940, 42-47.

Faunce, Frances Avery, and Frederick G. Nichols. *Secretarial Efficiency*. McGraw-Hill, 1939.

Gilman, Charlotte Perkins. *Women and Economics: A Study of the Economic Relation between Men and Women as a Factor in Social Evolution* (1898), www.digital.library.upenn.edu/women/gilman/economics/ economics.html. Accessed 22 May 2019.

Gitlin, Todd. *Inside Prime Time*. University of California Press, 1994.

Hall, Stuart. *Representation: Cultural Representation and Signifying Practices*. Sage, 1997.

Harrington, Mildred. "Too Much Dictation." *The American Magazine,* September 1930, p. 57.

Harris, Paul. "How Condoleezza Rice Became the Most Powerful Woman in the World." *The Guardian,* 15 Jan.200, www.theguardian.com/world/2005/jan/16/usa.paulharrisl. Accessed 22 May 2019.

Hatfield, Heather. "The Office Spouse: Rules of Engagement." *WebMD,* 2019, www.webmd.com/sex-relationships/features/the-office-spouse-rules-of-engagement#1. Accessed 22 May 2019.

Intini, John. "She's My Office Wife," *MacLean's,* 2006, archive.macleans.ca/article/2006/1/23/shes-my-office-wife. Accessed 22 May 2019.

Kessler-Harris, Alice. *Out to Work: A History of Wage-Earning Women in the United States.* Oxford University Press, 1982.

Khazan, Olga. "How Pence's Dudely Dinners Hurt Women." *The Atlantic* 30 Mar. 2017, www.theatlantic.com/science/archive/2017/03/pences-gender-segregated-dinners/521286/. Accessed 22 May 2019.

Kipnis, Laura. "Condi's Inner Life—What Freudian Slips Do—or Don't—Tell Us About Politicians." *Slate* 26 Apr. 2004, www.slate.com/articles/arts/culturebox/2004/04/condis_inner_life.html. Accessed 22 May 2019.

Kittler, Friedrich A. *Gramophone, Film, Typewriter.* Translated by Geoffrey Winthrop-Young and Michael Wutz. Stanford University Press, 1999.

Krieger, Liz. "Why You Need a Work Wife." *New York Magazine,* 12 Nov. 2015, nymag.com/thecut/2015/11/why-you-need-a-work-wife.html. Accessed 22 May 2019.

Lipton, Lauren. "Office Wife? Time to End the Workplace Relationship." *CBS News Moneywatch,* 31 Mar. 2011. www.cbsnews.com/news/office-wife-time-to-end-the-workplace-relationship/. Accessed 22 May 2019.

"Making Miss Office Wife into Mrs. Home Wife." *Literary Digest.* 6 Dec.1930, pp. 34-40.

Marcellus, Jane. *Business Girls and Two-Job Wives: Emerging Media Stereotypes of Employed Women.* Hampton Press, 2011.

Martin, Catherine. "Adventure's Fun, but Wouldn't You Rather Get Married?: Gender Roles and the Office Wife in Radio Detective Dramas." *The Velvet Light Trap,* Sept. 2014, pp. 16-26, *Research Gate,*

www.researchgate.net/publication/301701082_Adventure's_Fun_
but_Wouldn't_You_Rather_Get_Married_Gender_Roles_and_
the_Office_Wife_in_Radio_Detective_Dramas. Accessed 22 May
2019.

Motion Picture Production Code. 31 Mar. 1930, www.asu.edu/courses/
fms200s/total-readings/MotionPictureProductionCode.pdf.
Accessed 22 May 2019.

"My Husband Had an Office Wife." *Coronet*. March 1949, pp. 118-122.

Naugle, Wendy. "Why Everyone Needs a Work Wife." *Glamour*, May
2016, p. 138.

Noah, Timothy. "Prexy Sks Wrk Wf." *Slate*, 17 Nov. 2004, www.
primary.slate.com/articles/news_and_politics/chatterbox/2004/11/
prexy_sks_wrk_wf.html. Accessed 22 May 2019.

O'Konski, Alvin Edward. "My Office Wife." *American Magazine*, July
1946, p. 49.

"Office Wife." *Oxford English Dictionary*. 3rd ed. Oxford, 2004.

Owen, David. "Work Marriage." *David Owen*, 1987, www.davidowen.
net/files/work-marriage-2-1987.pdf

*Perry Mason*. Prod. Gail Patrick Johnson. CBS. 1957.

Pillsbury Flour ad, *Ladies Home Journal*, March 1934, p. 106.

Prince, Tom. "Do You Have an Office Wife?" *Gentleman's Quarterly*, 14
Feb. 2005, www.gq.com/story/office-wife. Accessed 22 May 2019.

Ragan, Elizabeth Hilliard. "One Secretary as Per Specifications."
*Saturday Evening Post*. 12 Dec. 1931, p. 11.

Rayne, Mrs. M. L. *What Can a Woman Do? Or Her Position in the Business
and Literary World*. 1898. Arno Press, 1974.

Rayner, Olive Pratt (Pseudonym of Allen Grant). *The Type-Writer Girl*.
Arthur Pearson Ltd., 1897.

Rosenbury, Laura A. "Work Wife." *Harvard Journal of Law and Gender*,
vol. 36, 2013, pp. 345-404.

Royal Typewriter ad. *The American Magazine*. July 1928, p. 103.

Shellenbarger, Sue. "Does Your Work Wife Get a Valentine?" *Wall
Street Journal*, 9 Feb. 2011, www.wsj.com/articles/SB100014240527
48704364004576132132977327262. Accessed 22 May 2019.

Stephenson, Seth. "How to Score an Office Wife." *Gentleman's Quarterly* March 2013, p. 120.

*The Beverly Hillbillies.* Prod. Paul Henning and Al Simon. CBS. 1962.

*The Mary Tyler Moore Show.* Prod. James L. Brooks and Allan Burns. CBS. 1970.

*The Office Wife.* Dir. Lloyd Bacon. Warner Bros., 1930.

"What Do the Women of America Think About Office Wives?" *Ladies' Home Journal* March 1940, p. 40.

Willard, Frances. *Occupations for Women: A Book of Practical Suggestions, for the Material Advancement, the Mental and Physical Development, and the Moral and Spiritual Uplift of Women.* 1897, www.archive.org/details/occupationsforwo00will. Accessed 22 May 2019.

"Women in Business II." *Fortune.* August 1935, p. 55.

"Work Spouse Memes." *Memes*, me.me/t/work-spouse. Accessed 22 May 2019.

Chapter Four

# Abused Wives and Divorce Mediation in Ontario: The Perspectives of Thunder Bay's Mediators

Robyn Pepin

In September 2011, mediation was introduced in Ontario's divorce process for common law or married couples seeking a divorce. Mediation is defined as "the intervention in a negotiation or a conflict of an acceptable third party who has limited or no authoritative decision-making power, but who assists the involved parties in voluntarily reaching a mutually acceptable settlement of issues in dispute" (Smith 853-54). Many legislators in the Ontario government believe that mediation is appropriate in the divorce process. However, many feminists, lawyers, academics, and numerous professionals acknowledge that mediation may be harmful for wives and their children who are, or were, in abusive homes (Rosnes 36; Chewter 99). In order to understand the Ontario court system and the current amendments that have been made to the Family Law Rules under the Ontario Courts of Justice Act, the implementation of family law in Ontario needs to be analyzed. Understanding the mediation process matters because there are many families for whom abuse occurs, but it is hidden. If abused wives can seek a divorce, then divorce mediation may be a route they are directed to take. Thus, this chapter may be helpful for people who know and counsel abused wives.

In this chapter, mediation is defined and critiqued in the context of the history and implementation of Canada's Divorce Act as well as the history of wife abuse in Canada. Political issues in Ontario are also discussed. I conducted interviews with seven mediators in Thunder Bay, Ontario, about the potential implementation of the Mandatory Information Program sessions and about how mediation potentially affects abused wives and their children. The following is a synopsis of the key research findings. I argue that it is important to analyze and critique the shift to include mediation in the Ontario family law system because abused wives who are divorcing do not hold the same amount of power as their abuser. These flaws need to be revealed because they impact the way abused wives may be treated and the way mediation may be practiced in Ontario. If the Family Law Rules are not consistent, how are mediators supposed to be?

## Methodology and Methods

I used a qualitative feminist approach when conducting the interviews to obtain a deeper understanding of the mediation process while I critically analyzed the social consequences of the Family Law Rules for abused wives. As a feminist researcher, I am deeply implicated in this research because my "personal history is part of the process through which 'understanding' and 'conclusions' are reached" (Maynard, 16). My interpretation is by necessity my own, and it can never be neutral because it aims to look critically at the dominant perspective. Positionality is, thus, important.

I chose to conduct semi-structured interviews. Interviewing is a "conversational practice where knowledge is produced through the interaction between an interviewer and an interviewee" (Brinkmann 471). It is short-term interaction between two strangers (or more) with "the explicit purpose of one person obtaining specific information from the other" (Neuman 342). I selected the research participants through convenience sampling. I approached seventeen potential participants in Thunder Bay, Ontario, who were listed on websites that provide direction to those looking for legal assistance or for mediators. Potential participants were approached via mail, which included an introduction to the study. The seven participants interested were interviewed. Three of the participants are lawyer-mediators, one is a legal aid lawyer, one is a private mediator, and two are social workers. Four of the participants are male and three are female. All are white, highly educated, and middle-to-upper-class Canadian citizens. They all have more than ten years of professional work experience outside of their mediator role. The mediation experience among the participants ranged from two to twenty or more years. Formal approval for this research was obtained through Lakehead University's Research Ethics Board.

## Woman Abuse in Canada

Wife abuse[1] has been recognized as a problem in Canada. When leaving an abusive relationship, wives and their children often have difficulty finding and/or staying in a safe space while obtaining assistance and proceeding with divorce because abusers are good at manipulating their spouses, and, thus, a cycle of violence usually recurs (Chewter 120; Krieger 244; Johnston and Ver Steegh 68). For example, during the early stages of separation or divorce, many wives are frightened. Abusers can recognize opportunities to get their partners back by showing remorse and declaring their love for them. Because abuse is recognized as a cycle of recurring events, many believe this time their partners will change. Ultimately, many wives are manipulated and walk back into a home with "a ticking time bomb." These problems can be reinforced, not mitigated, when abused wives are forced to attend an information program, with the potential of agreeing to attend divorce mediation. Thus, if some choose to attend mediation in lieu of court, they have no choice but to sit across from their abusers who then could manipulate them, which continues the cycle of abuse.

Understanding the complexities in domestic violence[2] cases is important. Lenore Walker describes a model of the cycle of violence as having three separate and distinct phases: tension building, when the tension builds until there is an abusive incident; acute battering incident, when a wife is abused and possibly leaves or calls the police; and loving contrition by the abuser, when the batterer is remorseful, apologizes, and may send flowers to his partner and court her (525). The problem with this model is that an abuser may appear remorseful until he has his wife back; at which time, the cycle of abuse most likely continues. This cycle covers up instances of abuse, as the loving contrition phase may make the abused wife believe he cares about her, and any domestic violence charges may then be dropped, only for the cycle to continue again. Kimberley Crossman et al. also describe a coercive control model, in which both physical and violent control mechanisms are used to control one's partner (455). They outline the following tactics to exert power over ex-partners: "physical assault, sexual coercion, intimidation, isolation, or any means to get one's partner to do something they do not want to do" (455). No matter its exact method, domestic violence affects many people. It does not matter what culture, class, race, or religion individuals are from. Poverty creates stress that makes abuse more likely and more common, but any wife, from any social class, ethnic or racial group, can find herself in an abusive situation.

Beyond the issue of the immediate danger faced by wives and children, "there is a link between spousal abuse and an abuser's ability to parent" (Chewter 114). Despite significant evidence of the harm caused to children by violence in the home, many family judges still operate under the assumption that wife abuse is not relevant to parenting. It is believed by many judges that: (1) wife abuse is only between the husband and wife and does not influence the abuser's relations with other intimate family members, including his children; (2) wife abuse is not harmful to children; and (3) wife abuse ends when the relationship breaks down (Chewter 115). All three of these assumptions are false. A man who abuses his wife may dominate, control, and coerce his children rather than be a positive father figure. A spouse who controls the other through "manipulation, violence, threats and verbal or other types of abuse to undermine the mental and physical health of the children's primary caregiver should be acting knowingly contrary to the best interests of the children" (Chewter 116). Research shows that young boys who grow up in homes where their mothers are abused are more likely to become batterers themselves and young girls are also more likely to be abused in their adult relationships (Cherlin and Morrison 801). This reveals that husbands and wives potentially maintain power imbalances in their relationships if they were exposed to abuse as children, informally allowing the cycle of abuse to continue.

## Divorcing Wives and the Legal Framework

These beliefs are evident in Section 16 of the Divorce Act itself, which disregards violence in marriage. Sections 16(9) and 16(10) of the Divorce Act oppress wives (Rosnes 42). Section 16(9) states that: "In making an order under this section, the court shall not take into consideration the past conduct of any person unless the conduct is relevant to the ability of that person to act as a parent of a child." Section 16(10) also states the following: "In making an order under this section, the court shall give effect to the principle that a child of the marriage should have as much contact with each spouse as is consistent with the best interests of the child and, for that purpose, shall take into consideration the willingness of the person for whom custody is sought to facilitate such contact." Together, these sections legitimize male violence. Section 16(9) allows judges to ignore past violence if it is believed to be irrelevant to parenting. Violence is not irrelevant to parenting, but many judges still act as though it is. Additionally, Section 16(10) is extremely problematic because it states that: "The custodial parent must facilitate contact regardless of past conduct (including violence)" (qtd. in Rosnes 42). The fact that wives will have to continue to see their abuser during transfers of children may deter them from leaving abusive relationships. Remaining in an abusive relationship provides the opportunity for abuse to escalate.

Disregarding violence in the home keeps wives and children in abusive situations and relationships. For example, abused wives and children are vulnerable when they do not leave a relationship out of fear (Rosnes 40). To make matters worse, some wives who do seek divorce are strictly advised by their lawyers not to mention abuse in court because it will complicate the case, as it leads to the issue that many judges do not recognize wife abuse. Furthermore, this may be an issue with lawyers because abused wives may not have enough money to pay for their legal bills in the first place, let alone prolong a case and make more work for the lawyer. However, if wives do mention abuse, "historical ideologies of women provoking or being responsible for the violence, or deserving it, are reproduced through legal discourse, and thus women are often blamed for their own oppression" (Rosnes 45). Blaming divorcing wives is problematic; blaming divorcing abused wives is even more troublesome—divorce is no-fault[3], even though the language in the Divorce Act complicates it.

Laws ignoring violence in marriage contradicts the notion that the law protects victims of abuse. The Divorce Act discourages wives from bringing these issues forwards in court, which shows that old attitudes and beliefs that wives are to remain submissive to their husbands are reiterated in law (Rosnes, 60). Abused wives are ultimately trapped by the Canadian legal system, regardless of the route taken. At least these incidents, when reported, are on the public record to be challenged as a social problem. The Mediation Information Program, mandated since 1 September 2011, is an information session in which divorcing wives and husbands are offered the opportunity to attend mediation. Most mediation sessions are private and leave no public record for review or critique.

The Ontario government is attempting to eradicate the high volume of court case backlog through the new mediation legislation. The passage of "Rule 8.1 Mandatory Information Program" in the Courts of Justice Act mandates that all wives claiming support, property and/or custody of children must attend a mediation information session (Lay, slaw.ca). Although the objective of reducing wait times and backlog is laudable, in this context, it becomes important to understand when and how mediation is used and whether mediators have the skills and knowledge necessary to exclude cases of violence from mediation or to protect battered wives during the process of mediation. Alas, mediation as a form of dispute resolution may harm wives and children in abusive relationships.

Mediation in family law gives the impression that courts want to "help separating or divorcing couples ... by [persuading them to] use non-adversarial, private dispute resolution procedures" (Johnston and Ver Steegh 66). But many judges and lawyers believe that high-conflict family law cases should not be mediated but argued in court because "financial issues are inextricably entwined with custody and visitation issues" (Perry et al. 444). Mediation may, in fact, worsen the divorce process for abused wives. The potential inability to afford a lawyer indicates that these women may then be revictimized because they are forced to sit across from their abusers without representation: "The potentially tragic irony is apparent: a woman who has been unable to protect herself from physical assault and abuse ... [may now be persuaded] to engage in face-to-face, honest, direct, open discussion and negotiation with her abuser to reach a 'mutually acceptable agreement'" (Geffner and Pagelow 156). The agreement is not necessarily what the ex-wife is legally entitled to but what is agreed upon outside of court. Abused ex-wives may be provided with fewer resources, and in this instance, it is acceptable. The lack of resources provided to ex-wives can harm their children.

Professionals who are assisting divorcing couples must understand and recognize the consequences of joint custody and mediation in abusive relationships (Geffner and Pagelow 151). In this study, mediators were asked to define domestic abuse; however, no one had a clear definition. Rather, their interpretation of the relationship that was described to them by each mediating party was their indicator of abuse. One mediator noted the following: "Domestic abuse covers such a wide range of things. A lot of people see domestic abuse as just hitting somebody, but it's not; it can be hitting, slapping, spitting, pushing ... it can be verbal abuse, it can be just eye-looking [staring down the other person]." Another participant stated that "quite often, in family situations, there's a power imbalance, and where there's a power imbalance, mediation can cause more harm than good." Participants, thus, appeared to recognize power imbalances prior to mediation if disclosed to them, yet they continued to push forwards with offering their services.

One of the problems that may arise with the continuation of mediation is that children may be at risk of being harmed. Children may also be harmed when they see their mothers suffer further trauma through the events that take place before, during, or after mediation, which affect their ability to parent; the mediation process "may subject an abused [wife] or child to psychologically harmful confrontation with the abuser" (Geffner 156). Even though there is much literature on the negative effects of mediation in high-conflict cases, the mandatory information program highlighted the benefits of mediation and was implemented in Ontario.

All participants disclosed how divorce affects children for the separating parties. One participant advised clients to "leave a legacy to their child" by trying to get parents to work together on the outcome of their separation. This outcome is most likely difficult for abused wives. Another participant noted that "children from a home where domestic violence [takes place] might suffer academically or they might do well. Also, their behaviour might change whereby a child might become quiet or might become aggressive." Recognition of abusive behaviour and its impacts in the family are important; however, it is not beneficial for abused wives and their children to remain in an abusive environment or be required to attend a mediation session across from their abuser.

## The Potential Implementation of Mediation in Family Law

In theory, mediation may appear beneficial for divorcing couples; however, not all divorcing couples can mediate. Wives who choose to separate from their abusive partners can be stuck when applying for divorce. Implementing mandatory information sessions on mediation and attempting to persuade divorcing couples into mediation may make this worse. The information session is mandatory in cases involving children or division of property, so wives are often left in a lose-lose situation: "Sometimes an abused wife is so concerned with the custody of her children that she may not adequately assert her financial and property needs" (Geffner and Pagelow 157). One participant who went ahead with mediating a couple where abuse was present noted the following:

> The parties ... seemed capable of mediation, but [it all] became clear in the second or third session ... the woman was ... not at all ready to ... start her rights or entitlements. ... I would stop and say, "Okay, can you leave us?" and I would talk to her and say, "Look, there's a fine line between a mediator trying to give legal advice ... [trying] to fill that role and also trying to be ... objective."

This participant acknowledged the power imbalance in front of them and tried to assist without crossing ethical boundaries; however, not all mediators would attempt to validate a wife's legal position during a divorce.

If abused wives want to avoid mediation and have little or no access to legal entitlements, they are essentially required to claim a cheaper no-fault divorce. By claiming a no-fault divorce, they cannot request any rights to net family property or the matrimonial home under the Family Law Act or support under the Divorce Act or Family Law Act (Courts of Justice Act, Section 21). If wives do not claim any alimony or money from assets, abusers are not obligated to provide any support. This reveals that even split of matrimonial property becomes, in practice, null and void. No-fault divorce is not an option for wives with children. These women are forced to undergo the mandatory information session and, potentially, may agree to mediation even when there is no property to divide. The mediation process may not be beneficial for abused wives because it ignores the psychological and safety issues they face when they try to remove themselves and their children from abusive relationships.

Although the fact that mediation may be harmful to abused wives has been acknowledged publicly by Ontario Chief Justice Warren Winkler, the Ontario government still chose to implement mediation as part of the judicial process. For example, in 2011, one year prior to the implementation of mediation in Ontario family law, Winkler acknowledged that "every case can't be mediated ... there are some cases that involve spousal abuse" (qtd. in Schmitz, thelawyersweekly.ca). The mandatory information program, nonetheless, was implemented because divorce was thought of as a lengthy time-consuming process that took up provincial judges' time. Without examining the full effects of mediation on abused wives and children, the Family Law Rules were amended (Kauth, canadianlawyermag.ca). This amendment, however, does not acknowledge or facilitate a safe divorce process in the event of an abusive relationship (Krieger 257).

## Mandatory Information Program Session

In Thunder Bay, the mandatory information program sessions are conducted twice a month. One session is held for applicants and the other for respondents. The sessions are conducted by lawyers and mental health professionals, who provide alternatives to litigation in addition to community resources (Pottinger, weilers.ca). The program is "designed to help families understand the effects of separation on children and adults and to discuss the options that are available to help the parties resolve their disputes" (Pottinger, weilers.ca). However, there is no clear understanding if the information provided discusses the potential effects of violence on children.

The content of the family information session can be problematic. Wives who have endured abuse for a long period of time and have young children with their abusers may question why they are proceeding with a divorce. They may question their actions when they hear the effects of divorce on children in the mediation program. Wives may start to question if the abuse was that bad and wonder whether they could live the rest of their lives in an abusive environment for the sake of the children.

Based on the cycle of violence described by Walker, wives are forced to listen to the Ontario government's plea for reconciliation just as their abuser may be in the loving contrition phase. The mandatory information program is considered a plea for reconciliation because the program is based around having a smooth divorce by conducting mediation, yet it teaches parents the effects that divorce can potentially have on their children. This program, thus, contains a hidden curriculum: children will potentially suffer if their parents get a divorce. To advise an audience of individuals that children will suffer because of divorce without knowing the various backgrounds of the attendees is problematic. The mandatory information program is the first step in the divorce process, but the information provided may not speak to violence or abuse witnessed by children or committed against children unless an involved party specifically asked. An abused wife would most likely not feel comfortable asking questions regarding an abusive spouse in public. Thus, the following question needs to be asked: is the attendance of the participants confidential? If not, what happens if the issues discussed publicly become misconstrued and repeated to the ex-spouse? The mandatory information program session must be sensitive to the presence of abused wives. The period between separation and divorce is the most dangerous time for an ex-wife.

In Thunder Bay, the information program sessions are held on different days, which is one of the recommendations provided to keep the divorcing parties separate. There should be safety plans and security personnel on site, before, during, and after the session. The areas where the sessions are conducted "should be held in well lit, public places with easily accessible parking" (Brown 470). Also, attendance lists must be kept confidential so that victims cannot be located.

A confidante should attend the education session with an abused ex-wife. The confidante might recognize information provided during the session that may help or hinder the ex-wife's decision to divorce. Also, the confidante may hear things differently and, thus, give a different perspective on what is being discussed during the education session. For example, any information that is not sensitive to abuse may normalize instances of violence and be confusing, which could potentially influence the ex-wife to drop the divorce proceedings. Having a confidante may help the ex-wife not only continue with the divorce but also change the course of action from divorce mediation to court proceedings so that she does not have to mediate with her abuser.

## Issues of Mediation with Abusers

Echo Rivera et al. argue that "mediation is neither effective, nor safe when [wife] abuse exists" (322). The theory of mediation recognizes that it is voluntary and cooperative; parties can discuss their needs without feeling intimidated. Lee and Lakhani argue the following:

> Mediation is unlikely to be effective if it is imposed on unwilling participants…. mediation only yields fruitful outcomes in low-conflict cases where parties are [on equal ground and are] willing to mediate. If mediation [appears to be] forced on the parties, it is unlikely that mutual agreements can be reached, which leads to the parties ending up in litigation and unnecessarily prolonging the divorce process. (343)

Mediation sessions with abusers raise concerns about women's safety; intimidation prior to, during, and after a mediation session; revictimization; and the inability to negotiate fairly with the abuser. Most abused wives "internalize their abusers' exceedingly rigid rules and expectations and/or comply with their demands in an effort to avoid experiencing abuse" (Watson and Ancis 167), which demonstrates that abused wives, when persuaded to mediate with their abusers, will most likely give in to their abusers' demands rather than negotiate their own needs.

Sitting across from an abusive ex-spouse can be traumatic. Rivera et al. reveal that emotional abuse tactics will occur more often than physical violence in mediation (321). Since emotional abuse tactics can go undetected, abuse can be masked. This is one of the ways abusive ex-spouses can manipulate the mediator and revictimize their ex-wives. Furthermore, abusers are believed to "perform well under observation" (Rivera et al. 323), which further masks their abusive behaviour.

A mediator is also supposed to be an impartial third party. There are doubts whether mediators can be unbiased (Lee and Lakhani 344), particularly in cases with a history of domestic violence (Landrum 468). Also, it might appear beneficial for mediators to mediate all cases referred to them, even if it is not in the best interest of the parties involved, which is a problem. Divorcing parties are placing their trust in the mediator they are referred to. Divorce mediation that continues when domestic abuse is a factor may be problematic, and it puts not only ex-wives and any children in danger but also the mediator. Safety for all should be top priority.

## Regulation of Mediators and the Mediation Process

In Ontario, there are a few institutes that mandate and hold guidelines for family mediation. The institutes that monitor family mediation consist of Family Mediation Canada, the Alternative Dispute Resolution Institute of Ontario, Inc., and the Ontario Association for Family Mediation, Inc. Generally, these institutions define mediation as the use of an impartial third party to assist individuals in solving a dispute.

There is no explanation provided by the Ministry of the Attorney General as to why not all mediators to be accredited. The fact that mediation is unregulated in Ontario is disturbing and places abused wives in potentially dangerous situations if they try to divorce. Kari Boyle and Deborah Zutter, as well as Gráinne Dennison, are also critical of this state of affairs. In 2005, concerns were raised about regulating mediation in Ontario (Boyle and Zutter, 1). Bill 14, Access to Justice Act 2005, was introduced with "Amendments to the *Law Society Act,* intended to provide a framework ... which moved from a 'membership' model to a 'licensing' model, authorizing the Law Society to license persons by class to practise law or to provide legal services ... which included activities that could be associated with mediation" (Boyle and Zutter 1). It was argued by Ontario alternative dispute resolution service providers that "Bill 14 'over-reached' ... and mediators should be exempt from the Act" (Boyle and Zutter 1). How did this slip through the cracks? Regulating mediators "protects the public ... ensures the competency of the mediators and, thereby, the integrity of the court process" (Boyle and Zutter 1). Why are these provisions not in place, particularly since the government and courts are trying to persuade divorcing parties to mediate? Instead, mediation accreditation and mediation guidelines are not required for mediation to commence (Madsen 62). Rather, it is up to the mediator and the parties to determine what type of guidelines, if any, will be used during mediation (Madsen 66). The lack of regulation leaves abused ex-wives vulnerable. How can an abused ex-wife voluntarily agree to mediate on equal terms? These issues need to be thought of by the mediator before proceeding with mediation.

## Mediation Screening, External Experts, and Safety Planning

Most, if not all, mediators screen parties prior to mediation. Each participant was asked how he or she screens potential parties for mediation. All participants acknowledged that they interview each party prior to mediation and that there are multiple techniques and questions used in these interviews. It was further acknowledged that the answers provided gave them insight into the relationship and whether or not deeper questions were needed. All participants said that they interviewed potential parties by asking questions based on their previous mediation experiences. Only one participant recognized that abused women may fall under the radar if they fail to disclose instances of abuse during the initial mediation screening because their version of normal had been skewed.

Another participant acknowledged that if, after screening, mediation goes ahead and abuse in the relationship was not initially an issue, other power imbalances are sometimes recognizable:

> The way they speak ... you can see that there's been that control in the marriage, and sometimes in marriage one person controls more than the other, not necessarily considered or called domestic violence ... and that, as a mediator, when you see that it starts to become unbalanced ... you shift that back and balance it out ... by politely reinforcing that what you are hearing is correct. The realization sometimes makes people shift their attitude in mediation.

A further participant elaborated and stated that they must "observe their behaviour and body language to determine whether or not there is more to it than meets the eye."

Participants were then asked how they dealt with mediation when an imbalance of power became clear after speaking with clients. Some participants advised that external experts—such as counsellors, social workers, and property or financial experts—would be contacted for additional support. A question that followed was who incurs the fees for these external experts? The response was the parties to the mediation, which makes mediation a costly endeavour, contrary to the belief that mediation is a cheaper alternative to court.

Furthermore, when an imbalance of power is recognized, six of the seven participants suggested that they would consider conducting the mediation using shuttle mediation—a technique used when parties cannot mediate face to face. One participant defined shuttle mediation as follows: "when there are staggered arrivals ... with two offices available [in the same building]; so one parent is in one, and one's in the other, and they have no idea where the other office is ... and the mediator goes back and forth between the offices." Shuttle mediation may still intimidate an abused wife to agree with their ex-spouse. Fear of repeated abuse is one example of why an ex-wife may agree to their ex-spouse's requests, even though mediation is not occurring in-person. The after effects of shuttle mediation need to also be considered. Once the parties leave, the mediator is not responsible for any post-mediation behaviour.

## Shift from the Voluntary Mediation Process to the Mandatory Information Sessions on Mediation in Ontario Divorce Proceedings

Participants had differing opinions whether mediation helps or disadvantages abused wives. Three participants were not sure if divorce mediation was good or bad for abused women. Another participant warned that being persuaded into mediation may create an "artificial mediation": "Mediation is only as good as the parties participating in it are willing to make concessions ... and to empathize with the other party and those types of things are prejudiced when it is a forced thing. I think it is ... too blunt of an approach to a problem." If mediators themselves are unsure of whether mediation should take place with abused parties, why do mediators go ahead with it? Why are external sources potentially brought in? Is there only a monetary gain (i.e., employment) for mediators in these circumstances? What ethical standards are implemented in these instances? These questions must be continually revisited prior to agreeing to mediate.

## Mandatory Information Program Sessions Are Not Mandatory in Thunder Bay

As of 1 September 2011, the Family Law Rules were amended in Ontario: however, the mandatory mediation information sessions were not implemented and remain unimplemented in Thunder Bay. One participant acknowledged the following: "Judges are strongly reco-mmending mediation [...] if parties are separated, they have more freedom about following the process of mediation. So, up here [in Thunder Bay...], there is the preliminary step [...] both sides attend with the mediator for the intake interview [at different times]." Another participant further elaborated on whether the requirement to attend the information sessions will be implemented in Thunder Bay. In 2011, he believed it was at its trial stage: "Mediation has only just come to Thunder Bay [where it is highly recommended by judges that parties attend, but it is not mandatory]. I don't think it is the best thing, but I think it is always going to be that way because we're constantly finding problems in family law that we're trying to combat." The question remains as to whether mandatory information sessions should be implemented in northwestern Ontario.

Just as the mediation information sessions are not fully implemented in Thunder Bay, mediators also do not have full access to training. Two participants acknowledged that mediation training is minimal in Thunder Bay: "[Mediation training] is out there ... but it doesn't come to Thunder Bay. You have to spend [a large amount] of money to get down there to Toronto to get it. ... As a lawyer ... [training] is available, but as a mediator, [it isn't]." These two anecdotes indicate that there are problems ensuring mediators are properly trained. Private mediators are not required to have training, and some may, therefore, be inadequately trained to acknowledge abusive behaviour and its effect on abused wives.

## Family Mediation and its Impact on Ontario Law

The final component of this research was a discussion of how these changes impact the law. Participants were asked whether mediation privatizes court proceedings. Two participants were not sure how to answer this question specifically, whereas two others agreed that by definition, mediation privatizes court proceedings. One participant stated the following about the system: "Moves matters out of the judicial system into an alternative dispute resolution system, and that's obvious because that's what they're trying to do. But the issue then becomes are you selling the participants or one of the participants short by ... requiring that they attend mediation ... and, particularly without counsel." Legally, this is a problem, as agreements made in mediation are private; therefore, they are not recorded on public record. Since the agreements are not publicly known, they are also not subject to public scrutiny. This becomes not only a legal problem but also a social problem—one that requires careful consideration when moving forwards with legal matters outside of court.

## Conclusions

The results of this study reveal that Ontario Family Law rules are not universal in Ontario because the mandatory information program on mediation is not fully implemented in Thunder Bay (and presumably other areas in the province as well). It is also unclear whether attendance at these sessions by every divorcing couple will ever be mandatory in Thunder Bay. The inability to implement mandatory legislation displays funding inequalities in northern Ontario. Whether divorce mediation is in fact a desired outcome is doubtful in the case of abuse. Currently, this void in implementation gives mediators and judges in areas such as Thunder Bay authority over how rules are interpreted. This could be either positive or negative and, as it stands, there still is much potential for the revictimization of abused wives.

Also, mediators are unregulated by the government and may lack the training and skills necessary to screen individuals who are referred to mediation. Although accrediting bodies self-regulate their members, there is no government-created body overseeing how mediators conduct screening or other parts of the mediation process, including shuttle mediation. Abusive couples may slip through the cracks of pre-mediation screening. Are mediators blamed when abusive parties slip through the cracks and problems for women and children escalate? Mediators also need to remain conscious of the fact that children are directly or indirectly involved in the divorce process.

Overall, the results of this study suggest that the implementation of the divorce mediation process province-wide was premature. Thus, I recommend the following: a government-run body needs to be implemented to oversee mediators and the mediation process. One requirement of mediators must be to provide initial and ongoing mediation training, and it should be up to the overseeing body to ensure that training is accessible across the province, not just in large cities in southern Ontario. Mediation training should provide mediators with the tools to recognize power imbalances during pre-mediation screening. If wife abuse is suspected these screenings, mediation should not continue. Cases that do not show power imbalances, however, have the potential to work.

## Endnotes

1. Abuse of women who are not wives is also common, but it is not the focus of this chapter.
2. Domestic violence has multiple meanings and interpretations, depending on a victim's perception and others' beliefs about what domestic violence is. There is not one clear way to define it. It is important to assess every family matter involving domestic violence on a case-by-case basis.
3. A "no-fault divorce" means that the reason for divorce is not relevant; entitlement to property division, custody, and/or access to children and to support is not affected.

## Works Cited

Boyle, Kari, and Deborah L. Zutter. "Regulation of Mediation: How Could this Impact your Legal Practice?" *Canadian Bar Association— British Columbia Branch*, www.issuu.com/cbabc/docs/bartalk_04_06. Accessed 24 May 2019.

Brinkmann, Svend. "Could Interviews Be Epistemic? An Alternative to Opinion Polling." *Qualitative Inquiry*, vol. 13, no. 8, 2007, pp. 1116-38.

Brown, Cassandra. "Ameliorating the Effects of Divorce on Children". *Journal of the American Academy of Matrimonial Lawyers,* vol. 22, no. 2, 2009, pp. 461-82.

Cherlin, Andrew J., and Donna R. Morrison. "The Divorce Process and Young Children's Well-being: A Prospective Analysis." *Journal of Marriage and Family,* vol. 57, no. 3, 1995, 800-12.

Chewter, Cynthia L. "Violence against Women and Children: Some Legal Issues." *Canadian Journal of Family Law,* vol. 20, no. 1, 2003, pp. 99-178.

Courts of Justice Act, R. S. O. 1999, c. C. 43, O. Reg. 114/99.

Crossman, Kimberly, et al. "'He Could Scare Me without Laying a Hand on Me': Mothers' Experiences of Nonviolent Coercive Control During Marriage and After Separation." *Violence against Women,* vol. 22, no. 4, 2016, pp. 454-73.

Dennison, Gráinne. "Is Mediation Compatible with Children's Rights?" *Journal of Social Welfare and Family Law,* vol. 32, no. 2, 2010, pp. 169-82.

Divorce Act, R. S. C., 1985, c. 3 (2nd Supp.).

Geffner, Robert, and Mildred D. Pagelow. "Mediation and Child Custody Issues in Abusive Relationships." *Behavioral Sciences and the Law,* vol. 8, no. 2, 1990, pp. 151-59.

Johnston, Janet R., and Nancy Ver Steegh. "Historical Trends in Family Court Responses to Intimate Partner Violence: Perspectives of Critics and Proponents of Current Practices." *Family Court Review,* vol. 51, no. 1, 2013, pp. 63-73.

Kauth, Glenn. "Family Law Reforms Roll Out Across Ontario Today." *Canadian Lawyer Magazine,* July 2011, www.canadianlawyermag.com/legalfeeds/352/Family-law-reforms-roll-out-across-Ontario-today.html. Accessed 23 May 2019.

Krieger, Sarah. "The Dangers of Mediation in Domestic Violence Cases." *Cardozo Women's Law Journal,* vol. 8, 2002, pp. 235-59.

Landrum, Susan. "The Ongoing Debate about Mediation in the Context of Domestic Violence: A Call for Empirical Studies of Mediation Effectiveness." *Cardozo Journal of Conflict Resolution,* vol. 12, 2010/2011, pp. 425-70.

Lay, Geneviève. "Mandatory Family Mediation Information Session." *Slaw Online Legal Magazine.* 19 July 2011, www.slaw.ca/2011/07/19/

mandatory-family-mediation-information-session/. Accessed 23 May 2019.

Lee, Yuk Ki., and Avnita Lakhani. "The Case for Mandatory Mediation to Effectively Address Child Custody Issues in Hong Kong." *International Journal of Law, Policy and the Family*, vol. 26, no. 3, 2012, pp. 327-50.

Madsen, Lene. "More than 'Hanging Out a Shingle': Qualifications for Family Mediators in Ontario." *Canadian Family Law Quarterly*, vol. 30, 2011, pp. 49-70.

Neuman, W. Lawrence. *Social Research Methods: Qualitative and Quantitative Approaches*, 7th ed. Pearson Higher Education, 2010.

Perry, Sandra J., et al. "Stumbling Down the Courthouse Steps: Mediators' Perceptions of the Stumbling Blocks to Successful Mandated Mediation in Child Custody and Visitation." *Pepperdine Dispute Resolution Law Journal*, vol. 11, no. 441, 2011, pp. 441-65.

Pottinger, Fhara. "The Mandatory Information Program for Family Law Disputes: What Does It Mean for You?" *Weilers Barristers and Solicitors.* 15 Sept. 2011. www.weilers.ca/article/the-mandatory-information -program-for-family-law-disputes-340.asp. Accessed 23 May 2019.

Rivera, Echo. A., et al. "Abused Mothers' Safety Concerns and Court Mediators' Custody Recommendations." *Journal of Family Violence*, vol. 27, 2012, pp. 321-32.

Rosnes, Melanie. "The Invisibility of Male Violence in Canadian Child Custody and Access Decision-Making." *Canadian Journal of Family Law*, 14, no. 1, 1997, pp. 31-60.

Schmitz, Cristin. "Top Judge Proposes Free Court-based Mediation, AG says 'No Money'." *The Lawyers Weekly*, Oct. 2010, www.lawyersweekly. ca /index.php?section=article&articleid=12 64. Accessed 23 May 2019.

Smith, G. "Unwilling Actors: Why Voluntary Mediation Works, Why Mandatory Mediation Might Not." *Osgoode Hall Law Journal,* 36, no. 4, 1998, pp. 847-85.

Walker, Lenore. "Battered Women and Learned Helplessness." *Victimology*, no. 2, vol. 3-4, 1977, pp. 525-34.

Watson, Laurel, B., and Julie R. Ancis. "Power and Control in the Legal System from Marriage Relationship to Divorce and Custody." *Violence against Women*, vol. 19, no. 2, 2013, pp. 166-86.

Chapter Five

# Birthing a "Jewbilly" Identity through Wife-Work and Mothering: The Lineage of Family Narrative from Appalachia to Suburbia

Hinda Mandell

The gutter extension outside our house was my daughter's siren call. Mirabelle and I were having such a pleasant time outdoors one weekend afternoon, kicking around a Dora the Explorer ball in the backyard. She was being a good listener. I was being a patient mother, and her three-month-old baby brother was asleep in his car seat on the lawn. Perhaps we were all reveling in the fifty-degree and sunny weather, which is practically tropical for Rochester, New York, in February. The year was 2017.

Then it was time to go back inside the house. There was dinner to prepare, bottles to wash, and a husband to rouse from his basement office. So, I gathered my charges, and we trundled to the side entrance, when Mirabelle spotted the black piping that carries water from the gutter down the driveway. It never before caught her interest, but today she found it irresistible.

Like a bat out of hell, she grabbed it in one fell swoop and ran down our two-hundred-foot driveway—the hollowed length of the tubing was longer than her three-and-a-half-year-old body. And she kept running with it, across the road, and down the street and into a grassy knoll, which separates our street from a busy thoroughfare.

"Mirabelle!" I bellowed, as I hastily placed the baby (still in his car seat) back on the grass and left him as I chased after my daughter, who was now four houses down from ours. By the time I caught up, her cheeks were flushed, and she was as much out of breath from laughing as she was from her gutter-pipe-carrying sprint. I fumed, angered as much at her wildness and willfulness as I was at my inability to have her see the danger of her rebellion. What was I going to do—threaten her with a timeout? Take away TV for the night? Withhold her nightly Popsicle? She was not even four years old and already knew those were empty threats anyhow. Besides, it was much more fun to toy with mother and disassemble something. Any punishment wielded at her would be worth the havoc.

By the time I corralled her back onto our property—reunited with my son, who was now crying in his car seat, rudely awoken as he was from his slumber—and I reattached the piping to the siding of the house, the happy-go-lucky air of fifteen minutes' prior was sullied. My daughter was no longer a good listener, and I certainly was not a patient mother, yet my husband was still enjoying the peace and quiet that his basement office allowed.

"Your daughter is a hillbilly hellion," I hissed at him once inside, his cheeks slack from a relaxed afternoon. "She grabbed the gutter piping and ran down the street with it!"

"Did you put it back?"

"She could have been killed," I countered in disbelief at his primary concern. "And she's a horrible listener."

***

It was certainly unfair of me to castigate my daughter as a "hillbilly hellion," especially since such a derogatory label came from a place of parenting frustration. And by calling her such I was placing the blame of her wildness on her father's rural, Southern, and working-class lineage— and most assuredly not on my Jewish, solidly middle-class, and Boston-suburban roots. But this was clear: ever since hints of my daughter's bulldozer personality began to emerge, I labelled her obstinate traits as Appalachian—a direct product of my position as a woman married to a man whose family hails from West Virginia (even if my husband himself never stepped foot in the state of his family homestead). And by doing so, I was—to use the language of Rebecca Bromwich and Lynn O'Brien Hallstein in the introduction to this book—demonstrating that identities relating to wife-work and mother-work are totally enmeshed, at least for me. In sharing the personal anecdotes that follow, I am inspired by psychologist Dan P. McAdams's assertion that personal stories and the act of storytelling reveal "what is true and what is meaningful in life" (11). What has become so clear to me, as I elevate this revelation to a personal truth, is that the trials and tribulations of mothering my daughter are enmeshed with the emotional wife-work I constantly negotiate in my relationship with my husband considering our different family backgrounds—culturally, economically and ethnically.

When I married Matt, I knew that our family backgrounds had obvious differences in terms of socioeconomic class, geographic location, political viewpoints, education level, and religion. But I assumed that those differences would be contained except when visiting his family, who live two hours away by car, during the occasional barbeque. Ignorant to the way marriage actually functions, and the way family baggage is passed down through the generations like a type of cultural DNA, I thought I was marrying Matt as an independent entity. I did not realize I was becoming the wife to a man whose culture, inherited through his grandfather's Appalachian origins, is "very reluctant to accept authority," and who values self-sufficiency and independence as paramount to his existence (Barker). Months before marrying Matt, I had defended my doctoral dissertation focusing on political wives. Therefore, I had done the reading about "wife-work" and understood it in an academic sense as the emotional and physical labour associated with how society expects a wife to act (Mandell 49). But now, I was doing the living of wife-work and mothering in unison, and I saw a convergence of these two responsibilities: when frustrated by my daughter's oversized independence and lack of respect for authority, I became the wife responsible for our genetic offspring heavily influenced by the father's authority-shirking genetic input.

In Mirabelle's *Bubbe,* my mother, I had a natural ally—a product, as I am, of her familiar cultural milieu. So the "hillbilly hellion" label began to colour not only the way I framed Mirabelle's truculence but also the way my own mother made sense of her granddaughter's stubborn traits. And, in so doing, it enforced that in marrying my husband, I did not adopt his background and traditions (nor did I take his last name). Rather, I doubled down on my own traditions by seeing the truth in my mother's comments about my daughter. I was never worried about a cultural gap, though, between my daughter and me. After all, according to Jewish law, the child of a Jewish woman is considered Jewish as well, regardless of the father's background. Mirabelle simply had to be acculturated into my traditions.

During a snack, my mom made this comment: "She looks like a well-nourished Appalachian child."

And then, my mom made this quip when Mirabelle, who notoriously fights sleep, stomped around her bedroom as the clock closed in on 9:00 p.m.: "She's too busy making moonshine."

There was also the time when Mirabelle woke up her Bubbe, the day after my mother arrived from Boston, with a pressing declaration: "I want them presents!" Her twang was so perfectly Southern she must have learned it through genetic osmosis.

The descriptor "Appalachian" technically refers to "the cultural area along the Appalachian Mountains in the eastern United States from western New York state to Northern Alabama and Mississippi" (Russ 2). It's a major swath of the country, to be sure, but in my mind, it's synonymous with the rural parts of West Virginia that house my husband's geographic roots—a reductionist approach, but who ever said that spouses play fair and are opened-minded with each other? We use whatever is available in our respective arsenals to make our point, feel good about ourselves, shift blame, and recuse ourselves from responsibility. In this case, it was responsibility for a child with more energy than a college kid doped up on Red Bull and Ritalin.

Perhaps not surprisingly, my husband resists the "Appalachian" label of his daughter, battling his stereotypes of his family's rugged, rough-and-tumble roots. He counters it with his own assertion, posed as a question: why do you blame Mirabelle's wild ways on my side of the family, when your own dad, a Jewish Brooklynite, has his history of shenanigans?

And he's right. It's clear that my cultural allegiance isn't with my husband; it's with my family of origin, and as a result, I like to make my husband responsible for Mirabelle's rambunctiousness. After all, I married my husband at age thirty-one. That's three decades worth of approaching the world through a certain standpoint that feels comfortable to me. Some may say this makes me a bad wife. I like to think it makes me a good daughter.

It's true that my dad had a proclivity for climbing neighbours' fences starting at age four, trespassing into their backyards for the purpose of stealing pies. They were homemade, after all.

Matt's defense is clear: wildness is a trait running strong on both sides of the family. Yet the wife only holds his side responsible for Mirabelle's unrestrained qualities.

It's also true that my father was no angel. When he moved with his family to Long Island at age seven, he often wandered the streets so late at night that his parents were forced to call the cops in search of him.

Yet my dad, also not surprisingly, paints a bright description of his younger self as "scrappy and adventurous," assuring me, "I wasn't willful. I wasn't truculent"—implying, by extension, that Mirabelle is. My mom cuts in on the phone, offering her own explanation for her husband's childhood expedition: "He's the wandering Jew."[1]

And I laugh, as I always do, at my parents' stories of long ago and their retelling of these memory gems. This begs the question of why I attribute quaintness to my father's childhood antics in contrast to the frustration from which I judge Mirabelle. Perhaps it's because his stories are rooted in the past and I'm experiencing his anecdotes as family lore rather than lived experience. Or maybe it's the contrast between my intellectual, quiet dad with the rambunctious nature of his youth that I obviously never witnessed. I doubt it was quaint when my dad, in his elementary school classroom, dipped the braided blonde pigtails of the girl sitting in front of him into his inkwell, forcing the girl's mother to chop off her daughter's stained locks.

\*\*\*

My phone conversation with my parents cemented what I already knew: when I link Mirabelle to Appalachia, I'm othering my daughter and making my husband the cause of less-desirable traits that are nothing but typical in so many little kids, including, apparently, my dad back in the day. But then it sinks in when I hear my mom describe my dad as a "wandering Jew," thereby recasting his childhood adventures within a familiar ethnic frame. This story isn't about Mirabelle or even Matt. It's really about my trying to make sense of the rural, working-class family I married into, a family that is both white and White (the last name), whereas I'm white and Other (Jewish). By doing so, I draw on my own stereotypes of those who call home the Appalachian region, even as my family and I have been profoundly shaped by stereotypes and bigotry directed at us. For me, it seems that "wife-work"—the term coined by writer Susan Maushart (11)—has as much to do with my effort to reframe how I approach my daughter and husband's "hillbilly hellions" as it does with the manual labour of doing the laundry, making lunches, and buckling kids into car seats. Wife-work refers not only to the physical labour associated with how society expects a wife to act but also to the emotional and mental efforts as well. The narrative I constructed for my daughter, as an extension of the relationship to my husband's family background, is wife-work and mother-work at work synchronously.

"It is a commonplace to note that human beings both live and tell stories about their living," writes narrative inquiry theorist Jean Clandinin (44), and she adds that "The truth about stories is that's all we are" (51). It is through the examination of narrative that we can poke at family lore and how we frame stories not as entertainment tales but as substantiation of life circumstance, as products of our standpoint, and as evidence of individual perspectives that are shaped by family dynamics but cast by personal experience.

\*\*\*

My identity is moulded by the persecution of my relatives in the Holocaust and extends to my parents' experiences in the middle of the twentieth-century and even to my own interactions with ignorant kids who attempted to bait my Jewishness when I attended middle school and high school in Minnesota in the 1990s. ("Are you wearing a ponytail because you're Jewish?" was one such nonsensical and memorable instance). If the narrative in my household with my husband—to explain the exuberant tornado that is our daughter—is Mirabelle's Appalachian roots, the narrative of my youth was a birthright of dark humour stemming from an inherited history of anti-Semitic oppression, torture, and death.

No family heirlooms? That's because the Cossacks took them all and, besides, they would only weigh us down when making a break for it during a pogrom. Anxious about a big test? At least, you're not in a cattle car. Want to cut your own bangs? They'll look like "Hitler crusts." Desiring a pair of Doc Martens? If you want to wear overpriced Nazi boots, knock yourself out. My husband's family doesn't have family heirlooms either. But I attributed that to economics rather than to ethnic persecution.

So when I met Matt and his family and began to think about being a wife, I had to confront my own notions of non-Jewish whiteness, which for me meant interacting in a world without concern for how others perceive you and without the burden—or, sometimes, the benefit—of ethnic baggage. Storytelling shifted in one generation from "Jewish outsider" to "wild hillbilly" with the birth of Mirabelle, a product of our two families' union.

"Maybe," my mom said, "She's a Jewbilly," applying her trademark effort to make sense of a loved one within a Jewish frame, an act of love itself. And if there is such a marvel as a Jewbilly, Mirabelle would be the perfect poster girl. One of my favourite Mirabelle memories is when she grabbed a harmonica from her underwear drawer and asked me to listen to her playing the *shofar* in between gulps of air. This child could only have come about because of the union between her Jewish mother and West-Virginia influenced father. As the wife of a man who never had to worry about persecution or bigotry, who never had to be the butt of a joke because his family background was a peculiarity, I wonder whether our daughter will inherit my neuroses associated with belonging and cultural acceptance or whether she may escape the burden of feeling like an outsider—thanks to my husband.

\*\*\*

It's not just my husband's "hill people" (Vance 19) roots that's prompted me to link Mirabelle to West Virginia, nor is it her uncontainable energy and physical stamina that lend themselves to a stereotype of a rugged kid running loose on the homestead. It is her physical appearance, which does not resemble mine or my family of origin's, not a whit. I know I birthed Mirabelle because I have strong memories of her shooting through my birth canal. But there's little physical resemblance. Mirabelle has blue eyes and sandy blonde hair, a marked contrast from the brown eyes and mostly brown-haired folks in my family. She resembles a kewpie doll. But the features in my family of origin are less trademark cute. My father once abruptly remarked during a family dinner when I was in high school: "Well, I wouldn't call this a pretty family." When my sister and I balked at his comment, he embarked on a lecture that one can be beautiful without being pretty. It was a weak attempt to comfort his image-conscious teenaged daughters. One need not make that distinction with Mirabelle.

\*\*\*

When I met Matt in 2010, there was no question that I was drawn to the overarching family story that propels its existence: Matt's grandpa, Rick, a one-time coal miner in West Virginia, enlisted in the U.S. Army in 1941. Now that I am Matt's wife, this powerful narrative continues to nurture the connection between my family's background and his. Rick fought in the Battle of the Bulge, the last major German military campaign during World War II, and was taken prisoner by enemy forces, spending four months in captivity. As the family patriarch, Rick's influence is so great that his descendants all speak with a West Virginia twang, even though they were all born in Upstate New York, where Rick relocated to after the war. It appears that Matt is passing on that intonation to our daughter.

In Rick's story, and in Matt's commitment to preserving family-story-as-legacy, I saw parallels to the dominant event in my family: the escape of my mother's father from the Nazi invasion of Poland. My union with Matt, in becoming his wife, helped heal the trauma from that event, still present generations after the destruction, in part, because the story was so feel good— the Jewish granddaughter of a Holocaust survivor marries the grandson of a World War II prisoner of war. In fact, one of my favourite games that Matt and I still play is one of the imagination: if we were to face another Holocaust-like event, how would Matt save his Jewish-born wife, daughter, and infant son?[2] His loyalty to family as the cornerstone of his moral code is one of his most attractive qualities. But whereas narrative as lived experience helps us make sense of a chaotic world, and restores a sense of safety and kismet among the random disorder that defines life, it doesn't serve us well when we fall prey to its seductive patina that whitewashes complex identity dynamics.

\*\*\*

The stories out of Matt's family are spectacular; indeed, he's a second cousin to the unlikely stars of the documentary, *The Wild and Wonderful Whites of West Virginia,* which chronicles the drug use, gunfights, and family feuds for that distant part of the family. In Matt's immediate family in Upstate New York, there are tales involving fistfights, car crashes, and bruised egos leading to epic rows. In contrast, the memorable stories I inherited are just as dramatic but were often more moral oriented and involved the fight for civil rights and social justice. It's as if—in my family—the act of passing on stories was a lesson in itself as opposed to the sheer thrill of entertainment that categorized the tales to come out of the White memory box.

White stories often involved cars and tempers. And although the story about Rick during World War II reinforces a profound connection to the White family that I feel as a wife, the tales of cars and tempers create a division, which reinforces that as a wife, I am still an outsider in my husband's family. Insulting one's car could ignite rage, and commenting on one's driving skills could push someone over the edge. Pushing someone off the road could lead to an all-out brawl.

*\*\*\**

One of the first conversations I ever had with Matt's grandpa Rick was about cars. He asked me what type of car I drove. No one ever asked me that question directly before. Sure, it came up in conversation, but "What type of car do you drive?" was never a conversation starter. Instead, a friend's grandparent might ask where I went to college or where my parents are from. But now I found myself talking cars when I usually played the popular game of "Jewish geography." Yet Rick seemed pleased with my answer. Sure, my 2007 Corolla was foreign made, but it was dependable and practical without a showy curve to its frame. I felt like I passed some type of unspoken test to become Matt's wife.

*\*\*\**

Once, in the 1950s, Rick—who would have been in his thirties—was convinced that the local department of public works was intentionally plowing in his car when clearing the roads of snow. His car was stuck in the driveway—snowed in. So Rick later confronted the department director with a sucker punch. Another time, Rick's family members had to hold him back when he lunged after a guy who insulted his parking job.

Clearly, respecting Rick meant respecting his car, and respecting Rick's car meant respecting Rick's autonomy. With the car as an extension of the person, Rick had no tolerance when his own kid, RD—Matt's dad and Mirabelle's grandpa—got caught throwing stones from an overpass at oncoming cars. He took off his belt to discipline his son.

Both RD and Matt inherited the don't-mess-with-my-car gene, which translates to the "don't-mess-with-me" gene. When RD was once chauffeuring around his family when Matt was a kid, another driver cut him off by making a right-hand turn from the left lane. RD drove off the road to prevent a crash. The other guy did too—why, I'm not sure, although there was chatter that he was fooling around with his girlfriend while driving. RD burst out of his car and pulled the offending driver from his seat—dragging him over the girlfriend in the passenger seat—and lay into him.

Thanks to a gentleman's deal with the local cops, no charges were pressed on either side.

More recently, an afternoon drive with Mirabelle turned dramatic when a driver also cut off our car by making a right turn from the left lane, prompting Matt to swerve to the right, nearly driving us off the road to prevent a collision. Matt shouted expletives forcefully, put the car in park, and took off his seatbelt. His intentions were clear: he was going to confront the driver who almost crashed into us. But, in this case, such a prospect was absurd, since the driver was by now hundreds of feet down the road, securely in his car.

"What are you going to do, chase after that car on foot?" I yelled. Was I the nagging wife in this instance or an injection of common sense and therefore the family protector?

Matt quickly snapped back to reality and buckled in his seatbelt. But his instincts were clear: Must. Confront. Driver. The basis of Matt's road rage is not only the other driver's dangerous maneuver but also the driver's arrogance that his needs surpass those of others on the road. If there is one thing that enrages Matt over anything else, it is arrogance. And when you mix self-importance with vehicular misbehaviour, it's enough to send Matt into an apoplectic fit.

\*\*\*

My dad, too, views cars as identity markers and as sites for a moral code, but for him, it's about his Jewishness. Growing up, my parents only drove two types of cars: Saabs and Volvos. My dad said they were safe cars, but I think he also liked the European design. Even though he worked as a corporate executive in the financial services industry, and was successful in his business, he would never buy the "brand-name" Mercedes or BMW, even if those were the chosen cars of his professional peers. I grew up learning through ethnic osmosis that Jews don't drive blacklisted cars—a type of unofficial boycott of the German automobile industry because it was "deeply complicit in the work of the Nazis" (Goldberg). Of course, it is ironic that both Saab and Volvo originated in Sweden, a country known for its neutrality during the World War II, and we all know that a position of neutrality during mass slaughter of Jews as state policy isn't neutral practice at all. However, perhaps purchasing Saabs and Volvos is better than buying a Ford, which might be American made but whose founder was a notorious anti-Semite (Rudin).

Yet, during my senior year of high school, my father did a vehicular about-face when Mercedes released its first SVU. My father made the purchase. "The assembly takes place in Alabama," he said, offering his justification to halt his decade's-long boycott.

***

I was a daughter for thirty-one years before I became a wife. Therefore, I will always have a soft spot for my mother and her unintentional mischief "makery," and I will never think of her as wild and unlawful as I do for some members of my husband's family, even if her mischief sometimes crosses a legal line. Rather, when she goes "beserk" with her own car antics, I interpret her actions as merely demonstrating her outlandish *chutzpah*. No harm done! Besides, she's my mom, so I'll always forgive her antics. When I reflect on these stories I'm about to share—about my mother and cars—it becomes clear that family narrative is all about framing, even when there are competing frames that play into the same story.

For my mother, cars are sites of stress. She's never met a one-way sign she's respected or a lane designation she's found agreeable. She plows over curbs and thinks looking in her rear-view mirror—or, God forbid, over her shoulder—is for wusses. She once smashed her driver's side door when backing out of her own garage because she forgot to close her car door.

"So?" she says whenever I bring up the thirty-year-old incident.

But for a woman who labels every categorical thing, experience and person as Jewish or not (and there are certainly non-Jews who are bestowed the prized Jewish categorization and Jews who are deemed unworthy), it is ironic that my mother's vehicular orientation is rather like her daughter's "wild" in-laws: she is antagonistic, accusatory, and deeply defensive when it comes to her driving skills, even if she holds no allegiance to the actual car.

As a kid, I protested vocally as she drove through red lights, careened over curbs, and veered off the highway. She certainly did not welcome these comments from "the peanut gallery." But it was not just me taking offense to her street moves. Her reckless driving, though unintentional, got her Volvo badly keyed. Repeatedly. Even as an adult I would return home to Massachusetts and find new keyed markings on her car. When I would bring it up, she would regale me with stories about confrontations in the parking lot of her chiropractor, Marshalls, Whole Foods, or her physical therapist.

To understand my mother is to imagine a female version of Larry David, the star of HBO's *Curb Your Enthusiasm*. Both Larry and Karen, my mother, are connected by a strong personal sense of what is just and right—a moral code that most others view as *meshuganah*. This creates major social awkwardness most of the time.

My favourite Karen car story took place in the Jewish Community Center parking lot in Boston. My mom will not let me reveal the full details here, but she did consent to my writing this: on a particularly busy day without a spot to be had, my mom parked illegally near the front entrance. Her calculation was clear: she was going to be late to yoga class, and, besides, she had a physical therapy appointment for her strained neck that day so she felt entitled to that illegal spot.

Another driver, no doubt annoyed at the lack of available parking, saw my mother sprightly step out of her car and head towards the gym's entrance, mere feet away.

"You can't park there!" he yelled at her.

My mother, as you now know, is never one to tolerate an attack on her vehicular code, even if the accusing party is in the right. Therefore, she shot back: "I could have brain cancer!"

To which the driver snarled, "I hope you do."

Shaken but not deterred, my mother continued into the building. After yoga class, she returned to a car more keyed up than it was that morning.

When my mother retells this story, there is always a glint of pride, not that she gamed the system without consequence (which she did) but that she stood up to an alpha man, who, in her opinion, should have minded his own business. She was the object of his rage so this became a feminist moment for her. She transformed from a woman scorned to a woman who stood up to a chauvinist who verbally assaulted her. It was as if she was making a statement about personal freedoms: do not tread on mine or I'll bite back! Her retelling of the story meshes with the White view of the car as an extension of the self—an attack on my car is an assault on me. Sometimes, if I need to muster up compassion for my husband or my husband's family, I am able to do it by finding linkages between my family of origin and my family by marriage. As a wife, I find strength and sense making in the grounding relationship I have with my mother, so it helps when I can find similarities between her and the Whites.

***

If I were to apply the textual analysis technique known as the commutation test, I would see assumptions embedded in my view of my family's storytelling (McKee): everything relating to my side of the family is justified, quaint, or humorous, and everything related to Matt's is less refined and more questionable. To do this test, I switch the subject's identity by swapping out my mom for one of my in-laws with West Virginia roots. Suddenly, from my perspective, the narrative transforms from a funny story to tell at dinner parties about my mom's parking antics to something wilder.

In addition, that is when I realize the intersectional connections between Appalachia and Jewishness because it is not so much about the story itself but who is telling it, who interacts with it, and who witnesses it.

***

Now that Mirabelle is almost four, she delights in picking out her outfits and dressing herself. One morning, as she stuck her legs into a pair of Dora the Explorer underwear, she had a question.

"Mommy, what's a '*tuchas*?'"

"A *tuchas*," I said, "is a tushy."

A simple nod demonstrated comprehension. In addition, it became clear that I had just defined one Yiddish term with another. My Appalachian daughter has a Jewish *neshama*, confirming that Jewish markers are passed down from a Jewish mother to her children.

However, according to Grandpa RD, this is not necessarily the case. During a visit over the winter holidays, Mirabelle exhibited her fullest display of energy by shrieking at full capacity while running around the living room in circles until she collapsed. She huffed the obvious: "I am dizzy."

The adults were still digesting dinner to this most discordant of soundtracks. As he looked on at the Tasmanian devil who is his granddaughter, RD said over his last bites of chicken with rice, "Wild like a White." Unlike his son, RD does not oppose the overlay of Mirabelle's wildness on his side of the family. Maybe he is less self-conscious of its roots.

***

My perspective of my parents as the more innocent party shifted during a winter windstorm in 2017 that felled thousands of power lines in Rochester, leaving us without power for six days. I was obviously still their daughter, but in this instance, I could not turn to them as a source of strength because they live 360 miles away. Our shared cultural background did not offer much assistance in a house without heat. My identity as a wife took over in the immediacy and urgency of the crisis created by Mother Nature.

When the lights first went dark in the afternoon, Matt was eager to buy a generator.

"Are you crazy?" I said, thinking of my husband as an overly proactive mountain man. We're not going to spend $1,000 for something we'll use once." Having grown up in the suburbs, I had never seen a generator. In my mind, they were lifesavers for hospitals during natural disasters and were used in displaced persons' camps in faraway lands.

They were not needed in the suburbs.

I had never been without power for more than a few hours. However, for Matt, it was different. Since he had grown up in the "North Country" (the northernmost part of New York that is just miles away from the Canadian border), extended power outages were common enough that they were not an occurrence to fear. However, one had to be prepared. In the Boston suburbs of my youth, a power outage meant the inconvenience of not being able to use the electric appliances for an hour before we were back on grid.

The morning after the windstorm, when we woke up to a cold house still in the dark, it was clear that a generator was needed. The only problem was 150,000 other people without power were also in search of one as the "windstorm of the decade" prompted the worst outages in fourteen years in the region (Orr). Yet by 5:00 p.m. that day, Matt secured a generator and had less than an hour of light left in the day to install it. He called on his good friend, a contractor, and they got to work.

My parents voiced their concern all the way from Boston: "You cannot be in the house while that generator is going. You will die!"

I did not want to die. I had a baby. I did not want him to die. And Mirabelle had too much life in her to be snuffed out. I felt myself, as their daughter, getting pulled back into their orbit at the risk of alienating my husband who was attending to the very practical business of keeping our house—and his family—warm.

It did not help that the house stunk of gasoline. I thought the generator—positioned about twenty feet outside our garage on the driveway—was causing the fumes. I did not realize until much later that the smell of gas, necessary to run the machine, lingered on Matt's shoes and gloves inside the front door.

Therefore, I took Mirabelle and her baby brother, and we found refuge at a friend's house.

When I returned home the next morning, our house was toasty warm inside, but I ran to the bedroom, expecting to find an unresponsive husband.

"Matt!"

He rolled over. "Yeah?"

The house smelled like a house. There was no catastrophe. Yet.

"Aren't you glad you have a blue-colour husband?" he asked.

And I was. Although previously it was convenient to live with a bona fide "mountain man" (my nickname for him), it was now about much more than convenience. It was about safety and physical wellbeing. However, my parents were petrified: "You cannot stay in a house with a generator running," my mom reiterated her new mantra. "I swear to God I'll call the police and have them evacuate you."

The soundtrack to this phone call was chainsaws in our neighborhood as crews and homeowners attempted to clear brush, fallen debris, and trees.

My dad, who never met an appliance he could fix, applied more pressure: "You're tired so you're not thinking clearly. Get in the car now and go back to your friend's house with the kids. You are not staying at your house. It's not safe."

And, for the first time in my life, I was a woman pulled between two identities and relationships, which were at odds with each other. I was a daughter accustomed to following parental decrees. I always described myself as a beta personality; I may put up an initial fight, but once my parents apply pressure, I fall into line. Nevertheless, I am also a wife, and when it came to this windstorm, my husband took offense that I left the house the night before as he was connecting the generator to the furnace. It demonstrated that I did not trust his ability to keep his family safe. However, what did my parents and I know of a generator and its safety? *Bubkas.* That is what. Therefore, fear won out that first night. Exhaustion and concern for my relationship with my husband took over the second night. In that moment, my wife-work became exerting the emotional and mental effort to make a leap of faith in trusting my husband and seeing the situation from his perspective—and not from the perspective of my parents, who serve as my default safety net.

"Your parents are crossing a line," said Matt when I indicated I might take the kids for a second night at a friend's house. "I'm about to blow a gasket! Your parents do not even have a functioning fire alarm in their house. And they're telling me how to manage this situation?"

Therefore, I made the decision to stay in a house powered by that fearsome generator. It was clear that if I left, my husband would view the departure as an act of betrayal and as a signal that I held no regard for his capabilities to care for his family and to man the generator that would keep our family safe and warm (or dead, according to my parents).

I decided to pack an emergency bag in case catastrophe erupted in the house at night. (After all, my ethnic heritage instructed me to think about worst-case scenario.) Into a backpack went a bottle, formula, diapers, a change of clothes for my daughter, sanitary pads and Tylenol. I put the car seat by the front door and the keys by the table. Everyone's jackets were ready to go, as were two blankets, one for each kid. If I did not feel better about staying in a house powered by a generator, at least I felt better prepared.

My mother tried once more: "People die all the time from carbon monoxide positioning caused by generators. You're going to die!"

Therefore, I went to bed with my heart pounding and with the window opened a crack in my infant baby's room. Mirabelle is tough, I thought. She can handle this.

The next morning, I actually woke up. And telling from Matt's snores, Eddie's cries, and Mirabelle's "Mommy, is it a school day?", my family was all right as well.

When all my family's basic needs were met, I called my mother to give her the third degree.

"Mom, your hysteria really doesn't help in crisis situations," I chastised her over the phone.

"So you're alive?"

Later that day, she sent Matt a text, an effort to patch his ego scuffed from the assumptions, allegations, and inferences that he is incapable to care for his family.

"I want to thank you for all the work you've done taking care of the family!" she wrote. "As you know, I'm very nervous about generators and gas leaks. But you did a great job connecting it, which in a million years I could not do or imagine doing. You are our rock. Thank you and all my love!"

With that text, my mom acknowledged not only her limitations but also her awareness that her word is not gospel, and that sometimes her daughter—as a wife—has to do things for her own marital relationship beyond *Bubbe's* control. That text acknowledged that there is life beyond uncertainty and fear. That worst-case scenario doesn't always transpire. That a son-in-law with mountain roots can disrupt a family narrative built on fear and catastrophe. And that such grit—determination in the face of chaos—can be a very Jewish trait after all.

***

It's now clear that I waiver between affection and antagonism in my label of Mirabelle as my Appalachian daughter. I admire her grit. I envy her boundless energy. I marvel at her embrace of life at full speed. Yet these traits can drive me bonkers when they work against me.

"Are you my baby?" I like to ask her in moments of tenderness.

"No, I'm Mirabelle," she answers without hesitation. That sentence contains multitudes. Through her sheer force of personality, Mirabelle will establish herself as a person without derivative. There is only one response to her assertion.

"Yes, you are."

## Endnotes

1. My mother lives life in a Jewish–not-Jewish binary. I grew up in a household I'd describe as abundantly, culturally Jewish. There was never any talk of God, but we observed all of the holidays, kept kosher, and saw the world through a Jewish narrative that pitted the wrong way of doing something against the Jewish way (i.e. the right way). Since, according to my mother, some things (not just someone, but objects, ideas and, experiences) are either Jewish or not Jewish, they are by default either acceptable or questionable. She applies this rule down to even the most mundane and random experiences like how to burp a baby— such as the time my mom once accused my sister of burping her son in a goyish manner. In this instance, "goyish" was simply a euphemism for "wrong." Of course, there's an explanation for my mother's binary worldview. Her father fled Poland in 1939 just as the Nazis were invading the country. Although he made it safely to the United States via a seven-year stay in Panama, his entire family—immediate and extended—was murdered in the Holocaust.

2. I later learned that there's a short story with a remarkably similar storyline in this beautiful short story (Englander).

## Works Cited

Barker, Bill. "Appalachian Culture: Sharing the Gospel and Ministering in the Appalachian Region." *Appalachian Regional Ministry,* www. christianmountain.org/resources/Appalachian Culture %20and%20 preachingPP.pdf/. Accessed 23 May 2019.

Clandinin, D. Jean. "Narrative Inquiry: A Methodology for Studying Lived Experience." *Research Studies in Music Education*, vol. 27, no. 1, 2006, pp. 44-54.

Englander, Nathan. "What We Talk About When We Talk About Anne Frank." *The New Yorker*, 12 Dec. 2011, www.newyorker.com/magazine/2011/12/12/what-we-talk-about-when-we-talk-about-anne-frank/. Accessed 23 May 2019.

Goldberg, Jeffrey. "Why I'm Ending My Boycott of German Cars." *The Atlantic*, 29 Aug. 2014, www.theatlantic.com/international/archive/2014/08/why-im-ending-my-boycott-of-german-cars/379310/. Accessed 23 May 2019.

Mandell, Hinda. *Behind Every Man: Media Construction of Wives at the Center of Political Sex Scandals*. Dissertation. Syracuse University, 2011.

Maushart, Susan. *Wifework: What Marriage Really Means for Women*. Bloomsbury, 2001.

McAdams, Dan P. *The Stories We Live by: Personal Myths and the Making of the Self*. Guilford Press, 1993.

McKee, Alan. *Textual Analysis: A Beginner's Guide*. Sage, 2003.

Orr, Steve. "Rochester's Windstorm of the Decade Wreaks Havoc." *Democrat & Chronicle*, 8 Mar. 2017, www.democratandchronicle.com/story/news/2017/03/08/rochesters-windstorm-decade-wreaks-havoc/98919752/. Accessed 23 May 2019.

Rudin, James A. "The Dark Legacy of Henry Ford's Anti-Semitism." *Washington Post*, 10 Oct. 2014, www.washingtonpost.com/national/religion/the-dark-legacy-of-henry-fords-anti-semitism-commentary/2014/10/10/c95b7df2-509d-11e4-877c-335b53ffe736_story.html?utm_term=.5fde1760cd8c. Accessed 23 May 2019.

Russ, Kathryn A. "Working with Clients of Appalachian Culture." *VISTAS Online*, 2010, www.counseling.org/resources/library/vistas/2010-v-online/Article_69.pdf/. Accessed 23 May 2019.

Vance, J.D. *Hillbilly Elegy: A Memoir of a Family and Culture in Crisis*. Harper Collins, 2016.

# Part II

## Wife-Work in Different Cultural Contexts

Chapter Six

# *Mujeres Trabajadoras:* Examining the Role of Mexican Immigrant and Transnational Wives

Ariadne A. Gonzalez

On a hot South Texas morning, the workday begins bright and early. It isn't uncommon for workers to begin their day in the early hours of the morning, but for immigrant and transnational working women, in particular, their daily routine is different and influenced by varying occupational conditions that speak to their challenging reality. Their work begins before leaving their homes, as they cook breakfast, get the children ready for school, and even clean their homes so that the workload is less intense than when they arrive from work in the afternoon or evening. At the same time, for immigrant and transnational women working along the South Texas–Mexico border, however, getting to and from work is challenging enough considering that many must undergo the daily trek of leaving their home in Mexico and entering into the United States (U.S). For many transnational workers, the laborious routine of leaving, entering, and re-entering two countries is done on a daily basis. Along the South Texas—Mexico border, women walk into the U.S. and set foot onto a local bus that takes them to their job sites. The local bus system is their lifeline as they attempt to break away from poverty and create their space in today's global economy. Once they cross the Texas border, their daily routine begins in the downtown area of Laredo,

Texas and serves as the central location by way of the local bus transit system. The sun is glaring and scorching, and as it rises, dozens of women initiate their trek into the most affluent residential communities to begin their duties as domestic workers. Most of the neighbourhoods where domestic workers are employed are surrounded by long winding roads where the only shade is provided by several large trees.

Transnational and immigrant domestic workers make up a portion of the border employment sector, yet little is known about their occupational lives and experiences while working in the U.S. and maintaining ties to Mexico. This chapter focuses on studying actual work practices rather than abstract representations of work by centring the working immigrant wife and the meaning of work that is created and negotiated. It also focuses on the variability of domestic work, which is juxtaposed with issues of gender, immigration, work, and life on the border between South Texas and Mexico. The focal point of the immigrant-working wife is vital, since it recognizes a meaning of work that is negotiated by this interesting ongoing tension between what it means to be a good wife and a good provider. In this regard, immigrant-working wives discern their work as a growing family necessity and as a sacrifice made in the name of the family. At the same time, however, even though work is accepted as a productive way to provide for the family, it is also reconstituted as a way in which immigrant-working wives remain proud and dignified in the quality of work they accomplish.

For decades, thousands of women have entered the U.S in search for work, and even though large numbers of women migrate from Central America, studies show that most women are from Mexico (Hondagneu-Sotelo and Avila; Mattingly 74). In 2016, the Pew Hispanic Center reported that 11.6 million Mexican immigrants resided in the United States and of that number, 51.5 percent were women ("Pew Research Center"). Women who enter the United States from Mexico are more likely to hold jobs in low-paid service industries and work in homes, factories, farms, restaurants, and hotels. They are also likely to settle close to or on the U.S-Mexico border after migration.

Transnational workers, and specifically daily border crossers, who cross between Mexico and the U.S. experience different occupational conditions. The border represents a diversified sector of domestic workers who approach their occupational lives differently since many step into the U.S. legally but cannot legally work. The constant presence of border patrols means taking on the daily practice of eluding and escaping them in an effort to avoid getting caught working in the U.S. without the proper worker documentation and being potentially deported. There are also material conditions that complicate their daily migration experience. The issue of traveling long distances by bus or foot, when there is no transportation, makes arriving to work on time and being back into Mexico before sundown incredibly difficult. The border between U.S. is also a volatile space, particularly due to the ongoing violence in Nuevo Laredo, Mexico. The Laredo-Nuevo Laredo border is unique in that it has recently drawn much attention because of the ongoing turf war between two drug cartels in Nuevo Laredo: The Zetas and The Gulf ("Nine Bodies"; Timoshenkov). This group of domestic workers face complex circumstances since the women must live under such uncertain circumstances in Nuevo Laredo, whereas another sector of the population comprised of documented and undocumented immigrant domestic workers work and live on the U.S. border—each group has varying circumstances yet both attempt to make it into the U.S. workforce.

## Literature Review

The following literature review examines the domestic work literature through an examination of the historical and organizational factors of women and domestic work in the U.S. I draw on the dirty work and identity literature in organizational studies to develop an understanding of domestic workers' ongoing process of identity construction and negotiation, and to have a more focused grasp on how wives as immigrant domestic workers grapple with identity negotiation. This focus draws our attention to the ongoing call for the dislocation of the organization of work.

Because of an increasing low-wage economy, female labour migration to the U.S. from Latin America and Asia has increased. The number of mothers entering the labour market has increased, as has the time children spend in daycare or after school care (Hagelskamp et al. 336). More immigrant women are seeking employment outside the home, yet not much is known about how this work affects their wife role. Even though immigrant women hold a diversity of jobs, this research study focuses on immigrant domestic workers.

## Domestic Work as Wife-Work

The job duties of domestic work—caring, cooking, and cleaning or care work—have been historically regarded as women's work, attempting to naturalize these tasks to women, specifically wives who earn a wage for the same type of work they perform in their own home on a daily basis. Thus, wives must grapple with a double burden they negotiate their occupational identity. Domestic work is a gendered occupation within the division of labour. On the one hand, productive labour is designated as work that is practiced outside the home and is paid a wage; it is also recognized as work to produce and distribute good and services, which is mostly seen as men's work. On the other hand, reproductive labour sustains the home. It is work that is practiced in the home and facilitates productive labour. It is undervalued and unpaid, and is dominated by women.

Domestic work in the U.S. has been historically regarded as invisible and is only made visible when it fails to get done. Cooking, cleaning, and caring for children have been regarded as the ways in which women naturally express their love for family—thus, essentializing domestic work. The actual work practices and the workers who accomplish such tasks continue to go unnoticed, but it is also equally important to understand that a particular sector of women enter this line of work. Domestic work is not only wife-work; it is also classed-work.

## Domestic Work as Classed, Raced, and Immigrant

Women who are retained as domestic workers are employed in such jobs because they are in dire need of paid employment (Mattingly 66). Middle- and upper-class women can "maintain their bodies and professional images," whereas the domestic duties are accomplished by poor women (Trethewey et al. 134). Whereas white feminists, in particular, sought to recognize the division between the private sphere and access to the public one, women of colour focused on "improving their working conditions and opportunities, as they ha[d] been generally confined to secondary labour markets and to positions at the bottom of the organizational hierarchy" (Holvino 252). As Evangelina Holvino affirms, "women of colour have always worked and been seen as workers" because of the demanding need to provide necessary income and other family expenses (252). Being a housewife and having a supportive husband were considered luxuries only afforded to white women (Holvino 252). This distinction forces us to come face to face with the vast differences between white women and women of colour and to distinguish between the different forms of oppression each faces.

Not only is domestic work gendered and classed (Acker; Flanagan; Holvino), it is also racialize. In the past, second-wave feminists sought help from African American women employed as domestics or from their male counterparts; but today, border crossers and immigrant domestic workers perform much of the domestic work (Ehrenreich and Hochschild; Flanagan; Hondagneu-Sotelo; Romero). Angela Trethewey et al. maintain that the U.S. and other developed countries have seen a surge of immigrant domestic workers. To a greater extent, women from the Global South and immigrants hold these types of jobs today (Glenn; Hondagneu-Sotelo; Romero; Trethewey et al.). Many are young women who enter the country as a way to earn money to send to their families in various developing countries, yet many are also married women who leave their families in their home countries in an effort to provide for them.

## Domestic Work as Dirty Work

Dirty work is defined as occupations that are physically, morally, or socially tainted (Ashforth and Kreiner; Hughes). The nature of such work is deemed demeaning, immoral, distasteful, high risk, or labour intensive (Ashforth and Kreiner 414). Dirty-work occupations, such as domestic work, are challenging when trying to construct and maintain a positive identity (Hughes 50), which is intriguing, since many women who perform domestic work are immigrant wives who encounter similar identity negotiation tensions. Furthermore, previous research on dirty work suggests that due to these jobs' negative associations with, workers are compelled to separate themselves from the work, yet they are aware of the stigma associated with these occupations' taint (Ashforth and Kreiner; Ashforth et al.). Blake Ashforth and Glen Kreiner argue that a worker's ability to negotiate the taint associated with their occupation is vital to their sense of self and occupational and organizational goals (414).

## Identity and Work

The process and implications of ongoing identity construction for low-paid service industries, such as domestic work, have not been theorized in great detail. Research has generally focused on white-collar workplaces and what Karen Ashcraft and Brenda Allen refer to as an overall "whiteness" towards organizational research (6). Because organizational scholars have been particularly interested in managerial, professional, organizational, and occupational identities and how they understand and negotiate issues surrounding the self in varying workplace settings, the actual work practices and experiences of immigrant-working wives engaging in low-paid dirty work must also be examined in an effort to better understand identity negotiation from a different yet important standpoint (Alvesson et al.; Tracy and Trethewey).

For poststructuralist scholars, the identity-construction process is a "site of struggle over individual and collective meanings" (Tracy and Trethewey 168). Because occupational life plays a significant role in identity construction, organizational scholars have been particularly interested in occupational identity, since the self is manifested through subjectivity and is tied to values and beliefs. With this in mind, many scholars have explored how individuals make sense of their "complex and often ambiguous and contradictory experiences of work," yet the invisibility of immigrant workers, specifically working wives, remains acute (Alvesson et al. 12).

This chapter examines how wives as immigrant domestic workers construct and negotiate their occupational identity, which has particular implications for Mexican immigrant and transnational wives who leave their homes, husbands, and children in an effort to build economic vitality and upward mobility for them and their families. The central research question examines how wives as Mexican immigrant and transnational domestic workers construct and negotiate the meaning of their work in relation to their occupational identity.

## Methods

As I left my home one summer morning, I came across a busy intersection that quickly turned into traffic chaos. A city bus was causing much of the standstill, and as I waited patiently for the bus to gain traction, I noticed dozens of women exiting the bus and walking into my residential community. I have lived in the same city for most of my life, but until recently, I lived in a vastly different community. I grew up on the side of town where domestic workers were more likely to be my neighbours rather than the side that hired them. These women were domestic workers entering some of the most affluent communities in Laredo. I followed them, thus beginning my journey into this research study.

This study took an ethnographic approach by maintaining the tenets of engagement and being precisely positioned to observe and experience what is being studied. Even though other scholars have noted that recent ethnographic work have taken form in more continual and succinct encounters, the importance of remaining connected with members of domestic communities and subcultures remains invaluable (Atkinson; Hammersley and Atkinson; Lindlof and Taylor 135). According to Harry F. Wolcott, time does not solely "guarantee the breadth, depth, or accuracy of one's information," (70) and because of the level of familiarity of the city and its inner workings, I have upheld the canons of ethnography.

Laredo, Texas is located in the South Texas region and it borders Nuevo Laredo, Tamaulipas, Mexico. It has an estimated population of 236,000 inhabitants of which 95.6 percent are Hispanic or Latino ("United States Census"). I began my fieldwork by traveling to the city's main transit location in downtown Laredo and several surrounding neighbourhoods for four months. Because domestic workers are usually mobile workers and are essentially in constant movement, I realized that participant observation and interviewing would function as the principal data collection procedure. Even though I was not able to enter most of the domestic workers' actual job sites, I rode the city bus alongside many of the women to and from their job site. A transnational worker I have known for more than a decade also became my informant, and the information she provided regarding the city transit system and the times and days most workers cross into the U.S. and back into Mexico was priceless. Most importantly, she put me in contact with several domestic workers she knew.

I completed a total of twenty-nine interviews with Mexican immigrant domestic workers, which varied between fifteen and seventy-five minutes in length. I interviewed many of my participants during short interactions at the bus station and at multiple bus stops. Most of the women did not speak to me or acknowledge my presence. These are focused women. They pay close attention to who enters and exits the bus, and an unfamiliar face is quickly noticed. However, as the weeks went by, they became friendlier, and I had plenty of small conversations pertaining to the weather or the long workday. Eventually, we even discussed family and varying work-related issues. This initial engagement with my participants enabled me to have deeper conversations, as I managed to gain trust, which produced more meaningful and richer interactions. My fieldwork specifically yielded sixteen interviews, yet I also engaged with key transit staff, other transnational workers, and domestic workers, who did not have the time to engage in more than a few minutes of conversation.

I also chose semi-structured interviewing as a second form of data collection, since this form of data collection allowed my participants to express themselves freely and fully (Mishler 233). These were in-depth interviews that took place in their homes, small local restaurants, and their job sites. Thirteen in-depth interviews were completed during the data collection process. I asked questions that evoked stories. I asked the same questions to all of my participants, yet depending on my participants' responses, I asked further probing questions. Examples of my semi-structured interview protocol include the following questions: Can you tell me what led you to begin crossing the border for work? How would you describe the work you do for other people? What does your husband think about you working outside of the home? How does having a job make you feel? In total, I interviewed twenty-nine domestic workers, and all twenty-nine participants self-identified as Mexican or as Mexican immigrants; eighteen participants were transnational workers who travelled to and from Mexico at least three to five times a week, and eleven lived and worked in Laredo, Texas. The women ranged between nineteen and sixty-six years of age. All interviews and related conversations were held in Spanish.

In keeping with the research question about how wives as Mexican immigrant-working wives construct and negotiate their occupational identity, I employed a narrative thematic analysis in order to analyze their stories and lived experiences. A thematic analysis calls for all data to be coded where it is sorted and categorized (Lindlof and Taylor 252). Catherine Riessman suggests this form of analysis is a way to capture the meaning of words, to explain what function they serve, and to discover what stories emerge from these encounters. Through this form of analysis, common themes and connections began to emerge from the data where thematic clusters formed. Domestic workers negotiate the meanings of work that are directly aligned with being a good wife. These meanings are marked by the importance of familial and financial responsibilities.

## Findings: The Meaning of Work

My analysis revealed that immigrant domestic workers negotiate a meaning of work directly aligned with their roles of wives. For my participants, negotiating the meaning of their work meant that being a good and productive worker meant being a good provider for the family. This good worker–good provider narrative is juxtaposed with a need to work and make sacrifices for the family. Thus, the meaning of work shifts out of necessity and sacrifice; as a result, for my participants, a wife's work is continual. Twenty-six of the twenty-nine women privileged being a good worker–good provider. The findings draw attention to how immigrant domestic workers negotiate their role as wives and position themselves in the public sphere while grappling with the ongoing duties of the private sphere. For my participants, the meaning of their work is directly aligned with necessity and sacrifice. All twenty-nine participants constructed an occupational identity that aligned with the need to work and make sacrifices in an effort to substantially contribute to their family's upward mobility. The following is an analysis of the two overarching themes found in this study: good worker-good provider and *necesidad y sacrificio* (necessity and sacrifice).

### Good Worker–Good Provider

In Nuevo Laredo, Isabel's[1] day begins at 5:00 a.m. and doesn't end until 6:00 p.m. or 7:00 p.m. She works for her children from the moment she awakes. Isabel, a transnational domestic worker for four years, works because she doesn't have a choice. With three children living in Nuevo Laredo, she describes her thirteen-hour work day, including the two hours of travel each way, for six days a week: "*Todo lo que hago—todo lo que me arriesgo es para ellos, pero no es facil. No paro*" ("Everything I do—all of the risks I take is for them, but it's not easy.

I don't stop"). Like many transnational workers, she can legally cross into the U.S. yet she cannot work. This is what she refers to as the *"arriesgos"*—or risks she faces every single day. She understands her occupation is not the best paid, but Isabel looks beyond the laborious work, treatment, and the risks she encounters while travelling to and from work because she recognizes that having this occupation is the only opportunity her children have to live a better life in Mexico. Isabel's husband works in Nuevo Laredo, but since she is the only one who can cross into the U.S., she sees herself as the main provider. As she earns dollars rather than pesos, Isabel brings in more money into the household than her husband. However, she positions herself as a wife whose primary role is to provide; and even though her husband works long hours, she understands the complexity of working long hours for little money. This discernment allows her to employ an occupational identity of a working wife, but first and foremost, she describes herself as a *"trabajadora,"* a worker, and she hates the names people often use for her occupation. Regardless of the occupational constraints, she is a *"trabajadora y aguantamos tanto porque tenemos que hacerlo. Esta dificil para aguantar tanto"* ("worker and we endure so much because we have to do this work. It's difficult to endure so much"). In this particular context, *"aguantar"* is translated into English with such words as "endure" or "tolerate." At different points within the interviews and quick conversations at the city bus stops, domestic workers continuously discuss their experiences of *aguantar.* Whether associated with laborious efforts, the complicated relationship between employer and employee, or the strenuous travelling to and from work, *aguantar* is a constant theme, but it is mostly coupled with perseverance. A good worker *"aguanta"* or endures the difficult work in order to ensure their family's economic stability. In this case, Isabel is a good provider undeterred by multiple occupational constraints and executes her primary duty of a good wife, which is to provide for her family.

Isabel recounts a time she felt mistreated by her employer. After working for her employer in one of the most affluent Laredo communities for three years, she remembers once when her employer invited her to a birthday party in her home. She was opposed to the idea because it was her only day off and she thought it would be strange, yet she didn't want to disrespect her employer and accepted the invitation. She walked into the home feeling *"extraña"* or strange and uncomfortable but managed to make the best of it and even appreciated the invitation. However, the invitation as a guest was short lived when her employer asked her to work the party after her other worker fell ill and would not attend. Even though her employer paid her twice as much, she was upset and disappointed. For her, this incident was an insult. Initially, she was not pleased to be there but accepted the invitation because she didn't want to disappoint her employer and after spending her own money to cross the bridge, she was asked to work: "I didn't even want to go but I felt bad and I did it so I could stay in good terms with her and that is how she repays me? Well that's how it is. One has to endure and keep on giving it your all because this is my job and that is the reason I have what I have for my children. Just keep moving forward, but that is how they repay us." The employer-employee relationship is complex and difficult to navigate because even though employees, such as Isabel, believe they have formed a friendship or perhaps have become part of the employer's family, they are otherwise reminded of the contrary (Hondagneu-Sotelo; Romero). As Isabel recount this incident, her friend Maria eagerly supports Isabel's point:. "*Nosotras somos empleadas; eso esta muy claro!*" ("We are workers; that is very clear!") She asserts the fact that they are workers first and quotes her mother saying that she is "*la muchacha de la limpieza—eso métete en la cabeza*" ("*the cleaning girl—get that thought into your head*"). According to Maria's mother, it should be clear to Isabel and Maria that they are employees and not part of the family.

What is interesting is Isabel's willingness to discern what the occupation provides and, at the same time, to recognize the poor treatment by her employer. This tension between the positive and negative aspects of the occupation exists and is managed by underlining the importance of the job. She endures the treatment and is resolute in providing for her children, but it is also important to note that her role as a wife means she must endure and accomplish her job tasks to provide for her family. She discursively negotiates between the negative and positive aspects of her work. In the end, she underlines the importance of persevering by "*echándole ganas al trabajo*" or "keeping at it." Isabel mentioned that it is a "*deber como madre y esposa*" ("duty as a mother and wife"). Regardless of the treatment or hard work, her children are first, and as a mother and wife, she must provide for her family, regardless of the occupational hardships she continuously endures. It is the construction of this work-related identity that provides a sense of meaningfulness.

Eager to help her family, Araceli has lived in Laredo for a year and for the past eight months, she has worked six days a week and for three different families. At nineteen, she is undocumented and young, but she clearly understands the reality of hardship. She is the youngest of eleven children and recently married, and although most of her family remains in Veracruz, Mexico, they rely on her to send money. Araceli is quiet, soft spoken, and rarely looks up when speaking, but that should not be confused with a lack of assertiveness. During our conversations, she insists on discussing her experiences.

Araceli describes the substantial amount of work she undertakes in each home. She characterizes her job as exhausting, and to make matters worse, she objects to returning home only to do the exact tasks once more. The double burden of managing a workload outside the home coupled with unpaid domestic labour inside the home is ubiquitous on the border and throughout the United States. Today, wives are spending more time working outside the home, yet according to the U.S. Bureau of Labor Statistics, 49 percent of them are performing household duties in their homes, whereas 20 percent of men will do the same. Like Araceli, most of my participants express the ever-consuming realization of the "second shift" (Hochschild), not only from a physical standpoint but from a creative standpoint as well. Even though wives enter the workforce and work equal to or more hours than their husbands, they perform second-shift work for their husbands as well. This directly aligns with women's role as wives, whose job it is to accomplish care work first and foremost, which attempts to essentialize care work as wife-work. With the exception of one participant, domestic workers talk about the physical exhaustion and strain as they describe the laborious demands of the job and explain the literal and figurative lengths they undertake in order to accomplish their job. At the same time, they explain the continuous responsibility of the second shift. A tension exists here, as wives positions themselves as good workers and providers—a role that extends from the job site to the home. Being responsible as well as a good wife isn't only accomplished by supporting their husbands with additional income and completing their duties at work; it is also accomplished by second-shift work. Similarly, Amalia, an undocumented domestic worker, explains that even though her husband didn't want her to work initially, it was a necessity. However, her husband was quick to remind her that it was also important for her to perform her work duties in their home. Interestingly, Amalia says that taking care of the home is a responsibility that no one else but her should undertake: "*Es muy importante porque la mujer es la cabeza de un hogar. Eso va primero*" ("That is very important because a women is the head of the household. The home comes first"). Her children help her at times, but being a good worker and provider means she can provide extra income for the family, yet the responsibility of accomplishing second-shift work still falls on her.

Araceli understands the reality of her family's financial standpoint and realizes she is the only one who can turn things around for her family back home. During the most exhausting parts of her day, she thinks about her mother and wonders exactly how her mother's life would change now that she has the financial backing of her daughter. While sweeping the floor, she constantly reminds herself of the benefits of her occupation, the financial freedom, which she hopes to use to return one day to her mother. An interesting shift takes place as she tells me about her mother. Araceli realizes the negative aspects of her work, and she even admits she would attempt to find another job if she could legally work in the U.S. She continues to negotiate her occupation's long hours and monotonous routine with being aware she is her family's lifeline to financial sustainability. The meaning of work for Araceli surpasses the understanding that a worker's occupational identity is "constituted at work" (Ashcraft; Wrzesniewski et al.). Of course, her occupational identity is constructed and negotiated through different occupational possibilities that may relate to the workplace; however, as Araceli's experience demonstrates, it certainly transcends and overlaps with other locations. For these domestic workers, these other locations usually relate back to the family's financial and relational circumstances as well as to the emotional and physical strain of the actual work. Together, these said influences affect the work accomplished in the workplace.

## Necesidad y Sacrificio (Necessity and Sacrifice)

Cecilia, a domestic worker, has been working hard ("*darle duro al trabajo*") in Laredo for over twenty-five years. Necessity is what kept her in a job with a former abusive employer for over a month, as she was still able to send that money back to her family in Mexico. This need to push through the work is tied to necessity and sacrifice for many domestic workers. The necessity to work in order to move their family forwards is tied to the sacrifices women make to shift their family, especially their children, parents, and even husbands into a better economic position. Cecilia has endured through the work despite the sacrifices she has made, yet she knows her job provides medical care and access for her family living in Mexico, but it still comes at a price, as she was unable to care for or visit her father while he was dying in Mexico:

> Of all my experiences of taking care of elderly men, I was not able to take care of my father the same way. My father needed me for a long time just like the elderly men I cared for. My mother would console me by telling me that if it wasn't for me, my father would not be well taken care of. I was not there to give him his medicine or to bathe him, but I was there with the resources to purchase the medicines he needed. Yes, and my mom would tell me, "No my child, you weren't there to care for him physically, but you were there for these other resources." And, yes, my father would have had me to care for him physically, like my sisters, but he wouldn't have had the resources to purchase the cremes and medicines he needed and all of that. That came from me. It took some time for me to finally understand that. I wanted to be with him but it wasn't possible.

Cecilia could not be with her family when he passed away. It took her time to understand that even though she was unable to be in Mexico when he fell ill and when he died, her job as a domestic worker provided his entire medical care. She was relieved her job allowed for prompt health access and medical care for her father, but because she had to work, she could not spend the last months of her father's life in Mexico with the family. Cecilia describes herself as a good worker willing to sacrifice her time with her family in order to sustain their lives. Her mother often reminds her that a good daughter provides for the family, even though she may spend too much time away from them. With her mother's help, she continuously attempts to remind herself of the positive aspects her job brings.

Not only does Cecilia take care of her family back in Mexico, she also cares for her husband who lives in Mexico. For Cecilia, being a good wife and daughter means working for the financial needs of her entire family. Working creates opportunities and opens the door to a better future for her husband and family. Her husband does not have a steady job in Mexico, and together, they decided she would continue living in the U.S. in order to have a steady income. Cecilia tells me she visits him once every two weeks, and even though it isn't an ideal situation, the money she earns compensates for the separation. For Cecilia, being a good wife means she makes sacrifices to secure financial stability.

Lupita, fifty-nine, has worked as a domestic worker for over thirty-five years and even though she is now in a much better financial position, the need to work for her children and husband has often kept her from quitting undesirable jobs. Lupita never loses sight of why she works and never dwells on the social and physical taint of the work. In our conversation, she describes the dirty work but mainly focuses on the importance of family: "I had to do a lot of things. There were many things that I had to do, and I did them. My boss would tell me things and the work was too much for what she would pay me. I had to stop and think ... about making sacrifices. I had to think about my children, the necessities at home, and my husband." Lupita makes that necessary shift. She adjusts her focus from the arduous work and poor treatment to the outcome of that same job: upward mobility for her children and ending their economic hardships. Even though the money was not comparable to the work, she stayed. Lupita understands her job is her livelihood, and even though she does not make enough money, the decision to ultimately stay in that job is tied to necessity. The necessity to provide for her family extends to who she is as a wife and mother. Accomplishing these laborious job tasks for her family has given her ample reason to focus on the outcome of her labour (helping her children and husband) rather than only on the strenuous work.

At thirty-seven years old, Veronica, an undocumented single mother of five, has lived through her share of difficult times. She has always believed in working outside of the home and making money for her family. According to Veronica, a good mother knows how to take care of her family by providing what they need. She was married to a U.S. citizen but is now separated. During her marriage, her husband refused to work on her citizenship papers, thus failing to secure her citizenship status. Her husband believed she married him because of her citizenship status even though they were married for more than fifteen years. She never understood why her husband refused to let her work: "*Yo hubiera querido trabajar en esos tiempos. Él no me dejo y lo decia que porque no. Él tenía miedo que no hiciera el quehacer pero yo le decia que no tenía nada que ver, pero no, nunca me dejo*" (I would have worked during that time. He didn't let me work and I would ask him why. He was afraid of not doing the housework but I told him that would not happened, but no, he never let me"). During the time Veronica was with her husband, there was a financial need to work, but he refused to let her work. Even though she wanted to work outside the home and addressed his concerns of becoming too lax with her household duties, and he didn't allow it. Veronica understood that being a good provider would not interfere with accomplishing her husband's understanding of her role as a wife.

Her husband recently started paying child support, something he stopped for years because he refused to work and provide any financial support for his children. Veronica has fallen ill many times, but she never misses a day of work: "It can rain, and I have to get the bus or even if it's cold, and I get sick, and I still go to work because they won't pay the day. They won't pay, and I need it. I get strength, and I tell myself that I can't miss work. I have to go. I have to go. I have to do the impossible sometimes, and it's all for them. As a mother, I have to make money in order for my children to have a place to live."

## Discussion: Constructing and Negotiating the Meaning of Work

My participants' lived experiences highlight an interesting understanding of how they construct and negotiate the meaning of work. Drawing attention to the material conditions that influence their occupational identity, my participants' occupational concerns move them to deploy a meaning of work that is closely influenced by areas of nonwork such as strong familial responsibilities, as they experience in particular their roles of wives, mothers, and daughters. This focus on the material conditions, which are external to the work site, influence the ways my participants reacted, negotiated, and redefined themselves as the backbone of their families. Most research on occupational identity has centred on how the organization and profession influence occupational identity (Ashcraft; Wrzesniewski et al.), whereas my research highlights the need to explore how nonorganizational and nonprofessional factors influence the construction of an occupational identity tied to being a good worker and a good wife, emphasizing both the work accomplished outside and inside the home.

My participants desire a positive identity in their job performance and integrate it to their roles of wives and mothers. Much of the research on occupational identity maintains that workers construct an occupational identity focusing on the workplace and not beyond it. Their meaning of work is constructed in and around the workplace, which means their occupational identity is influenced by the work performed. However, new research suggests that workers construct their occupational identity in and beyond the workplace, which means that like other recent studies focusing on identity construction, domestic workers on the border construct and negotiate their occupational identity by recognizing the negative job attributions while also acknowledging and focusing on the positive attributes the job produces. This is important because my participants acknowledge these negative job features of the domestic work discourse by drawing attention to the work being difficult or tough, which captures the laborious aspect of their occupation. On an individual level, my participants create meaning out of their work in order to make a better life for their families (Broadfoot et al. 157). Creating meaning out of their occupation is important to them because when their job is difficult, unfair, or laborious, they look to the tangible value it provides. Their construction of being a good worker is deeply connected to their responsibilities at home—especially for the family members they financially support in and outside of the United States.

Creating a meaningful sense of work that is indicative of their laborious occupation adds to the ongoing conversation about the relationship between work and life. For more than two decades, scholars have sought to understand the ongoing interest in work-life (or what falls within nonwork) balance in relation to the demands of work and the quality of life (Clark; Cohen, Duberley, and Musson; Guest; Hochschild; Nippert-Eng). At least six outlooks of work-life balance are employed to describe the relationship between work and life: segmentation, spillover, compensation, instrumental, conflict model, and border theory. Each model or theory centers on how people navigate in or between the work and life domains. However, Laurie Cohen et al. study focuses on the lived experiences of home-work dynamics and argues that people do not inhabit ideal types of segmenting and integrating as ways to maintain order at work and/or at home. Interestingly, they argue that people utilize the notion of importing, which is described as "purposeful and drawing on roles, identities, and activities of one sphere to achieve projects in another" (235). This is important because importing brings in particular "material artifacts as well as ideas, feelings, and identities from home into work and from work into home to achieve particular things" (235). This dynamic interplay of work and life is seen as a management strategy for these two domains. Likewise, my participants negotiate an identity that is infiltrated or, in this case, imported to the family-life domain. There are no clear work-life-balance boundaries per se; consequently, they construct a meaning of work that draws from their nonwork life, whether it be familial responsibilities that help them redefine the work as necessary. In particular, my participants understand that sacrifice and the need to work are aligned with being a good wife and a good provider for the family. The meaning of their work enables wives to persevere and, in that effort, they are create an occupational identity around determination and commitment to their families.

## Conclusion

My participants' lived experiences capture an interesting under-standing of how immigrant and transnational worker wives are redefining the meaning of work. Usually, the role of wife is that of a support system, whereas the male figure of the family is known as the breadwinner and backbone of the family. However, my participants negotiate a meaning of work that directly aligns with being a good wife. Rather than as the support system, they are positioning them-selves as workers who provide and sustain their homes and families, which makes their meaning of work one of need and sacrifice. They do not detach or distance themselves from the stigmatized work. Rather, they enact new meanings of that work and align it with their lived experiences of being proud and productive working wives who are integral to their families. Their purpose does not waver, as they are mindful of a promising future and are tenaciously responsible for their families.

## Endnote

1. Please note that all participants' names are pseudonyms in order to protect their privacy. Also all Spanish to English translations are my own.

## Works Cited

Acker, Joan. "Hierarchies, Jobs, Bodies: A Theory of Gendered Organizations." *Gender & Society*, vol. 4, no. 2, 1990, pp. 139-158.

Alvesson, Mats, et al. "Identity Matters: Reflections on the Construction of Identity Scholarship in Organization Studies." *Organization*, vol. 15 no.1, 2008, pp. 5-28.

Ashcraft, Karen Lee. "The Glass Slipper: "Incorporating" Occupational Identity in Management Studies." *Academy of Management Review*, vol. 38, no. 1., 2013, pp. 6-31.

Ashcraft, Karen Lee, and Brenda J. Allen. "The Racial Foundation of Organizational Communication." *Communication Theory*, vol. 13, no. 1, 2003, pp. 5-38.

Ashforth, Blake E., and Glen E. Kreiner. "'How Can You Do It?' Dirty Work and the Challenge of Constructing a Positive Identity." *Academy of Management Review*, vol. 24, no. 3, 1999, pp. 413-34.

Asforth, Blake E., et al. "Normalizing Dirty Work: Managerial Tactics for Countering Occupational Taint." *Academy of Management Journal*, vol. 50, no. 1, 2007, pp. 149-174.

Clark, Sue Campbell. "Work/Family Border Theory: A New Theory of Work/Life Balance." *Human Relations*, vol. 53, no.7, 2000, pp. 747-70.

Cohen, Laurie, et al. "Work-Life Balance? An Autoethnographic Exploration of Everyday Home-Work Dynamics." *Journal of Management Inquiry*, vol. 18, no. 3, 2009, pp. 229-41.

Flanagan, Caitlin. "How Serfdom Saved the Women's Movement: Dispatches from the Nanny Wars." *The Atlantic Monthly,* vol. 293, no. 2, 2004, pp. 109-28.

Ehrenreich, Barbara, and Arlie Hochschild. *Global Woman: Nannies, Maids, and Sex Workers in the New Economy.* Owl Books, 2002.

Glenn, Evelyn Nakano. *Forced to Care: Coercion and Caregiving in America.* Harvard University Press, 2010.

Guest, David E. "Perspectives on the Study of Work-Life Balance." *Social Science Information,* vol. 41, no. 2, 2005, pp. 255-79.

Hagelskamp, Carlin, et al. "Negotiating Motherhood and Work: A Typology of Role Identity Association among Low-Income, Urban Women." *Community, Work & Family,* vol. 14, no. 3, 2011, pp. 335-66.

Hochschild, Arlie. *The Second Shift.* Avon Books, 1989.

Holvino, Evangelina. "Intersections: The Simultaneity of Race, Gender and Class in Organization Studies." *Gender, Work and Organization,* vol. 17, no. 3, 2010, pp. 248-77.

Hondagneu-Sotelo, Pierette, and Ernestina Avila. "'I'm Here, but I'm There': The Meanings of Latina Transnational Motherhood." *Gender & Society,* vol. 11, no. 5, 1997, pp. 548-71.

Hondagneu-Sotelo, Pierette. *Doméstica: Immigrant Workers Cleaning and Caring in the Shadows of Affluence.* University of California Press, 2007.

Hughes, Everett C. *Men and Their Work.* Free Press, 1958.

Lindlof, Thomas R., and Bryan C. Taylor. *Qualitative Communication Research Methods.* 3rd ed. Sage Publications, Inc., 2011.

Mattingly, Doreen. "Making Maids: United States Immigration Policy and Immigrant Domestic Workers." *Gender, Migration, and Domestic Service,* edited by Janet Henshall-Momsen, Routledge, 1999, pp. 62-82.

Mishler, Elliot George. "The Analysis of Narrative-Interviews." *Narrative Psychology: The Storied Nature of Human Conduct,* edited by T. R. Sharbin, Praeger, 1986, pp. 233-54.

"Nine Bodies Found Outside Home in Mexico's Nuevo Laredo." *Reuters*, 27, July 2017. www.reuters.com/article/us-mexico-violence /nine-bodies-found-outside-home-in-mexicos-nuevo-laredo- idUSKBN1AD00H. Accessed 24 May 2019.

Nipper-Eng, Christena E. *Home and Work*. The University of Chicago Press, 1995.

"Pew Research Center: Facts on U.S. Immigrants, 2016." *Pew Hispanic*, September 2018. www.pewhispanic.org/2018/09/14/facts-on-u-s- immigrants-trend-data/. Accessed 24 May 2019.

Riessman, Catherine Kohler. *Narrative Methods for the Human Sciences*. Sage Publications, Inc., 2008.

Romero, Mary. *Maid in the USA*: Routledge, 2002.

Timoshenkov, Miguel. "Cuellar: Degree of Violence Assessed." *Laredo Morning Times,* April 2013, www.lmtonline.com/articles /2013/04 /03/news/doc515bd643ccdc4232138221.txt. Accessed 24 May 2019.

Tracy, Sarah, and Angela Trethewey. "Fracturing the Real-Self ← → Fake-Self Dichotomy: Moving Toward 'Crystallized' Organizational Discourses and Identities." *Communication Theory,* vol. 15, 2005, pp. 168-95.

Trethewey, Angela, et al. "Constructing Embodied Organizational Identities: Commodifying, Securing, and Servicing Professional Bodies." *The Handbook of Gender and Communication,* edited by Bonnie Dow and Julia T. Wood, Sage, 2006, pp. 123-43.

*U.S. Bureau of Labor Statistics: American Time Use Survey: Household Activities. United States Department of Labor,* Oct. 2015, www.bls.gov/ TUS/CHARTS/HOUSEHOLD.HTM. Accessed 24 May 2019.

Wolcott, Harry F. *The Art of Fieldwork*: Alta Mira Press, 2005.

Wrzesniewski, Amy, et al. "Interpersonal Sensemaking and the Meaning of Work." *Research in Organizational Behavior,* vol. 25, 2003, pp. 93-135.

Chapter Seven

# Behind the Screens: Mary Elkinton Nitobe and Mary Dardis Noguchi

Suzanne Kamata

In the West, it is often said that behind every great man is a woman. In Japan, female supporters behind the scenes often go unacknowledged. Both Noguchi Hideyo, the renowned bacteriologist whose image appears on the Japanese 1,000 yen note, and Nitobe Inazo—the revered statesman, author, agriculturist, and former face of the 5,000 yen bill—were married to American women named Mary, which is especially significant in a country that has traditionally valued racial purity and in which marriages between Western women and Japanese men have been uncommon. Whereas the reputations of these men have remained secure and have perhaps even expanded, their wives are rarely mentioned. Ignored or not, these American women— and others, such as Therese Schumacher, the German bride of Nagayoshi Nagai, father of pharmacology in Japan—played a part in the success of their Japanese husbands. In this chapter, I attempt to illuminate the contributions of these two women, the wives named Mary, and to suggest some possible reasons for their erasure. I also argue that they should not be erased but rather acknowledged.

## Background

Japanese women have been subjected to the ideal of "good wives, wise mothers" since at least the Meiji Period (1868-1912), when the government established girls' schools throughout the country. As Jan Bardsley writes in her introduction to *The Bluestockings of Japan: New Woman Essays and Fiction from Seito, 1911-16*, the intended goal of these schools was to produce "thrifty, domestically skilled, good wives to the nation's leaders and wise, patriotic mothers to their children" (11). Some early Japanese feminists, such as the poet Yosano Akiko and Hiratsuka Haru, a graduate of Japan Women's College, used their education to rebel against these expectations by writing essays, stories, and poetry. They addressed issues such as sexual freedom, abortion, love, marriage, and the politics of prostitution. While they sometimes looked to the West, translating works by radical women such as Emma Goldman, their writings, published in the magazine, *Seito*, often confronted "the woman question," as it pertained to middle-class, educated Japanese women.

Later iterations of Japanese feminism concentrated upon the issues surrounding the so-called comfort women, women who were forced into sexual slavery by the Japanese Army during the Second World War. In the 1970s, *uman lib* (from "woman's liberation") took hold, promoting a more transnational view and incorporating a critical response to Western cultural imperialism. Furthermore, transnational feminism has considered the conditions of women of colour, women from the Global South, and postcolonial women; Japanese feminists also sought to atone for Japan's imperialist past, which was influenced by Western imperialism. More recently, Setsuko Shigematsu has advocated for critical transnational feminism—an anti-imperialist or decolonial" form of feminism.

In recent decades, feminist scholarship has tried to highlight women previously elided from history. I believe, however, that some Western wives of prominent Japanese men have fallen through the cracks, which is, perhaps, due to their in-between status. Not quite Japanese, and not quite foreign—who, exactly, is responsible for bringing them to our attention? Many such women fail to conform to the standard of "good wives, wise mothers," yet they might not have attracted the attention of transnational feminists, either. Nevertheless, as Sakiko Kitagawa argues, it is time for a mode of feminism in Japan that permits an understanding of "the complex interconnectedness of women's lives." I believe that includes Western women in Japan.

Even now, well into the twenty-first century, the percentage of marriages in Japan between Western women and Japanese men is small. As Diane Nagatomo notes in *Identity, Gender, and Teaching English in Japan*, less than 2 percent of the 21,488 marriages between a Japanese and foreign national registered in Japan in 2013 were between Japanese men and American women. In the late nineteenth century, such marriages were even more unusual. From 1639 to 1859, during the period that Japan had limited contact with the West, foreign women were prohibited by law from entering Japan entirely, and marriages between Japanese and Westerners were illegal. Between 1873 and 1897, there were 230 legally recognized marriages between Japanese and non-Japanese people; of these, only twelve were between Japanese men and Western women. One may expect that the sheer novelty of an American or European wife would render her memorable, especially if she were married to a well-known Japanese man. Yet this was not usually the case.

Two Western women associated with prominent Japanese men have recently gained recognition in Japan through their depiction in popular TV dramas or movies—such as *Leonie*, which introduces the American mother of sculptor Isamu Noguchi, and NHK's recent series *Maasan*, which is inspired by Scottish whiskey maker Rita Taketsuru, wife of Masataka. Surprisingly, however, the exceptional marriages between national heroes Hideyo Noguchi and Inazo Nitobe and their American wives have been barely recognized. Nor has the marriage between Nagayoshi Nagai and Therese Schumacher been given much attention, even in Nagai's hometown, Tokushima. The sudden posthumous fame of Scottish whiskey maker Rita Taketsuru suggests that early interracial marriages between Japanese men and Western women would, indeed, be of interest, if only Japanese people knew about them.

In 2016, I conducted a brief survey of 121 first-year students at Tokushima University, hailing from various parts of the country, and I asked if they had ever heard of six well-known men—Noguchi Hideyo, Nitobe Inazo, Nagai Nagayoshi, Sakamoto Ryoma, and current Prime Minister Abe Shinzo. Furthermore, I asked what, if anything, the students knew about their wives. I was surprised to discover that although all were familiar with Hideyo Noguchi, only five knew his wife's name and/or nationality, and although 108 of the 121 surveyed students responded that they had heard of Inazo Nitobe, only five knew that her name was Mary and only one student identified her as

American. Only one student, a female from Tokushima majoring in nursing, knew of both Nagayoshi Nagai and his German wife, Therese. Additionally, most students could not name the current prime minister's wife. Several did, however, know the name of the wife of folk hero Ryoma Sakamoto, possibly due to a recent TV miniseries, and several knew the name of the wife of popular writer Natsume Soseki. To be fair, Japanese wives of public figures tend to remain in the background, which may be a holdover from Confucian ideals promoted in Japan during the seventeenth and eighteenth centuries. The treatise *Onna Daigaku* (1729) prescribes that women be obedient and submissive to the men in their lives. Women, then, were meant to live their lives quietly, in service to men. Until recently, most Japanese people did not even know the name of the current prime minister's wife. As Yo-Jung Chen writes in *The Diplomat*, in Japan "a politicians' wife is mostly confined to an invisible, obedient, and supportive role." The prime minister's wife is considered a private citizen, and her activities are said to have no bearing on her husband's political career. From my own experience, I know that Japanese wives are often kept separate from men's work lives. For instance, I have never been invited to any work-related parties for my high-school-teaching husband.

Thanks to feminist movements in the United States and Europe, women are increasingly emerging from the shadows of their famous husbands. For example, many books have been devoted to the various wives and lovers of American writer Ernest Hemingway— such as *The Hemingway Women* by Bernice Kert (1998); *Hadley* (1982) and *Paris without End: The True Story of Hemingway's First Wife* both by Gioia Diliberto (2011); and the novel *The Paris Wife* by Paula McClain. Similarly, the life of Mileva Maric Einstein, a physicist and Albert Einstein's previously forgotten first wife, has been brought to light in biographies written by Milan Popovic, Ramila Milentijevic, and Christopher Jon Bjerknes as well as in the novel *The Other Einstein* (2016) by Marie Benedict. Additionally, Clementine Churchill, wife of Winston, has been the subject of several biographies. In contrast, although Japanese women and other women in Japan have made great strides towards equality in the past decades, wives often remain in the background, or behind the scenes, no matter what part they have played in their husbands' lives.

Gender certainly plays a part in this, but I believe that Schumacher,

Elkinton, and Dardis have also been ignored because of their nationalities. Although Japan has at times been open to Western influence, at many periods in its history, politicians and others have rejected white supremacy through encouraging a sense of Japanese superiority. Having to acknowledge the contributions of foreign wives, thus, would dilute the accomplishments of these national heroes. Additionally, some Japanese feminists have bristled against Western hegemony, seeking to focus on Asian issues.

In this chapter, I rely upon previously published books in Japanese and English, articles from journals and newspapers, films, personal experience, and surveys of Japanese college students and adults to attempt to answer to the following question: why are Japanese people not familiar with the foreign wives of national heroes Noguchi Hideyo, Nitobe Inazo, and Nagai Nagayoshi?

## Therese Nagai

I first learned of Therese Nagai while listening to a student presentation. I was teaching a class of first-year pharmacology students at Tokushima University. Their assignment had been to make a group presentation on something related to their major. One group chose to introduce Tokushima-native Nagayoshi Nagai, the father of pharmacology in Japan, and the founder of Tokushima University's Pharmacology Department; his statue overlooks a pond on campus. My ears perked when the student mentioned that he had married a German woman. How was it that I had lived in Tokushima for twenty-six years, yet no one had ever mentioned her to me?

My Japanese boyfriend had kept me a secret from his parents until we decided to marry. Even then, his parents tried to encourage him to marry a Japanese woman and confessed that they were worried about what other people would think if they had a foreign daughter-in-law, not to mention half-Japanese grandchildren. When we did actually marry, my name was not entered in the official family register but added as a mere footnote because I am not a Japanese citizen. Since there had been so much resistance to my own marriage, as an American, to a Japanese man, I had come to the conclusion that marriages between foreign women and Japanese men were a very recent development. When I had first arrived in Japan in 1988,

*Nihonjinron*—the notion of the uniqueness of the Japanese—was widespread. Books extolling the supposed superiority of the Japanese race topped bestseller lists. I'd met Western wives of Japanese who had been shunned by their in-laws because they were foreign, presumably for sullying the pure blood of their husband's family lines. In my own case, I'd once been invited to dinner by the principal of the school where I worked as an assistant English teacher. When I mentioned a dream I'd had, his wife remarked, "Oh, do foreigners have dreams?" as if I were an alien species and that dreams were unique to the Japanese. "Maybe you will decide to stay in Japan and get married," the principal's wife said later during the meal. "Perhaps to a Filipino." It was as if she couldn't conceive of the idea that I might actually marry a Japanese man.

Since marriages between Japanese men and Western women were so wildly exotic, I couldn't imagine that anyone, having heard of one, would forget, especially a marriage between a lauded native son and a German Fräulein. Didn't ordinary people know of her? I knew of Wenceslau de Moraes, the Portuguese sailor who'd settled at the foot of Mt. Bizan and who wrote about Tokushima in Portuguese. There was a museum dedicated to him at the top of the mountain. I also knew of the German prisoners of war who'd been interred in nearby Naruto during World War I. Because of these foreign men, the prefecture had established ties with both Portugal and Germany. But what about this woman, Therese? I'd been a member of the Association of Foreign Wives of Japanese for over a decade, and her name had never come up. I was determined to find out more about her and other foreign wives who had preceded me.

## Mary Elkinton and Inazo Nitobe

Mary Elkinton, the only daughter of a prominent Quaker soap-making family, met Nitobe Inazo in 1886 when he gave a lecture about Japan in Philadelphia. She was impressed by his views on women's education in Japan. Shortly thereafter he departed for Europe, however, the two deepened their acquaintance through correspondence (Mizenko 177). They fell in love, and decided to marry.

Their wedding, held on New Year's Day in 1891 at the Friends Meeting House in Philadelphia, was reported across the country. *The*

*Boston Post* called it "An Uncommon Union," whereas a sub-headline in the *San Francisco Chronicle* noted "The Romance of an Oriental Student and a Susceptible Young Woman." A few days after the ceremony, they sailed for their new home in Sapporo, then a frontier town on Japan's northernmost island. Once settled, Nitobe established the first night school in Japan. In addition to teaching, he wrote and self-published a biography of William Penn. Mary busied herself with leading Bible study classes and writing chipper letters home to Philadelphia. Later, when Mary inherited $1,000 from a lady who had been taken in as an orphan by the Elkintons, she used the money to buy a piece of property and start a private school. Nicknamed "Ragged School," its official name was *En'yu Yagakko*, meaning Far-off Friends School. The first graduating class was in 1899.

Mary, who went by "*Mariko*" in Japan, gave birth to a boy, Thomas, who died eight days later. She returned to Philadelphia to mourn and wound up staying for over a year. Later, the couple adopted Yoshio, the son of Inazo's sister, and still later, Kotoko, the granddaughter of another sister. Mary's parents sent a young woman named Rachel Read over to be her personal nurse. Rachel's cousin, Bryn Mawr-educated Anna Hartshorne, who became a teacher at the school for Japanese girls founded by Umeko Tsuda (which later became Tsuda College), also lived with the Nitobe family in Japan for several years.

Around this time, Nitobe suffered a nervous breakdown reportedly due to overwork. During his recovery, he began to work on the book for which he is most famous today— *Bushido: The Soul of Japan*, which has been long regarded by some as the definitive tome on the Land of the Rising Sun. In his preface, Nitobe writes, "the direct inception of this little book is due to the frequent queries put by my wife as to the reasons why such and such customs prevail in Japan" (qtd. in Oshiro 7).

Mary helped to get the book published in Philadelphia and handled related correspondence and proofreading. *Bushido: The Soul of Japan* became a bestseller when it was published in English in the United States. (Its reception in Japan was mixed.) Six years after its initial publication, a tenth revised edition was issued in English. In the preface to that volume, Nitobe notes that the book had gone through eight editions in Japanese. The book had also been translated into several other languages, including Mahratti, German, Polish, French, Chinese, and Russian. Nitobe writes the following: "Exceedingly flattering is the news that has reached me from official sources, that President Roosevelt has done it undeserved honor by reading it and distributing several dozens of copies among his friends." Again, he thanks his wife for "her reading of the proof-sheets, for helpful suggestions, and, above all, for her constant encouragement." As a result of the book's success and influence, Nitobe and Mary were invited to meet the Meiji emperor.

Although Mary once professed a desire to learn the "language, habits, and customs" (Oshiro 9) of the country, she never became fluent in Japanese. Except on special occasions, meals were Western, and she ate them with knives and forks. In an essay, published in *Quaker History*, writer George Oshiro remarks, "Her personality did not allow her to be humble to her servants and to other Japanese around her. She had always commanded awe and respect" (14). This assessment of her character would indicate that she was not demure and subservient—not an ideal Japanese wife.

After Nitobe's retirement, the couple returned to Japan where Mary, now almost seventy, helped to find the Japanese Humane Society, and was active in the YWCA and the Friends Girls' School in Tokyo. In 1935, she accompanied her husband on a trip to attend a conference in Banff, Canada. He collapsed and was sent to the Royal Jubilee Hospital in Victoria, where he died after an operation.

Mary returned to Japan to carry on her husband's legacy. In her remaining years, Mary Nitobe continued to collect and publish Nitobe's writings. She was engaged in editing his diaries at the time of her death. Nitobe's dream was to forge a bridge between East and West. Importantly, Mary was essential to Nitobe's success, as he wrote his bestselling book in response to Mary's inquiries. It was his wife, Mary, who proofread the book, endeavoured to find a publisher for it, and managed his correspondences. Without her, it's likely that he would not have achieved such enduring, international recognition. Although it's difficult to know just how much her ideas informed his writing, their work together clearly constituted a partnership. Mary should be recognized for her own part in expanding cross-cultural understanding.

## Mary Dardis and Hideyo Noguchi

And the other Mary? Hideyo Noguchi wed the Irish American Mary Loretta Dardis in 1912, but information about her is scarce. They met in New York City, where he was involved in research at the Rockefeller Lab. Noguchi kept to himself even in the laboratory where he preferred to work alone. According to a 1931 article in *Time Magazine* only a few of his friends knew more about "the tumultuous little scientist ... than that he was born in 1876 to a Japanese peasant, that he eventually reached the U.S. where he produced important discoveries on snake venoms, syphilis, infantile paralysis, rabies, smallpox, yellow fever, that nations gave him kudos."

Noguchi, a descendant of a samurai, is remembered in Japan for his intelligence, his courage, and his filial piety. Fukushima Prefecture's website includes a page devoted to its native son, who "devoted his life to mankind and died for mankind." There is no reference to his wife in this carefully crafted bio. The website of the Hideyo Noguchi Africa Prize also skips Mary but notes that her husband returned to Japan to visit his mother after a fifteen-year absence. Likewise, most children's biographies of Noguchi emphasize the relationship between him and his mother, Shika, whose hard work in the rice fields made it possible for her disabled son to thrive—a standard Confucian theme. (Noguchi's father and grandfather were said to be lazy drunks.) In the 2016 manga biography for children written by Yago Yasuo, Mary is featured in four panels. The first panel mentions her marriage with Noguchi but nothing about her background or how she met the Japanese man. In the second panel, she is exclaiming over a discovery he made at the kitchen table. In the third and fourth, she brings her husband a letter from Japan about his mother and urges him to go visit her.

*Dr. Noguchi's Journey: A Life of Medical Search and Discovery*, originally written in Japanese by Astushi Kita, also focuses more on the scientist's relationship with his mother and the object of his youthful unrequited love than it does with his American wife of seventeen years. In the first mention of Mary, Kita writes, "On April 10 Noguchi married Mary Dardis, whom he had met some years earlier, in a small quiet church ceremony" (173). In another account, by Nobuko Iinuma, the large-eyed, full-figured Irish American beauty and the scientist met at a piano bar near the lab, where they both liked to drink. Dardis was born in Pennsylvania in 1876 to an American father and Irish mother.

She had two younger brothers, John and Thomas. According to the 1930 United States Federal Census, she was literate but had little or no formal education. In Kita's unattributed account, "Mary was not the kind of woman who could take—or even fake—an interest in her husband's research" (174). At thirty-five, Mary was the same age as Noguchi.

According to Iinuma, Noguchi and Mary were married by a justice of the peace alongside the Hudson River in an impromptu ceremony, presumably while both were under the influence. In marrying Noguchi, Mary lost her American citizenship. According to the Expatriation Act of 1907 (also known as the Perkins Act, after the xenophobic California senator George C. Perkins, who sponsored the bill), American women who married foreign nationals were regarded as having expatriated themselves to their husband's nationality. Furthermore, under Japan's 1873 Great Council of State Proclamation, a foreign woman legally married to a Japanese man was considered Japanese (Nagatomo 83). Thus Mary, who had never been to Japan and could not speak Japanese, became Japanese.

Noguchi kept his marriage a secret from his colleagues at the Rockefeller Institute because, according to his friend Araki, "they might not be so quick to give full membership if he had a wife and they had to figure on her pension for the future, too" (Eckstein 184). However, Noguchi's reasons for discretion may have been more complicated. Supposedly, his mentor and employer Flexner did not like Mary, so Noguchi may have feared his mentor's censure. Also, according to biographer Gustav Eckstein, he told another friend that he didn't want news of his marriage "out among the Japanese of New York" (184). Perhaps he sensed that his fellow countrymen—and possibly his colleagues at the Rockefeller Institute—would disapprove of his union with an American woman. Although New York did not have anti-miscegenation laws as did some other states, marriages between whites and non-whites were controversial on both sides of the Pacific.

Whatever the reason their seemingly impulsive marriage remained hidden, by all accounts, they were affectionate towards one another. Noguchi nicknamed her "Maizie," and she called him "Hidey." While apart, their letters to each other were signed with love. For her part, Mary tended to her husband's appearance and wellbeing as much as he allowed. According to Eckstein, she learned to make Japanese dishes, such as sukiyaki, in addition to other foods he enjoyed, such as roast lamb, cabbage, and corn beef. When she came across his hidden liquor bottles, she poured the contents down the sink. She also helped to keep him entertained, reading to him from Tolstoy and Shakespeare, while he peered into his microscope at the kitchen table. They sometimes went to the opera.

In 1928, he announced to his wife that he would go to Africa for further research. Filled with a sense of foreboding, Maizie urged him to stay home. He set off for Accra to try to find the cause of yellow fever. Over the next several weeks, he kept Mary abreast of his research via post. In one of his last letters to Mary from Accra, dated 27 March, he writes the following: "I spend every moment of every day waiting for a telegram from you. When I am dispirited or tired, you are the one thing that raises my spirits. I am always thinking of you. It is rare that I dream but when I do, it is always of you" (qtd. in Kita 243).

Tragically, he contracted the disease himself and died in Africa just after writing to tell Mary of his impending return. After his death, many of his colleagues at the Rockefeller Institute awere surprised to learn of his marriage. With nothing to gain through continued secrecy, however, Mary emerged as the grieving widow. A California news-paper reported that she was "in a state of collapse following the receipt of the news of her husband's death in Africa" (qtd. in Kita 243). She later planted a rose bush at his grave. Although she never remarried, records show that she shared a house with her younger brother, Thomas. Two years after Noguchi's death, she regained her American citizenship. Atsushi Kita writes the following: "she maintained a connection with his family by sending Inu, Hideyo's sister, twelve dollars a month out of the bereavement allowance she received from the Rockefeller Institute. Mary lived on for almost another twenty years, dying on the last day of 1947" (251).

How did Mary spend those last twenty years? Or for that matter, how did she spend her first thirty-five years? Why did she marry at such a late age (for that time)? What compelled her to marry a Japanese scientist? Why did he choose her? In contemporary Japan, although Noguchi's mother is celebrated, his marriage is rarely mentioned, and these intriguing questions remain unanswered. Nevertheless, Mary Dardis Noguchi played an important part in the life of Hideyo

Noguchi over their seventeen-year union. One could argue that her assistance may have even helped to prolong his life. Although she deserves consideration in any account of the life of this complicated man, she is also an intriguing figure as a woman in her own right. Not just any woman would have surrendered her citizenship to marry a brilliant yet mercurial foreigner. The marriage itself defied convention yet was evidently founded on passion and mutual respect. In existing accounts, she is something of a cipher. She is credited with taking care of Noguchi's material needs, but very little is known about her. It's time that Mary Dardis Noguchi and other unsung foreign wives of notable Japanese men got their due.

## Conclusion

Considering that the wives of national heroes Inazo Nitobe, and Hideyo Noguchi were white women from the United States, it is possible that their contributions to their husbands' lives and careers as well as to Japan, more generally, have been downplayed due to their nationality. Even still, though, as this chapter shows, these women influenced their husbands' lives and careers.

Mary Nitobe promoted education through the founding of a private school. In addition to her work as a pioneering educator, her discussions with her husband inspired his most successful book, and she was responsible for publishing her husband's writings both before and after his death. Thanks to Mary, his work enjoys an international reputation.

Likewise, Mary Noguchi looked after the physical and material needs of her husband and gave him emotional support. As a native speaker of English, one would expect that she helped to make his life in the United States easier in various ways. As marriage in Japan at that time was typically more of a merger between families, it might have been easy to discount their union as a marriage of convenience, or desperation, since he needed someone to take care of himself. However, letters between them indicate affection, and by American standards, theirs seems to be a great love story. Because she was foreign born and did not conform to Confucian ideals, perhaps she was something of an embarrassment to the Japanese. It's likely that Japanese scholars and historians would rather forget that one of their highest achieving native sons spent most of his life abroad with a barren woman he met in a bar. Nevertheless, her identity remains a tantalizing mystery. Surely, she was far more complicated and interesting than her Japanese biographers would suggest.

While these women certainly deserve attention for their own accomplishments, public acknowledgment of their identities would also contribute to a more holistic understanding of their husbands. Additionally, openness about these early transnational marriages may also contribute to better intercultural understanding and acceptance in an era when prejudice against foreigners and biracial children endures in Japan.

## Works Cited

Bardsley, Jan. *The Bluestockings of Japan: New Woman Essays and Fiction from Seito, 1911-16.* Center for Japan Studies/The University of Michigan, 2007.

Chen, Yo-Jung. "The Changing Role of First Ladies." The Diplomat, July 8, 2014. www.thediplomat.com/2014/07/the-changing-role-of-first-ladies//. Accessed 28 May 2019.

Eckstein, Gustav. *Noguchi.* Harper and Brothers Publishers, 1931.

Fukushima Prefecture. www.pref.fukushima.lg.jp/site/portal-english/en05-03.html. Accessed 28 May 2019.

Hideyo Noguchi Africa Prize. www.noguchiprize.afro.who.int/en/home/. Accessed 28 May 2019.

Iinuma, Nobuko. *Nagai Nagayoshi to Terēze: Nihon yakugaku no kaiso* (Therese and Nagai Nagayoshi: Father of Japanese Pharmacology). Nihon Yakugakkai, 2003.

Iinuma, Nobuko. *Noguchi Hideyo to Merī Dājisu : Meiji Taishō ijintachi no kokusai kekkon* (Noguchi Hideo and Mary Dardis: Foreign Wives of Famous Men During the Meiji and Taisho Eras). Suiyosha, 2007.

Kita, Atsushi. *Dr. Noguchi's Journey: A Life of Medical Search and Discovery.* Translated by Peter Durfee. Kodansha, 2005.

Kitagawa, Sakiko. "Cultural Self-Understanding and Japanese Feminism." *The University of Tokyo,* www.utcp.c.u-tokyo.ac.jp/members/pdf/kitagawa_east_asian_feminism.pdf. Accessed 24 May 2019.

"Medicine: Funny Noguchi." *Time Magazine*, May 18, 1931.

Mizenko, Matthew. "Nitabo Inazo and Mary Patterson Elkinton: An International Marriage Made in Philadelphia." *Phila-Nipponica: An Historic Guide to Philadelphia & Japan*, edited by Linda H. Chance and Testuko Toda, Japan American Society of Greater Philadelphia, 2015, pp. 176-180.

Nagatomo, Diane Hawley. *Identity, Gender and Teaching English in Japan*. Multilingual Matters, 2016.

Nitobe, Inazo. *Bushido: The Soul of Japan,* 10th ed. Putnam, 1905.

Oshiro, George. "Mary P.E. Nitobe and Japan," *Quaker History*, vol. 86, no. 2, 1997, pp. 1-15.

Shigematsu, Setsu. "Rethinking Japanese Feminism and the Lessons of Ūman Ribu: Toward a Praxis of Critical Transnational Feminism." *Rethinking Japanese Feminisms*, edited by Julia C. Bullock et al., University of Hawai'i Press, Honolulu, 2018, pp. 205-29.

Yago, Yasuo. *Noguchi Hideyo*. Poplar, 2016.

Chapter Eight

# The Socialization of Fulani Young Girls as Good Wives: A Persisting Pedagogical Ideal in the Context of Social Change

Ester Botta Somparé

I n 2008, at the beginning of my research in the district of Tassara, located in the coastal region of Guinea and inhabited by a Fulani minority group, I talked with a man who had just asked a *waliou* to foresee the future of his children. According to local beliefs, *waliou* are wise men, who have not only a wide Islamic knowledge and a deep comprehension of local history and tradition but also some magic powers, such as the capacity to foretell the future. When fathers must make an important choice about their children, for instance deciding whether they should go to school or become shepherds, the expertise of *waliou* may be of great help. *Waliou* may predict if a young boy will become a Koranic teacher, a skilful craftsman, or a high public officer; they can also foresee whether a girl will be married to a man living in the same village or whether she should move to town or even abroad. This explanation intrigued me, as it underlined an important point: fathers are worried about the professional destiny of their boys, but they are more concerned about the marital life of their daughters, as if their future amounted to becoming a wife. Some weeks later, at the local primary school, my hypothesis was confirmed: during a speech directed to parents, who were being sensitized about the importance of providing children with schooling, the director said: "You never know what your child will become. If you send your child to school, you give a boy the opportunity to become a minister; you give a girl the chance to be married by a president." This teacher suggested that the fact of becoming a well-read woman may give a girl the opportunity to make a better marriage. Instead of sharing the hard life of a nomadic shepherd, she may move to the capital and raise her children in a beautiful house, enjoying the comfort offered by a wealthy husband. But then the teacher added: "And then, you know, times are changing ... and maybe your daughter may become a minister herself!"

## Theoretical and Methodological Framework

In French-speaking literature on African societies, it is very rare to find books explicitly centred on the identity and the experience of wives, with the exception of a book on polygyny called *La femme de mon mari* (Fanzaing and Journet Diallo). Nevertheless, anthropological and sociological literature does provide important information about wives, but it is generally embedded in more general publications concerning relationships within the family and rules that codify them. It would be impossible, here, to offer an exhaustive review of all the works that while dealing with African family offer ethnographic information on wives. One example is the classic book *La Famille Wolof* (Diop), which describes in detail the procedures used to select one's partner, the ritual celebration of marriage, as well as the behaviour expected from wives and husbands. Some of these publications seem to adopt, willingly or not, a feminist point of view, at least according to the definition given by Huguette Dagenais. For Dagenais, a feminist methodology insists on attributing to women a visibility often denied by describing their working conditions and by highlighting their point of view about the situations they experience. Such features are present, for instance, in Suzanne Lallemand's book *Une Famille Mossi,* where the author, a woman anthropologist, explores the point of view of two co-wives and how they co-exist as well as their opinions on men, love, seduction, and sex. A feminist methodology is also used, in a more explicit way, by Nehara Feldham in studying gendered social relations in Malian society. In a village located near the town of Kayes, she describes the difficult situations experienced by young women unhappy with their marriage and willing to divorce; they find themselves in a sort of no man's land—foreigners both in their own family and in their family-in-law, with virtually no place to go. While describing African families, all these studies point to the structural inequality between the two sexes and hint to men's domination. In a comparative study of men's domination in many societies all over the world, the feminist anthropologist Nicole-Claude Mathieu (1991) remarks that such an inequality is often rooted in myths or is presented as a natural condition. Women are socialized to consider men's domination as a matter of fact—as an established order that is not to be contested. Even though they may not like this situation, they feel compelled to conform to it and are not likely to think that such a hierarchy could be challenged. Mathieu explains that socialization plays an important role in wives' submission: for example, the mother's behaviour and comments provide their daughter with a model of marital relationships that they tend to adopt and repeat. The aim of this chapter is twofold: to see how the process of socialization of young girls tries to convert them into good wives, corresponding to a pedagogical ideal defined by men and to explore how Fulani women—and Guinean women more generally—experience a contradiction between their progressive access to education and paid work as means of empowerment and the imperative to stick to the traditional wife's role.

The concept of intersectionality—which refers to interacting forms of domination related to different aspects of individual identity (Creenshaw)—is important in understanding how Fulani girls and young women are submitted to a double process of domination, from both men and elderly people. As all youngsters, male and female, they have to cope with the necessity to conform to the elders' decisions in a gerontocratic society, where choices about children's future must take into account the interests of the whole family, even if they sometimes clash with individual aspirations. For instance, if the household needs a new shepherd to take care of its most precious capital, the cattle, a student may be obliged to leave school and go to the pastures, even if he regards this possibility as a nightmare. In this context, it is not astonishing that marriage results from a decision based on lineages, not individual choice. In the Tassara district, this is explained not only by the fact that "elderly people know better" but also by threatening beliefs, such as the idea that two young people in love who have already experienced a certain degree of intimacy will surely go to hell if they decided to get married, along with all their relatives. However, demographic studies suggest a new trend towards progressive participation of young people in the decision to marry, not only in towns but also in some rural areas as well (Hertrich 139). Postponing the age of marriage is the consequence of a redefinition of lifecycles (Locoh and Mouvaga-Sow 3), which has allowed the emergence of a new space of adolescence, marked by such occasions as school or apprenticeship. This period appears to be favourable to the consolidation of autonomy and to the increased participation in life choices. Nevertheless, as we will see later, there is still an asymmetry between boys' and girls' possibility to resist elder pressure as far as marriage is concerned. Autonomy, independence, and individual ization—which are conceived as a person's ability to establish a critical distance from one's family and community (Alain Marie 73)—seem to be important concepts to analyse modern West African societies, particularly transformations in the family structures. Alain Marie and his co-authors, in particular, focus on such aspects to describe how economic and social crises that disrupt individual solidarities within the lineage encourage individuals to struggle for their own living, instead of relying on family or community networks. In such a context, demographic and sociological studies point to an increasing tendency to choose one's partner, which may lead to a more intimate relationship for the couple, grounded on solidarity and mutual support. Nevertheless, Thérèse Locoh and Myriam Mouvaga Sow observe that despite the general reduction of age, which may favour more egalitarian relationships for the couple, the persistence of polygamy does not support this new direction.

Thus, this chapter questions the possibility for young women to partially challenge the two forms of domination to which they are exposed. It presents, at first, the pedagogical ideal of the good wife conveyed by traditional education, showing how such a model is transmitted and internalized during socialization. For the definition of a good wife, I shall use Durkheim's context of pedagogical ideal (1922), based on the conviction that every society, at a certain time, has a specific ideal of man and woman and that education is the effort to shape children so that they will correspond to such models.

Durkheim's pedagogical ideal is a complex concept that takes into account social differentiation and cultural dynamics: not only does it change over time, in order to adapt to social mutations, but it also presents some aspects shared by everybody and some others that are only typical of some social groups. However, Durkheim does not mention the process of formation of such an ideal, but it is likely to be influenced by the hegemonic group's representations of society and education. Thus, it seems probable that the ideal of the good wife corresponds to men's wishes about their spouses, and not to the women's own definition.

By adopting an intergenerational perspective, this chapter also describes the process of progressive inclusion of individual aspirations in decisions about marriage, pointing to the fact that boys and girls have different degrees of autonomy in existential choices. Finally, it considers education and paid work as tools of empowerment that must take place, so far, within socially acceptable limits so that they do not challenge male supremacy within the family. Particular attention is paid to mothers, who are the most important actors in in teaching girls about how to become a good wife. The chapter tries to describe the ambivalent reactions of these daughters, who for the first time, have acceded to secular knowledge and now aspire to paid work.

Concerning methodology, this chapter is based on eighteen months of fieldwork in the district of Tassara, in the coastal region of Guinea, which ended in 2008. As I have explained elsewhere (Botta Somparé and Vitale), during this anthropological research, I was unexpectedly led to use different methodologies to work with men and women, preferring interviews with the former and participant observations with the latter. Interviews were done in Pulaar and translated into French by my interpreter, who was also the school teacher; informal conversations with women also took place in Pulaar (that I had started to talk a little by that time), with the help of young girls attending the village school. I realized that interviews with women, made by myself and by a male interpreter, were perceived as inspections, as a way to scrutinize women's competence as educators and models for their daughters—a sort of examination to which they were already constantly submitted in their daily lives. That's why most of the material I collected with women comes from participant observation and informal conversations. In particular, teenage girls attending school in the Tassara district were not interviewed formally, as we established a close relationship that allowed me to spend a lot of time with them, as I followed them at school as well as during housework and leisure time. Furthermore, the research results presented in this chapter are also grounded on more recent observations concerning the girls met during my research, with whom I could keep in touch: some of them have already become wives, and others are just about to get married. I also had more recent conversations with female students at a university in Conakry in the spring of 2017 about their professional projects, which have also helped me reflect on their struggle to reconcile their professional expectations and the obligations of marital life. Without meaning to, my difficult and progressive integration into a women's social group made women become central actors of my research; thus, I paid a special attention to their role in society, the memories of their education, and their opinions on childrearing, school, and choices about their children's future.

## Fulani Girls' Education as Preparation for Marriage

The district of Tassara is inhabited by the Fulani—semi-nomadic cattle breeders, who at the end of the nineteenth century, migrated to this region from the mountains of Fouta Djallon. In this minority group— who maintain an ethnic identity based on a tradition of Koranic knowledge and on a pastoral lifestyle—the characteristic feature of gender relations is a deep separation of women and men; they perform different activities, related to the gendered division of work, and occupy different spaces. Men are considered superior to women: their pre-eminence is visible both in public life, as women cannot take part in public decisions, and in private life, since they are socialized to submit to their husbands. Parents, and especially mothers, educate their daughters to become good wives. Such an education requires practical training aimed at converting them into accomplished housewives as well as a moral teaching intended to provide young girls with the correct values when interacting with their husband and their family-in-law.

### Domestic Skills: A Wife's Knowhow

During primary socialization, from the age of four, some of the girls' and boys' games are different. The boys' favourite toys are minicars, which are built from a can of sardines; they joyfully drag them everywhere in the village with a rope, or hoops and tires. Girls, in contrast, prefer to imitate their mothers, who are usually busy with cooking: not far from their mothers, the girls use tomato cans as imaginary pots, to be filled by leaves or sand, while they pretend to light a fire made of little branches and stones. Women encourage them and ask such questions as: "what will you prepare today for your husband?" They urge them to "come and crush rice!" or demand if they have not prepared lunch yet. If a man comes around, he may give the little girls a small amount of money, telling them: "Please, cook a good meal for me!" Thus, they play the role of a husband who is giving his wife the "dépense"—a daily amount of money used to buy ingredients for cooking. Through these jokes, adults contribute to the socialization of the girls for their future role of wives, who are expected to prepare a meal for their family every day. Cooking is considered a woman's essential skill, and it is an important element in gender relationships, as serving a meal is the symbol of a wife's love and respect for her husband. Ideally, a wife should be able to serve her husband and, occasionally, his guests, a tasty meal; during the lunch, she will be around to offer more water, sauce, or rice. In the same region, in another ethnic group, the Landouma, I heard the story of a local chief's wife, who kneeled in front of him to serve him a lunch; he suddenly had to leave, but the woman remained. He found her in the evening: she was still waiting for him, kneeling in the same place. Her behaviour is still admired and described as an example of respect and submission, as a sort of prototype of a good wife's virtues.

A husband is always proud to say that his wife is a good cook, as it also appears in the oral tradition, for example in the epic of Soundjata Keita (Niane), in which a Mandinka warrior fights to recover a wife who had been abducted by a tyrant and who was said to be an excellent cook. It is interesting to note that the culinary skills of a young girl are cultivated throughout her childhood, as are other domestic skills: by the age of ten, a girl is expected to replace her mother in daily cooking activities, even though teenagers still need their mothers' assistance and supervision in preparing the most complex meals. A young girl learns to prepare every kind of Guinean meals, from the poorest to the richest ones, as she must be able to adapt to the economic condition of her future husband, who may be wealthy or poor. As teenagers in their village associations, girls will occasionally organize parties, where they will cook for the boys, who must finance the meal.

Besides cooking, young girls are expected to acquire other domestic skills that correspond to a rigid sexual division of work, in which women are loaded with a heavy burden. They must ensure the order and the cleanness of the house as well as the upkeep of the vegetable garden; if they are born in a family of cattle breeders, they must also learn to milk cows. These skills are taught by mothers and other women in the neighbourhood, whose practical lessons, mostly based on imitation, have the double purpose to enable girls to help their mothers with housework and to prepare them to become good wives. Cleanliness is considered an important virtue of a wife and is seen as a symbol of self-respect, resulting from good conduct. Fulani women who can keep tidy homes and beautiful vegetable gardens are highly appreciated in the whole region; they are also expected to take care of their personal hygiene, especially in the kitchen, and to provide fresh, clean clothes to their husband and children. And, finally, they are also required to be hardworking, to wake up early every morning, and to possess a high-level of endurance, resulting from being accustomed to intense work from the age of six.

## A Good Wife's Virtues

In addition to domestic skills, a young girl also has to internalize a good wife's moral virtues. Since their infancy, young girls have been socialized to be present in the domestic space and to keep close to their mothers. As mentioned above, their first games fix them in a precise place, namely a fictive kitchen, where they imitate the activities of adult women. The idea of "not walking" (*ne pas marcher*), is considered as an important educative value, as expressed by Adama Bah,[1] a forty-year-old wife: "A girl mustn't get used to walking a lot; otherwise, when she gets married, she will not accept to stay still in her husband's home. She will say: "My parents used to let me go everywhere; I will not stop it now. That's why you meet women who, as soon as they finish to cook the lunch for their husband, immediately run away, to another man's place." This belief, also shared by other Guinean ethnic groups, appears even in the games that fathers play with baby girls; for instance, they will tenderly hit their feet while saying "Stop walking! You walk too much!" Boys are raised in a completely different way, as they are encouraged to move and explore their village. In a pastoral society, boys will be required to move a lot in order to follow the herds or to go and try one's luck in towns or abroad. In a more general way, if boys have to leave the women's world to assume their masculine identity, detaching themselves from their mother, girls are not encouraged to act in a similar way (Pierre Erny 231). On the contrary, their proximity with adult women allows them to profit from their wisdom, to imitate their examples, and to better integrate into their sexual group. These girls' movements are strictly controlled by mothers, aunts, and elder sisters out of the pervasive fear that they could have premature intercourse with boys, thus discrediting their families.

At the age of thirteen or fourteen, young girls start to receive explicit advice concerning their future marital life: these suggestions are a continuation of previous teachings aiming to transmit the values of respect and obedience towards adults. Helimatou Diallo, a forty-five-year-old-woman and a mother of four daughters, explained the following: "If my daughter comes back from school, telling that her teachers need wood, I tell her: 'you must go and get wood for them, you always have to listen to your parents and teachers. That's the only way to become a respectful and obedient wife." Respect is of great value in Fulani education: it indicates the correct attitudes that are expected towards a person having a superior status, due to age or social position within the lineage and the village community. A disciple, for instance, must respect his Koranic teacher; a son-in-law should show respectful attitudes towards his family-in-law. Respect implies obedience, helpfulness, politeness, and reserve: the child who kneels before his father and the woman who fetches a bucket full of water for her husband display respectful attitudes. I was often told by my informers that "for a man, the most important person to respect is the Koranic teacher; for a woman, it's the husband."

These explanations immediately convey the idea that husband and wife have different statuses; the wife's submission is an important dimension of their relationship. The pedagogical ideal of the good wife recommends helpful, warm, and welcoming attitudes towards the husband and his close relations, as well as polite and respectful relationships with the co-wives and the neighbours. During my conversations, I heard the following remarks: "wives should not forget that God put women a step behind men"; "women are very small compared to men's greatness'; and "in marriage, God puts man on the top and woman at the bottom." For this reason, women are incited to forgive men for his infidelities and to tolerate polygamy, which is almost universal in the district of Tassara. It is interesting to note that women contribute to the preservation of a pedagogical ideal based on submission, as they explain to girls that they will have to obey to their husbands' decisions and wishes. Even if elder women can express their solidarity to young wives unhappy with their marital life, they still encourage them to accept their condition, as submission to men is considered a natural exigency, something that is in the natural order of things—a sort of natural law that cannot be contested. During the fieldwork, I was often puzzled and even upset by women's adherence to a definition of a good wife that encouraged their total submission to their husband. Even though I tried to highlight the ideological and religious justifications of this attitude, I am still left wondering about such an adherence. I think that it is important to keep in mind some of Nicole-Claude Mathieu's warnings about women's consent to their domination. For Mathieu, consent can be a way to lead an "acceptable life" in a hierarchical order that is unfair and unfavourable to women, especially young ones. This adherence is more about adaptation than giving consent—a way to obtain gratifications and to avoid symbolic or real violence related to so-called deviant behaviours. Secondly, Mathieu considers that women—because of physical and mental tolls that wife-work takes, but also because they may have limited access to knowledge, information, and resources—may lack the adequate tools to question the ideologies and beliefs that justify their domination. In the following lines, I present examples of such justifications according to my interlocutors in the Tassara district, starting with Helimatou Diallo's remarks:

> At home, my husband takes all the decisions concerning his daughters' future. The father must always decide, in marital life and with children; otherwise, people will say that the husband is playing the wife's role and that the wife behaves like the husband. Such marriages often fail because a man must always be superior to his wife. For me, a good husband is a man who can lead the prayer. When the time comes to perform ablutions, he would say to his wife: "You see, it is time to pray, you will do like me …"

The man will step forward; the wife will stay behind. They will pray, and if, afterwards, the husband needs something, the woman will do it for him. Then, if time has come to lie together in bed …well, children born from such a union will be blessed.

In this passage, religious interpretation plays an important role in masculine supremacy, as in the prayer, men stand in front of women, as if to confirm that God dictated such an order of things. For Fulani women, Koranic education has become accessible only in recent years; before, women just celebrated the ceremony of admission into a Koranic school and would only learn the verses they needed to pray. Thus, in the previous generations, women considered their husbands as their guides and teachers in the religious practice. Many informers agreed that, for men, salvation depends on Koranic knowledge, whereas a woman just needs to respect her husband because if he is a good devotee, he will also show her the way to paradise.

However, besides religion, other beliefs push women to accept their husbands' domination and to transmit to their daughters the pedagogical ideal of a submissive and deferential wife. First of all, there is the attempt to root women's inferiority in nature in order to transform social inequalities into biological evidence. Such a sentiment is visible in the words of an old man, who told me the following: "I have noticed that, very often, when a woman expects a boy, her pregnancy is longer, up to ten months. For girls, only nine months are required. This means that, from the very beginning, God wanted to show us that men come first." As noted by Nai Kanté, in Guinean societies, mothers and daughters have a specular relationship: a girl is considered as her mother's mirror. Women often say that in order to prepare a girl for marriage, mothers must be a good example for her: the mother's behaviour towards the father as well as the mother's character is important to shape a well-educated girl and a good wife. Before marriage, the husband's family may enquire about the behaviour of the wife's mother because a woman's intimate nature is supposed to be transmitted to her daughter. A flighty woman is more likely to have inconstant, unfaithful daughters, who quickly shame themselves with an undesired pregnancy; a serious, faithful wife will probably have daughters who will preserve their virginity until their wedding day, thus filling their mothers with pride. If this happens, as said by an old woman, "a woman can walk with her head held high and never bow down to anyone" because this is the sign of a good education, strict supervision, and a fine example. In my interviews, I always noticed that women, especially young ones, were very tense and uneasy when I asked them about their daughters' education, as if they saw my questions as a kind of inspection. Whereas men told me all about their worries concerning their children's education, women were always on the defensive, like Laouratou, a mother in her early thirties: "I don't agree with other parents, who say that our children are impolite and badly educated and, especially, that girls tend to deviate from their mothers' recommendations. This is not everybody's case. Personally, I have educated my daughters very well, and I don't have any fear." I understood, later, that asking questions about a girl's education not only means to question her mother's talents as an educator but also to cast doubts about her example and her intimate nature. Actually, it is a common belief that the mother's morality as well as her capacity to set a good example may be judged through her daughter's behaviour.

Furthermore, the belief of *barakah* also plays an important role in making mothers aware of their alleged responsibilities in their children's and, especially, their daughters' behaviour. *Baraka* is a religious concept—a divine influx (Marie Vitale 234) that a Koranic teacher may transmit to his disciple by his spiritual influence, who may then transmit it to his offspring by blood. However, in Guinean society, the belief of *barakah* widely reaches beyond the religious sphere and extends to family life and working relations. Thus, wives, children, and apprentices must respectively seek *barakah* from husbands, parents, and masters. As with respect, *baraka* intervenes in the relationship with a person enjoying a superior social status and often (but not always) implies the idea of an eternal gratitude or of an inextinguishable debt, which has to be acknowledged and rewarded through proper behaviour. For instance, a man who builds a house for his parents, who endured many sacrifices to raise him, deserves their *barakah,* conceived as a powerful blessing, resulting from the satisfaction of the creditors towards the grateful debtor. Sometimes, *barakah* simply comes from a person who is feeling respected and honoured.

This benediction is so strong that it may bring success and help someone to live a blessed life. Thus, a respectful wife, who always displays impeccable behaviour towards her husband, deserves his *barakah*: the husband's satisfaction finds expression in his children's success. For instance, talking about a family whose members hold important working positions, a boy said to me: "This is because their mother deeply respected their father. That's why all the children succeeded. That's *barakah*; they are just blessed." This belief has a dark reverse. Children's success is attributed to both parents, whereas only mothers are blamed for their failures (Somparé 628). During the last ten years, I often met upset mothers at the university whose children had obtained bad marks and who asked me to do my best to improve this situation because they feared husbands' anger. They felt responsible of their children's failure, which may be attributed to their disrespectful or unfaithful behaviour. Recently, I met a man who was furious with his son because he had left school, started to smoke marijuana, and to steal: "That's my wife's fault. She has not respected me; she doesn't deserve my *barakah*. I told her: this boy is not my son. I don't know who is his father, but that's not me!" Thus, the belief in *barakah* helps to keep women in a condition of exploitation and submission ( Somparé). Hard living conditions are supported for children's sake so that *barakah* seems to preserve family cohesion.

## Three Generations of Young Girls on the Point to Marry: Has Anything Changed?

My research has showed that the socialization of young girls to their future marital life has not changed over three generations: the model of the good wife that is transmitted nowadays in the district of Tassara is similar to the education received by grandmothers sixty to eighty years ago. Despite these commonalities, there are some important differences. First of all, the decision to marry has evolved towards a progressive recognition of young couples' choices and agency, which challenges the elder's authority towards young people. This change is presented here through a comparison of stories collected about the preparation of the wedding day.

In the generation of the grandmothers, who are between sixty and seventy years old, early marriage was extremely frequent: a girl was considered ready to marry as soon as she developed breasts. In this generation, marriage was a family affair, usually arranged by fathers and uncles; thus, accounts about the wedding show the bride's total passivity. Unaware that the crucial day had come, she knew nothing about her husband's identity and was literally torn away from her family and her mother, whose tenderness was still important for a young girl. All this mystery was due to the fear that the bride would have fled and hidden if she had known that she was on the verge of being married. Such a situation was explained by Hadja, a woman in her late seventies:

> One day, I was coming back from the river with my calves, when I saw that there was a party at home. There was a lot of noise, people who were cooking. Some women took me. They led me to a room; they put a white dress on me and braided my hair. They told me that it was my wedding day, and, in the evening, they brought me to my husband.... I was extremely unhappy. I expected it a little bit; my breasts had blossomed, so I knew that it would happen. However, very slowly, I got used to my husband and my new condition, especially when I started having children.... The hardest, however, was to be separated from my mother. I left home when I married, and I just saw her again when she was about to die. If she met me at the market, she avoided me; she knew that the very fact of being close to her, of talking to her, would push me to escape. And everybody would have accused her if I had left my husband and come back to my parents' place.

Hadja's case is somewhat extreme because other old women were sometimes allowed to visit their parents, even though they always had to be escorted by a family-in-law member. It is also important to note that, if in these accounts, as in some stories concerning excision, brides appear very passive and are simply handed over to old women who dress them and accompany them to their husband's home, bridegrooms were also unaware of what was happening. In interviews, a lot of old men recalled their astonishment when in the evening, they had suddenly discovered that a woman had been sent to them.

In the accounts of women belonging to the mothers' generation, who were aged between thirty-five and fifty during my research, marriage still does not appear as a choice, but as an obligation; however, it is not anymore a sudden, brutal event. Parents try to prepare girls for this moment and to make them accept that they will have to leave home, as in the case of Kadiatou, who is in her late thirties:

> One day, my father told me: "You know that you are with us, now, but that one day, very soon, you'll have to leave. You have been promised to someone for a long time. Now, you have to be a model for all the girls in the village; you must keep an irreproachable behaviour." And three days before the wedding, he told me: "The time has come. Now, your husband will be your father and mother. You must listen to him and do all he wants because you cannot stay here. You have to leave my home, that's a constraint of life. You won't be able to help me anymore. I accept. I forgive. Now go and take care of your husband." That's how you go to your husband's place, because you want to honour your father's promise. And even if you are unhappy, if your husband beats you, you will stay and won't complain, because your parents may get angry and bring you back. However, they will surely be unhappy and upset.

Adama, who is a little older than Kadiatou, recalled the following: "My mother told me: we have met someone who would like you to become his wife. You have to listen and obey your family-in-law. You will leave your mother and father, but you will find our equivalent. Your mother will be your husband's mother. Your father will be your husband's father but, to be short—your father, your mother, your aunt, your everything is your husband." Marriage is presented to these girls as an inevitable destiny, which they need to accept. The fact of telling to the young girl that her husband will now represent her mother, father, and brother disrupts the teenager's affective world, as she must leave her reassuring family connections to go and live with an unknown man.

Nowadays, young people ask more and more for the possibility to choose their partner or, at least, to give their consent to their parents' choices and to be presented with some alternatives. Nevertheless, this is especially true for boys; girls may raise objections or propose another choice, but if their father insists, they usually feel morally obliged to conform to his will. However, in the Tassara district, many girls seek a kind of protection from early marriage by asking an influential man, such as the chief of the district, to negotiate with their parents in order to postpone the marriage or to reject the partner. They usually ask him to intercede, as they wish to continue, for some years, their apprenticeship or their school education. Mothers can support them, for instance by hiding girls when some relatives pay a visit to the village: paternal uncles are especially feared in this sense because they can easily ask their nieces to marry one of their sons; it would be very unsettling, for parents, to raise objections to such a demand.

It also happens that a couple of young people decide to marry and the boy asks for his family's support to accompany him in the process. However, as in the past, most Fulani families reject the idea of marriage between a boyfriend and a girlfriend: how could a boy respect a daughter with whom he has already established intimate connections? As explained by Helimatou. "You cannot marry your boyfriend. That's the tradition that was transmitted to us by our grandparents. Those who do that will go to hell, bringing with them all the relatives that authorized such a union." This religious explanation may conceal the fear that individual preferences can lead to the formation of new couples, instead of decisions taken inside the lineage that dictate marriages of convenience in order to establish alliances and tighten family bounds. However, young people sometimes struggle to impose their own choices, as affirmed by Amadou, a thirty-five-year-old teacher, about marrying a girl of his choice:

> People understand, at last, that the old method was not the right one. There were too many quarrels, too many divorces, when parents chose for their children, without listening to their opinion. With my fiancée, I behaved differently. I asked her: "Do you really love me? Are you ready to marry me?" It was only when she said "yes" that I started the procedures. Of course, in my family there are people who do not agree with my choice, but I think that lovers must be left alone.

Thus, as stated by Véronique Hertrich about the Bwa ethnic group in Mali, "change is more about dialogue and negotiation between individuals and families than opposition" (138). Families tend to recognize a "space of intervention and expression of the individual. Their role is not any more to organize marriages, but to express their approval about projects established by the couple and to manage the formal procedure that will lead them to marriage. This also reveals a new trend in intergenerational relationship, grounded on dialogue" (138).

Nonetheless, it is important to note that when we talk about "decisions taken by the couple," this may conceal an important asymmetry due to the age gap between the two partners. What if (as it sometimes happens) the bridegroom is a man in his mid-thirties who wishes to marry an adolescent who is half his age, for instance to one of his students at middle school? Can we really consider that both partners enjoy the same degree of freedom of choice or has the young girl submitted to pressure, either from her family or her future husband?

Girls' effective consent to marry varies from case to case and requires considering such factors as individual maturity and aspirations as well as the gaps between husband and wife related to age, education, social position, and the presence or the absence of co-wives. With the new importance attributed to the preference and the choices of the fiancés, a romantic and sentimental dimension, absent in past generations, has been introduced into the relationship: a man may now court the girl, pay her a visit in her parents' presence, offer gifts, and whisper sweet words. This romanticism surely helps girls to accept more easily their upcoming marriage, which remains the most important moment of their lives. As observed by Daniel Smith—who studies Nigerian girls experiencing sexual promiscuity during their adolescence—even though marriage corresponds to a restriction of individual freedom, it is also an extremely valued status for all young girls, as it marks the beginning of adult life and the passage to becoming a wife and future mother. Married girls feel that they are superior to their single friends: even if they are younger, they behave like elder sisters and may ask unmarried girls to make small services and commissions for them. Women who are older than twenty-five frantically look for a future husband and do not hesitate to see a *marabout*, a Muslim religious leader, in order to seek their magical help in their quest. However, marriage is also feared because, even nowadays, it often occurs too early in a girl's life and separates her from her family and friends; it also conflicts with their other objectives, such as the desire to study and achieve professional self-affirmation.

## Not Only Wives: Marriage and Self-Fulfillment

In the introduction to this chapter, I mentioned the speech by the director of a primary school, who tried to encourage parents to send girls to school through showing that times are changing and that now a girl can have the ambition to become a high officer, or even a minister. Indeed, even though the schoolgirls I interviewed did not show these kind of ambitions, they had professional projects. Unlike their mothers, they did not expect to become housewives, busy with domestic and agro-pastoral work; they wished to work in the modern sector, possibly in an office as a secretary or employee, or to become a doctor or a teacher. Girls study to improve their quality of life and to have a more comfortable and easier existence than their mothers—either by marrying an educated and wealthy man who would surely look for a well-read woman or by getting a good job in the modern sector. Some young girls who are illiterate, or have just attended school for some years, are also integrating into the world of work; for instance, as tailors or hairdressers. My research shows that girls are extremely attracted by the perspective of a professional career. Indeed, in a society where pastoralism is quickly declining and many families are losing their cattle, it is vital to find other sources of income. Even large cattle breeders do not expect all their children to become herders and want at least some of them to work in other sectors. The messages conveyed by teachers in school encourage girls to become more autonomous and to study and look for a job: thus, school is a vector of transformation, as stated by Jean-Claude Filloux in his comments about Durkheim's conception of school: "Durkheim insists many times on the capacity of the school system to produce change. From this point of view, school is not only a micro society reflecting social issues, but, most of all, a place where change can start" (86). Girls now consider work as the base of their future autonomy in marital life, which would help them to have more financial independence. It is important to note that this is not a completely new tradition: the desire of women to seek economic independence from their husbands—for instance through trade or participation in women's associations—has existed for a long time in West Africa. As stated by Locoh and Mouvaga-Sow, "women are both dominated in patriarchal societies and full of initiatives to ensure the living of their families, often without their husband's support. The tradition of polygyny has taught women not to count on their husbands, but to face, if necessary, their children's needs." This affirmation, which is surely true in many cases, must be balanced by taking into account other situations; for example, in many families, men are still the most important, or the only, providers of a regular income. My conversations with men are full of references to the stress they feel for having to meet the demands of wives, children, and other extended family members. Not only do husbands often finance the expenses of some their wife's young relatives, but they are also expected to buy gifts and make other significant contributions to their parents-in-law.

Nevertheless, in interviews, some young women expressed their mistrust towards men who could neglect or abandon them for a second wife. For example, Oumou, a young Fulani teacher living in the Tassara district said the following:

> When a man wants to marry you, he will promise that his love is eternal, that he wants to do everything for you. But after some years, he will start to be interested in other women. You can't count on men; they will spend money to marry a second wife, or use it to party with friends or girlfriends. If you have your own job, you can count on yourself. You can satisfy your own needs and take care of your children.

For another example, on the front door of a hairdresser's shop in the mining town of Kamsar, where many apprentices are receiving professional training, there is a panel that reads "A job is a woman's first husband."

For many women, employment is also important to preserve the husband's respect and consideration as well as to prevent neglect and bad treatment, as explained by Aicha, a 23 years-old student, who is studying to become a nurse: "If you have a job, you will be the most beautiful, the most respected girl, because you have your own autonomy. You don't have to ask money to your husband every day. But if you don't work, your husband won't respect you. He will think that he can do whatever he wants with you, that you are worth nothing." Kadiatou, a sociology student, also explained the following: "Nowadays, only money counts. Girls want to have a rich husband, but men also like being married to a woman who has a good job, or to a promising student, who will earn a good salary. In our society, if only the man works in a family, he will have a lot of problems to make a living. If the wife works, she can contribute and this is of great help." However, the ambition to work outside the domestic sphere may present some conflicting aspects with the pedagogical ideal of a good wife, especially because studying and working opens new spaces of freedom during adolescence and youth. For some, this is a threat that needs to be controlled. Saverio Kratli notes that pastoralists, who are often depicted as hostile to schools, especially for girls, are keen to provide them with formal education only as long as they do not go too far away and remain in an area where their mothers can control their movements.

Usually, in the Tassara district, when a girl expresses the desire to go to school, mothers are reluctant to accept, not only because their daughters are a great help in housework but also because they have to grant them a freedom that can be misused. Thus, mothers fear that for girls, school may become a pretext to meet boys and that they may have intercourse before marriage. Furthermore, in the Tassara district, there are only primary schools. Those who go on to secondary school have to go to Kolaboui, a big village five kilometers away, which means they would have to spend a long time far away from their mothers. During marital life, the freedom enjoyed by a working woman can also represent a problem. A lot of girls explained to me on the one hand, they were eager to marry and to become, at last, an adult woman, but, on the other hand, they feared that marriage would prevent them from studying and working. Fatoumata, who studies journalism, said the following: "I chose this job because it grants me a certain freedom. In our society, you don't usually have the possibility to move, to go and spend some nights out of home, but as a journalist, you have a sort of legitimation to do that…. But this becomes difficult when you marry, you have to find a very understanding husband, and that's not easy." Thus, these women hope to find an understanding husband, and often, in the Tassara district and elsewhere, they lay down their conditions: they accept to marry only if the fiancés agree to let them pursue their studies or professional training. However, even if the husband accepts, practical conditions are often difficult, as a married woman is the bedrock of the family and has to cope with the important burden of domestic work. In ten years of teaching, I witnessed many cases of students who had many difficulties attending classes during their pregnancies; they were forced to bring their babies to the university but finally had to abandon their studies, as it was almost impossible to balance them with their domestic obligations. Nevertheless, in other cases, women managed to find domestic support, often from within their own family, which allowed them to complete their studies and pursue their careers.

A traditional wife's submission is also challenged by the progressive integration of women in the world of work. According to the many women I interviewed in the Tassara district and in the capital, men appreciate educated women, but they do not wish to marry them because they would be too sharp and alert or because they would no longer be able to impose their supremacy. Women's access to school and also to Koranic instruction surely represents a step towards equality and a threat to male domination grounded on the monopoly of religious knowledge. Also, educated girls do not only learn from their mothers and elder sisters, as in the previous generations, but they can now teach them. For instance, mothers are particularly happy to explain that their daughters were able to teach them some Koranic verses, thus increasing their knowledge as well as their autonomy from the husband. The prayer and their relationship with God seem to become more accessible and personal as they are no longer completely mediated by the husband. Furthermore, the mothers I talked with are convinced that their educated daughters will be able to help them, either if they marry a wealthy man or if they find themselves a good job. They are convinced that a daughter, who grows up close to her mother and shares domestic work, is much more aware than a boy of her physical strain and of all her difficulties: thus, the daughter will do all she can to help her mother in old age so that she can rest.

I did not collect data on men's reactions to the increasing autonomy of young women. However, on International Women's Day, some Guinean male students and teachers shared on Facebook a picture of a bride who was kneeling before her husband and washing his feet with devotion. It was accompanied by this sentence: "Happy woman's day. I stand for objective equality at work, but I hope that women will always take good care of their husbands at home." This sentence suggests an anxiety about the reconciliation of women's ambition about professional self-fulfillment and the submission expected in marital life.

# Conclusion

In this chapter, I tried to show how the pedagogical ideal of the good wife is challenged by increasing aspirations of self-fulfillment and quests of autonomy, which leads to a desire to postpone one's marriage in order to have a longer adolescence and youth. I think that Guinean women in the Tassara districts and elsewhere try to reconcile two aspects of their identity. On one hand, they still adhere to the pedagogical ideal of the good wife, which suggests submission, but, on the other hand, they are enthusiastic about their future, as they desire wealth, freedom of movement, and even power. Mothers welcome the possibility that girls may work outside the domestic sphere, as they expect their economic help in their old age; they are also proud about their access to Koranic and French knowledge. As for young men, the pedagogical ideal of the young wife now involves "awakening," which includes literacy, adapting to an urban context, supervising the children's studies, being fashionable, and being able to interact with well-read people. This schism between a progressive self-affirmation in the public realm and the social imperative of submission to men in the private one, which is supported by religious beliefs, seems to be a feature of the identity of young Guinean wives.

## Endnote

1. I am using pseudonyms in the text to preserve the interviewees's anonymity.

## Works Cited

Bara Diop, Abdoulaye. *La famille wolof.* Karthala, 1985.

Botta Somparé, Ester. *Education familiale et scolaire dans une société pastorale guinéenne.* L'Harmattan, 2015.

Botta Somparé, Ester, and Mara Vitale. "Women and Anthropologists in West Africa: Comparing Two Research Experiences" *Women Researching in Africa*, edited by Ruth Jackson and Max Kelly, Palgrave, 2018, pp. 153-70.

Crenshaw, Kimberly. *Demarginalizing the Intersection of Race and Sex: A Black Feminist Critique of Antidiscrimination Doctrine. Feminist Theory and Antiracist Policy.* Chicago, University of Chicago Legal Forum, 1989.

Dagenais, Huguette. "Méthodologie féministe et anthropologie : une alliance possible." *Anthropologie et société,* vol.11, n.1, 1987, pp. 19-44

Durkheim, Emile. *Education et sociologie.* 1922. PUF, 1968.

Erny, Pierre. *L'enfant et son milieu en Afrique noire.* L'Harmattan. 1972.

Fanzaing, Sylvie, and Journet Diallo Odile. *La femme de mon mari : anthropologie du mariage polygamique en Afrique et en France.* L'Harmattan, 1988.

Feldham, Nehara "Relations familiales et rapports sociaux de sexe au Mali." *Journal des anthropologues,* vol. 1-2, no.124-125, 2011, pp.199-200.

Filloux, Jean-Claude. "Sur la pédagogie de Durkheim" in *Revue française de pédagogie,* vol.44, 1978, pp. 83-98.

Hertrich, Véronique. "Vers la construction d'un espace conjugal chez les Bwa, Mali." *Autrepart,* no. 2, 1997, pp.123-42.

Kanté, Nai. "Recherches sur la scolarité des filles en milieu rural." Master's thesis. Université Général Lansana Coté de Sonfonya, Conakry, 2001.

Kratli, Saverio "Education Provisions to Nomadic Pastoralists." IDS Working Paper 126. Institute of Development Studies, 2001.

Lallemand, Suzanne. *Une famille mossi.* CNRS, 1977.

Locoh, Thérèse, and Myriam Mougava-Sow, Myriam. "Vers de nouveaux modèles familiaux en Afrique de l'Ouest?" Congrès international de la population,18-23 juillet.UIESP, 2001.

Marie, Alain. "Du sujet communautaire au sujet individuel." *L'Afrique des individus,* edited by Alain Marie,. Karthala, 1994, pp.53-110.

Mathieu, Nicole-Claude. *L'anatomie politique : catégorisations et idéologies du sexe.* Editions Côté-femmes, 1991.

Niane, Djibril Tamsir. *Soundjata ou l'épopée mandingue.* Présence Africaine,1960.

Smith, Daniel Jordan "Promiscuous Girls, Good Wives and Cheating Husbands: Gender Inequality, Transitions to Marriage and Infidelity in South-Eastern Nigeria" *Anthropological Quarterly* vol. 83, n. 1, 2010, pp. 123-52.

Somparé, Abdoulaye Wotem. "Mobilité et reproduction sociale ou notabilisation dans les villes minières et ouvrières en Guinée." Dissertation. Ecole des Hautes Etudes en Sciences Sociales de Paris, 2006.

Vitale, Mara "Economie morale, Islam et pouvoir charismatique au Burkina Faso." *Afrique contemporaine* vol.3, no. 231, 2009, pp. 229-43.

# Part III

Resisting and Changing Wives' Roles and Lives

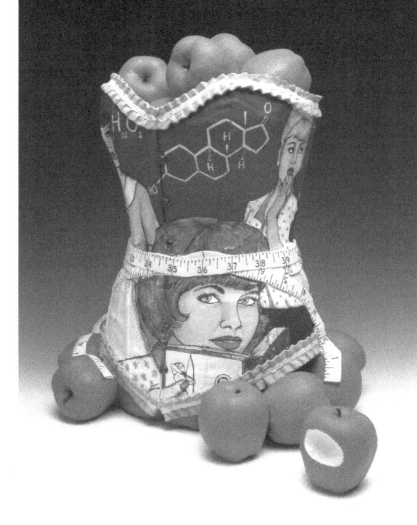

Chapter Nine

# Considering Family Law in Counting Wife-Work Apart from Mother-Work

Rebecca Jaremko Bromwich and Beverley Smith

I'm not sitting here—some little woman standing by my man like Tammy Wynette. I'm sitting here because I love him, and I respect him, and I honor what he's been through and what we've been through together.—Hillary Clinton, speaking about Bill Clinton in 1992

## Introduction

In May 2016, Sophie Gregoire-Trudeau, the wife of Prime Minister Justin Trudeau, attracted admiration and scorn, along with the sarcastic Twitter hashtag #prayforsophie, when she asked for more institutional support for her role as wife of the prime minister. The spouses of heads of state are telling instances of broader social trends. In the heteronormative traditional paradigm of Western nuclear family forms, woman spouses, or "wives," have long been helpmates—the supporters of husbands, the background to their foreground. They are the invisible unpaid labourers that make possible a capitalist income stream, a family life, and all the trappings of suburban middle-class success; they are the muses credited with inspiring their endeavours and art.

This chapter explores how the development of Canadian family law may better account for and value the unpaid labour that is traditionally understood to be wife-work. It explores the nuanced distinction between the overlapping roles of mother and wife. First, this chapter discusses the history of accounting for unpaid labour in Canada, documenting how less statistical tracking is done now as compared to a generation ago. We take the position that questions about unpaid labour should be reinstated in the annual long-form census. Then, this chapter offers suggestions towards mechanisms that could serve to ameliorate the precarious economic positions of women tasked with doing disproportionate amounts of unpaid labour relative to men. This labour, often relegated to the domestic sphere, is sometimes linked to having children, but not always. Much of it is specifically done for the advancement of their male spouses' careers. As such, these suggestions would have particular benefits for wives in traditional, heterosexual families, in which their husbands traditionally do less unpaid caregiving labour than they do.

Two caveats are necessary here: first, many suggestions offered here are not measures that would solely benefit wives. They would also benefit other categories of women, such as single mothers, who do more than their fair share of unpaid caregiving as well. Second, the proposals mentioned here start from the assumption of the unequal sharing of unpaid labour burdens between opposite sex spouses. They do not speak to the, rather obvious, complementary social change to be advocated for—that men do their fair share of housework and childrearing. It is notable, however, that wife-work is not co-terminus with mother-work, although the two are linked. Our position is not one of gender essentialism. As noted, the primary roles of women as caregivers are socially constructed. It is clear that younger generations do have different views about men's and women's roles in unpaid labour. Ultimately, as men do more and more unpaid labour in households, the counting of unpaid labour in economic valuation equations will not just benefit men indirectly but directly as well.

This chapter presents a doctrinal legal analysis of ways in which the unpaid labour of spouses (usually wives) in relation to childrearing, household tasks, and other labour have been accounted for in Canadian family law. This area of law provides an interesting example of valuation being placed upon wife-work, as it calculates spousal support as separate and distinct from child support. Thus, it draws a distinction between the roles of wife and mother, and separately calculates the monetary value of the role, income, and lifestyle benefits of one's tasks and life situation as a spouse. Spousal support is a legal determination that relates, doctrinally, not to the work of mothers but to the lives of wives. It looks at the law of unjust enrichment and how this equitable doctrine makes possible an accounting for caregiving and other labour traditionally conceived of as outside the capitalist valuation schemes, such as wife-work. At a minimum, family law shows that the quantification of unpaid labour by spouses is not only possible but routinely done. The fact that quantification of wife-work is possible in family law cases provides an example of how unpaid labour can be valued and accounted for—an example that could be used by analogy in prospective and ongoing ways in family units that remain economically unified. Such valuations could work towards what Marilyn Waring has suggested is necessary: making women count.

## Unpaid Labour and Inequality

Both statistical and qualitative evidence strongly support the contentions that women in Canada, as elsewhere, are socially unequal to men. Their disproportionate shouldering of the burden of care responsibilities—for their husband, children, and home—compromises their ability to fully participate and climb to leadership positions in the paid workforce. This caregiving work is understood in traditional and patriarchal social orders as the work of wives, which, of course, mothers are assumed to be; single mothers are largely invisible in the dominant narratives of the nuclear family form, although, statistically speaking, they most certainly do exist.

Women, understood primarily through their social statuses as wives and mothers, have traditionally been left by modern capitalist economics in a double-bind position: their unpaid labour is financially necessary for middle-class economic success by men, and crucial for middle-class aspirations for families in neoliberal societies to be achieved (60), yet this labour remains invisible in certain economic calculations, such as gross domestic product (GDP).

An economist and foremother of feminist economics Marilyn Waring has long pointed out, in their supporting roles, wives are considered non-producers and have no access to the distribution of money and other benefits flowing from the means of production except through their husband's income. Even in late capitalism, when women have largely entered into paid work, they face many challenges: a gender pay gap, glass ceilings that frustrate advancement, the social imperative to follow and support their husbands' career journeys, and the double-bind of child care burdens and paid work responsibilities. The invisibility of women's unpaid labour, performed by both single mothers and wives, perpetuates women's economic inequality. And as Susan Boyd has pointed out, "political equality and economic equality are inseparable issues" (60).

Based on the political economy of women's lives, it is not obvious that women's entrance into the paid work force has benefited wives. In 2016, even middle-class, otherwise privileged, wives are expected to pursue paid careers while continuing to perform a disproportionate amount of unpaid labour relative to their husband. Neoliberal expectations that women will be both breadwinners and homemakers create impossible scripts for wives to follow. More recent scholarship has advocated for a more nuanced and intersectional approach to assessments of women's economic situations—one that appreciates class, race, gender, ability, and other dimensions of embodiment (Merino and Lara). From Canadian statistical analysis, it is clear that racialization, disability, gender, and immigrant status tend to contribute to a person's poverty (Hatfield et al.). Even so, it is clear that, although women may experience different kinds of oppression, on the whole they remain, as a group, disadvantaged.

Even though access to remuneration, power, meaningful work, and education are important advances for some women, a large numbers of woman workers now balance paid jobs with domestic work in a social order where their roles as wives are largely invisible and not protected. Gone is the social condemnation husbands would have had to face had they abandoned their wives like in earlier generations. Cloaked in the guise of equality, and even subsumed under purportedly feminist language, is the idea that if marriages end, wives should move on and stand on their own two feet. The implicit claim that gender equality in spousal relationships has been achieved obfuscates and even makes invisible the socially and economically obligatory positions of dependence in which wives too often find themselves (Hough). In late modern societies, a fact too seldom acknowledged is that wives' financial disadvantage remains real and that wives' positions are incredibly precarious, particularly so when a wife does not work for pay outside the home. And when she does work, wives' jobs are still often less remunerative than those of their husbands, which does not help her vulnerability.

What we strive towards in this chapter is mechanisms that would allow the work of those in unpaid and supporting roles, most often wives, to be counted, which would make possible a way for those roles to be remunerated, compensated, and made more secure. Under the law of equity in relation to constructive trust, non-owners, often wives, can assert claims to an interest in property, despite having no formal claim to it. Furthermore, in Canada's regime for spousal support, upon the breakdown of spousal relationships, specific and precise actuarial calculations are made about what contributions spouses make to the lives of each other. In this chapter, we argue that concepts like those underlying the doctrine of unjust enrichment and methods analogous to those now used for spousal support determinations under Canadian family law should be more broadly utilized to make wives and wife-work count in economic calculations.

## (Not) Counting Unpaid Work

In Canada as elsewhere, women carry a disproportionate share of the burden of performing unpaid work both in households and in the paid labour force (Luxton; Luxton and Vosko). This work is often invisible and is not generally valued. As feminist scholars and economists have pointed out for decades, this happens because the term "work" is almost invariably defined in statistics as a term referring to paid activities linked to the market (Beneria). In the face of decades of work by feminists who have sought to ameliorate its marginality, women's unpaid work remains ignored or undervalued in dominant methods of measuring economic activity. Contrary to grand narratives of progress that are widely accepted, the Canadian government is further away from counting unpaid work systematically than it was twenty years ago, large because datasets are no longer collected annually. Although questions are occasionally asked about labour activities in the General Social Survey (GSS), the GSS poses questions to a small sample of Canadians. Established in 1985, this survey is not as reliable as the long-form census, which has a sample size of 25,000 Canadians across the country. Questions about unpaid labour were asked in the GSS in 1996, 2002, 2007, and 2012 (Statistics Canada).

Legal analysis was joined by grassroots activism in movements in Canada to ensure the collection of statistical data about the paid and unpaid work of women. Co-author Beverley Smith has worked for thirty-six years through writing letters, creating petitions, and conducting peaceful demonstrations; she also made four formal complaints at the Human Rights Commission and at the United Nation. Her 1997 complaint at the UN was met with some success. The working group of the Commission on the Status of Women found that there was an absence of women in decision making, that a high level of women and children lived in poverty, and that there were legal systems discriminating against women. Kids First, a national organization for caregivers, also pursued a court challenge at income tax court (*Boland*)—in which, discrimination was admitted. Her complaint was heard by the UN in 1999 (CBC).

Smith contended that the Canadian tax system at the time discriminated against families in which one spouse's labour was entirely unpaid. Smith's arguments were seized upon at the time by the Reform Party, as a means to advance conservative family values, but this was not Smith's own purpose in her decades-long advocacy career, which was also entirely unpaid. Indeed, the support from a far-right organization her advocacy is ironic, as Smith was seeking public redistribution of money by government to remunerate wives and mothers for unpaid labour—an undoubtedly socialist move.

Smith was trying to encourage the valuing of caregiving labour, which is quite a different agenda than that politicians seized upon. At the root of her advocacy, what Smith was upset about, was contradiction between the hours of work involved in her productive, socially sanctioned, and even culturally mandatory role as a wife and mother, and the lack of social recognition for her and for it. By doing the work she was socially expected to do, she lost a great deal of freedom and had no access to money. Thus, in specific tax-related relief focus of her argument should not be unduly focused on. Rather, the root of her argument was the invisibility of her unpaid labour when she left the paid labour force to care for her four children. What she fought against was her financial vulnerability, which was reported incidentally at the time as "the loss of social status and the fact that she couldn't get a credit card without her husband's permission" (CBC).

The 1990s saw the climax in Canada of decades of sustained and multifaceted advocacy about how unpaid work, especially parental caregiving, often done by wives, contributes to production. These challenges were levied at the government and in the courts. One challenge was an official 1991 objection by Carol Lees, a Saskatchewan farm wife, to the census wording that required her to exclude her unpaid roles in the tally of farm work. In 1993, Kids First Parent Association of Canada lodged an income tax court challenge and claimed unfair discrimination against at-home care of children. Canada along with all other member UN nations in 1995 signed the UN Platform for Action that promised to tally unpaid labour. Furthermore, in *Symes v. Canada* (1993), a lawyer mother unsuccessfully sought to claim her childcare costs as business expenses. In response to these and other challenges to traditional economic models that did not account for unpaid labour, particularly in the context of childrearing, Statistics Canada included an in-depth question about the amount of time individuals spent on unpaid work in the 1996 census (Luxton and Vosko). However, the unpaid labour questions were not included in the 2009 questionnaire. The long-form census in its entirety was abandoned by Canada's Conservative government in 2010, but when it was reinstated in 2016 by the newly elected Liberals, the questions about unpaid labour were not included.

## Canadian Family Law

### Unjust Enrichment

In the family law context, when spouses separate or divorce, the equitable doctrines of constructive trust and unjust enrichment have been used to account for indirect contributions (usually by wives) to the property of their families, whether in the context of a "joint family venture" or in relation to purely domestic work. When one party unjustly derives a benefit from the corresponding deprivation of another, including through the spouses' unpaid labour, a claim of constructive trust can be made.

Before the 1970s, it was the common practice across Canada for husbands to hold sole title to property (Steele). Laws dealing with the division of family property in Canada's provincial and territorial jurisdictions were decried and challenged in the last decades of the twentieth century for failing to consider unpaid work, especially in relation to childcare and housekeeping. Ultimately, the law in this area was changed by precedent to allow for claims of constructive trust, unjust enrichment, and, more recently, joint family venture to override the law's failure to consider unpaid labour.

In particular, two cases of the Supreme Court of Canada—*Murdoch v. Murdoch* 1975 and *Rathwell v. Rathwell* (1978)—contributed to legal change. The *Murdoch* case actually ended badly for the claimant wife, Mrs. Murdoch. After the breakdown in 1968 of her twenty-five-year marriage, Mrs. Murdoch, a ranch wife, was not entitled to a share in her family home, despite her labour both on the ranch and domestically. Mrs. Murdoch also sought support or, using the language of the time, "maintenance." She was awarded a lump sum for maintenance but no interest in the couple's property. This led to a public outcry and eventually to law reform around spousal support and matrimonial property.

The dissenting judgment of Justice Laskin provided the groundwork for the law of constructing trust to be applied to the context of unpaid labour by wives. After *Murdoch*, and in response to the public outcry that followed it, many Canadian provinces enacted legislation that valued and accounted for a spouse's indirect contribution to property when married couples separate (Mossman and Flanagan).

In *Rathwell,* a case based on a similar situation, the Supreme Court of Canada came to a different result. It held that a farm wife's unpaid labour, over the course of a twenty-five-year marriage entitled her to an equitable share in the family property by operation of the doctrine of "resulting trust" because the properties in relation to which Mrs. Rathwell claimed were paid for out of the couple's joint bank account, which reflected a "common intention" to share in the value of the property. The resulting trust was found because the Supreme Court ruled there was a common intention between parties to share in the benefits of the farm labour. However, as Justice Laskin did in *Murdoch*, a minority of the Supreme Court in *Rathwell* also suggested using the common law doctrine of constructive trust.

Then, in *Pettkus v. Becker* (1980), a common law wife was held to be entitled to half the share of the couple's bee farm property on the basis of constructive trust because her unpaid labour had resulted in a benefit to her spouse and to her detriment. This unjust enrichment was to be corrected equitably by the imputation of a "constructive trust," forcing the sharing of the farm property. Ms. Pettkus's nineteen years of unpaid labour on the family farm gave her a constructive trust in a 50 percent share of the property.

Soon after the decision in *Pettkus*, the Supreme Court subsequently clarified in *Sorochan v. Sorochan* (1986) that the basis of constructive trust is in unjust enrichment and that the deprivation need not be directly linked to the property at issue. Furthermore, the Supreme Court ruled in *Peter v. Beblow* (1993) that the value of the trust is not the "value received" but the quantum by which the property has improved. In *Peter*, the applicant common law wife was held to be entitled to the entire home. The existence of constructive trust was recently confirmed by the Supreme Court in *Kerr v. Baranow* (2011), and its scope of application was extended to what was called a "joint family venture," whereby married or common law spouses could share in property through indirect contributions.

## Spousal Support

Prior to the 1990s, the "clean break" model of divorce was dominant in no-fault divorce claims in Canada. However, the cases of *Moge v. Moge* (1992) and *Bracklow v. Bracklow* (1999) provide for an expansive and broad entitlement to spousal support. While the cases made clear that there would be an entitlement to spousal support in a wide range of circumstances, after *Bracklow*, lawyers and members of the public expressed concern about the uncertainty of outcomes when spousal support is awarded. In consequence, the first draft of actuarial Spousal Support Advisory Guidelines (SSAGs) was produced and released in 2005. The final version was produced and released in July of 2008.

Whereas other jurisdictions have child support guidelines, the quantification of spousal support is unique to Canada. These SSAGs came into being as a project of law professors Carol Rogerson and Rollie Thompson. They are not, in themselves, law. Their application is not mandatory. However, there is a growing body of precedent in which they are applied, and these decisions are law, so the SSAGs are progressively acquiring a more and more persuasive (and perhaps even binding) legal status. The SSAGs are intended to bring predictability and regularity into the awarding of spousal support.

Spousal support is awarded to married spouses upon matrimonial breakdown (or separation) pursuant to section 15.2 of the Divorce Act. Provincial and territorial statutes from across Canada provide for the awarding of spousal support to unmarried cohabitants. The exception is Quebec, whose regime does not accord rights to unmarried partners. It is significant that the determination of spousal support is distinct, constructed, conceived, and calculated as a separate category of remuneration under Canadian law, quite apart from child support, which is a more direct reflection of parental labour and the costs of childrearing, and is awarded to pay for the needs of children.

In the contemporary context across Canada, ten years after the publication of the final version of the SSAGs, spousal support is determined on the basis of mathematical calculations. There are limits of the extent to which spousal support is a redistribution of wealth. As the Supreme Court judgment in *Dumais-Koski v. Koski* (1997) points out, "marriage is not a legal institution created for the redistribution of wealth," and as the Alberta Court of Queen's Bench opined *V.S. v. A.K.* (2005): "A person does not acquire a lifetime pension as a result of marriage. Likewise, marriage is not an insurance policy." However, the statistical reality is that spousal support awards are frequently ordered on the basis of standardized calculations.

Married and common law spouses are not automatically entitled to spousal support. It is available for married spouses and formerly married spouses fall under federal jurisdiction and applies the same way across Canada under the federal Divorce Act. When spouses are not legally married, spousal support is available to spouses under provincial and territorial family law legislation. Since same sex marriage is legal in Canada, and because the law is formally gender neutral, spousal support is available to all spouses, regardless of gender, and can be required by a court order or under a separation agreement.

An entitlement to spousal support arises for one of two reasons:

1. Need based: to help the recipient spouse maintain or reasonably approach the standard of living enjoyed during the marriage after separation;
2. Compensatory: to balance the recipient spouse for the financial decisions and arrangements made between the parties during their relationship while it was ongoing.

A number of factors in relation to the spouses' relationship affect the amount and duration of the spousal support offered. Key questions relate to the payer spouse's ability to pay and the recipient spouse's needs. The amount is likely to be higher if the payer spouse and recipient spouse have a large difference in income. Furthermore, longer, traditional marriages in which one spouse (usually the wife) worked towards the family's wellbeing in an unpaid capacity are likely to result in larger amounts of support.

In essence, spousal support is now paid in a precise amount based on monetary calculations intended to reflect unpaid labour contributions. The SSAGs provide a number of mathematical formulas to be used in calculating the amount of spousal support payment; they can also be used to calculate the length of time during which spousal support should be paid.

## Application: Suggestions for Reform

We wish to suggest structural ways in which greater economic recognition and support can be provided to women, including wives, but not limited to them; a growing number of men are performing caregiving responsibilities and undertaking tasks traditionally conceived of as wife-work. We take aim at the privatization of the family and neoliberal privatization of the state. Advocacy to ameliorate the poverty of women often focuses on the challenges faced by lone mothers. However, we contend that women identified as wives face a similar kind of economic disadvantage to single mothers. Whereas single mothers are disproportionately poor, mothers who are wives often depend upon their husbands' incomes for security; therefore, they do not have access to the means of production.

It is neither impossible nor particularly difficult to imagine ways in which unpaid labour—still performed typically by wives, but also disproportionately by women who are single, married, widowed, or in a variety of partnership forms—could be calculated and counted in the GDP. Teasing out which aspects of a woman's labour are performed in relation to her role as a spouse, and which are incidents of parental unpaid labour, would be a nuanced but not an insurmountable task. For example, the SSAGs provide a model that may be useful by in the context of other household formations and the unpaid labour done in them. If math can be used routinely and successfully to value unpaid labour where separating spouses claim a constructive trust in property or claim spousal support, then math can be done in relation to unpaid labour contributions in households at times other than when a relationship breaks down. If the value of unpaid labour can be measured at any point in time, including at the point of divorce, then it can be measured at other junctures.

It is not our agenda to suggest that women should be doing unpaid labour or that wives are in some way more entitled to equality than single women—far from it. Our vision for a feminist utopia includes the equal sharing of men, women, and those who identify with neither gender in unpaid labour. We envision a world in which everyone can realize their greatest potential, both themselves and others, while sharing in the joys and burdens of childrearing and elder care.

Our suggestions towards quantification of "wife-work" and mother-work as distinct but related variants on unpaid labour are intended as intermediary steps towards achieving those ultimate, egalitarian goals. We are not recommending that the SSAGs be applied in their totality more generally to the context of valuing and quantifying unpaid labour. For instance, spousal support calculations factor in the income levels of the parties and are, by definition, larger amounts when paid by a higher-income spouse than a lower-income one. More consideration needs to go into precisely how to quantify and economically value unpaid labour. This chapter is intended to start a conversation towards such a mechanism: we are not proposing the final iteration of one. Finally, we also have a more modest, interim suggestion. Canada's federal government should reinstate the collection of data about unpaid labour in its census. Asking questions about unpaid labour is an important interim step towards recognizing its economic value: by making it visible, we can better ensure it is accounted for.

## Conclusion

Through analyzing the historical context of advocacy around unpaid labour in Canada, this chapter has highlighted the economic disadvantages often faced by women through their social mandated roles of wives and mothers and the unpaid labour associated with them. We have discussed how unpaid labour remains disproportionately done by women, including often wives, living in precarious economic circumstances. We have outlined some of the history of activism and advocacy concerning wives' unpaid labour in Canada. From this discussion, we have sought to open a space and initiate a new and renewed conversation towards imagining what practical mechanisms could be used to count and compensate the unpaid labour disproportionately done by women for them to attain more social equality as well as a more secure economic status. More specifically, we have argued for the reinsertion of questions about unpaid labour in the annual long-form census.

Furthermore, we have discussed how the specific actuarial calculations now routinely done in spousal support calculations pursuant to the SSAGs now in place in Canada provide an analogous model for how such calculations may be made. For an illustrative example, consider the very recent, and quite typical, case of *Fox v. Fox* (2017), in which the Ontario Superior Court considered in detail the monetary and unpaid contributions of spouses in determining the amount and duration of spousal support. There, a male spouse, who was a dentist, was required to pay spousal support to his former female spouse, who had reduced her hours of paid work to care for their three children over the course of a long marriage. Roles taken on in the marriage and the female spouse's primary role in caring for the parties' children were considered in the reasoning to allocate significant spousal support to her. Women and wives will benefit if a similar reasoning is employed in contexts other than family court.

Finally we have suggested that the common law of constructive trust provides an example of how women, mothers, and wives, can be shown to count.

## Works Cited

Boyd, Susan. "Is Equality Enough? Father's Rights and Women's Rights Advocacy." *Rethinking Equalitiy Projects in Law: Feminist Challenges*, edited by Rosemary Hunter Oxford: Hart Publishing, International Series in Law and Society, 2008, pp. 59-79.

*Bracklow v. Bracklow.* 1999, 1 S.C.R. 420.

CBC News. "UN Hears Calgary Mom's Tax Complaint" *CBC*, 11 March 1999, www.cbc.ca/news/canada/un-hears-calgary-mom-s-tax-complaint-1.171379. Accessed 27 May 2019.

Hatfield, Michael, et al. 2010. "First Comprehensive Review of the Market Basket Measure of Low Income." *Human Resources and Skills Development Canada*, SP-953-06-10, 2010, www.publications.gc.ca/collections/collection_2011/. Accessed 26 May 2019.

Hough, J. "Mistaking Liberalism for Feminism" Spousal Support in Canada." *Journal of Canadian Studies*, vol. 147, 1994, pp.158-59.

*Kerr v. Baranow.* 2011, SCC 10.

Luxton, M. "Friends, Neighbours, and Community: A Case Study of the Role of Informal Caregiving in Social Reproduction." *Social Reproduction: Feminist Political Economy Challenges Neo-liberalism*, edited by Meg Luxton and Kate Bezanson, McGill-Queen's University, 2006, pp. 263-92.

Luxton, M., and L.F. Vosko. "Where Women's Efforts Count: The 1996 Census Campaign and 'Family Politics' in Canada." *Studies in Political Economy*, vol. 56, 1998, pp.49-89.

Merino, G. A., and J. Lara. "Feminization of Poverty." In Shehan, Constance, ed. *The Wiley Blackwell Encyclopedia of Family* Studies, Wiley Blackwell 2016, pp. 1-4.

Mossman, M.J., and W. F. Flanagan, *Property Law, Cases and Commentary.* Emond Montgomery Publications, 2004.

*Moge v. Moge.* 1992, 3 S.C.R. 813.

*Murdoch v. Murdoch.* 1975, 1 S.C.R. 423.

*Pettkus v. Becker.* 1980, 2 S.C.R. 834.

*Sorochan v. Sorochan.* 1986, 2 S.C.R. 38.

Statistics Canada. "The General Social Survey: An Overview." *Statistics Canada*, 2017, www.150.statcan.gc.ca/n1/pub/89f0115x/89f0115x 2013001-eng.htm. Accessed 26 May 2019.

Steele, F.M. "The Ideal Marital Property Regime—What Would it Be?" *Family Law in Canada: New Directions*, edited by E. Sloss, Canadian Advisory Council on the Status of Women, 1985, pp. 128-131.

*Symes v. Canada.* 1993, 4 S.C.R. 695.

Waring, Marilyn, *Counting for Nothing: What Men Value and What Women are Worth.* 2nd ed. University of Toronto Press, 1999.

## Chapter Ten

# What Is a Wife?
# Partnering and Mothering in Freeform's *The Fosters*

Holly Willson Holladay

## Defining Family

T he traditional notion of "family" evokes an image of a married, heterosexual couple rearing their biological children, and the traditional notion of wife brings forth a stereotypical image of a heterosexual woman. Yet a number of societal and economic factors have called into question this nuclear family structure. As Wei Qiu et al. contend, ideological value placed on individualism "has led to changes in fertility, marital timing (delayed), a shift from marriage being arranged to free choice, a shift from marriage being viewed as a context for having children to a companionate arrangement, more open divorce (now seen as part of free choice), and acceptance of same sex relationships" (642). Furthermore, Rebecca Adams cites a recent Pew Research study that concludes "54 percent of kids in [America] don't live in a home with two heterosexual parents in their first marriage." Consequently, this shifting definition of "family" has been a central concern for scholars in a variety of disciplines, including communication, sociology, and family studies.

The growing acceptance of same-sex unions, both culturally and politically—and its necessary destabilization of the traditional, heteronormative family headed by a husband and wife—is perhaps one the greatest cultural turns driving this investigation. Powell et al. conclude that the 2008 referendums in California, Arkansas, and Maine, which sought to restrict marriage between same-sex couples, are evidence that public opinion plays an instrumental role in shaping the policy decisions that legitimate certain family structures and not others. Grounded in this justification, the authors engage in a comprehensive study "to explore people's definitions" of family and who fits under this umbrella (6); the majority of their interview subjects defined family as a traditional, heterosexual married couple with children, whereas only a quarter of their respondents defined it as a broader conception that includes unmarried, same-sex couples, both with and without children. Despite a minority willing to grant legitimacy to same-sex families, these families do, indeed, reflect the intimate and familial bonds that have helped define "family" for centuries, and the women in same-sex couples enact the spousal role of "wife" just as those women in heterosexual couples do. As such, scholarship has increasingly turned to the ways in which women in lesbian-headed families constitute their roles as wives and parents. As Jacqui Gabb indicates, although "motherhood and lesbian sexuality are antithetical to each other within Western culture ... lesbian mothers and their children appropriate and queer the traditional language and terminology of 'the family'" (9). Thus, while lesbian partnering and mothering offers a way to queer, or destabilize, notions of "the family," it simultaneously reifies the assumption of mothers as caretakers who are responsible for shaping how their children understand this societal institution.

It is paramount, then, to situate same-sex headed families—and lesbian-headed families in particular—within the changing landscape of the family. Given the historically blurred boundary between "wife" and "mother," both of which exist in the private sphere, in what ways may the contemporary configuration of lesbian wifehood and motherhood disrupt the masculinized public sphere? Furthermore, how might expectations of wifehood and motherhood change when contextualized apart from heteronormative constructions of partnering and parenting? In this chapter, I engage with these questions through an analysis of *The Fosters*—a televisual representation of lesbian wives and mothers.

## The Gendered Family on Television and Wives' Place in It

Domestic situational comedies, or those comedies that use some version of the family structure as a vehicle for its narrative, have been prominently featured in programing lineups throughout television's history. Between 1950 and 1990, 497 television series employed the domestic sitcom format, with subjects that included traditional nuclear families, extended families, and single-parent families (Skill and Robinson 449). Much like the popular conceptions listed above, the televisual representation of the family has historically colluded with the traditional, heteronormative structure, which emphasizes the presence of a husband and wife as well as a gendered division of labour that falls neatly in line with normative roles of masculinity and femininity, particularly for middle-class families. Beginning with representations in 1950s domestic sitcoms, Richard Butsch traces forty years of families on television and shows how middle-class parents are depicted as "a superb team ... of super-parents" (30), who are responsible for teaching their children moral lessons. Although these representations may seem to indicate an equitable relationship, Beth Olson and William Douglas's study of television families covering the same time period posits that even parents in the 1980s and 1990s "did not display more equality or less [masculine] dominance" (419), as one may expect given the changing social mores associated with gender equality throughout the late-twentieth century. In other words, wives' representation in the heteronormative television family remained relatively consistent in television's early history, with a sustained focus on reifying the traditional expectations of masculinity and femininity.

Given that scholarly attention has turned away from investigating the ways in which gender is reflected in domestic situational comedies in recent years, little research examines how traditionally masculine and feminine roles are embodied in more contemporary television. However, in their analysis of the 2005 to 2006 primetime television lineup, Martha Lauzen and her colleagues found that wives are more likely to inhabit feminized social roles associated with romance and family, whereas their male counterparts are more frequently contextualized within the masculinized public sphere of work (210). Furthermore, men, especially working-class husbands, are frequently contextualized as incompetent (Leistyna 345), especially regarding their ability to successfully contribute to domestic labour. Referencing

*According to Jim* and *Everybody Loves Raymond*'s titular patriarchs, David Petroski and Paige Edley contend that these types of representation "influence societal attitudes and perpetuate the Mr. Mom stereotype of the bumbling stay-at-home father," which works to "establish the mother as the primary caregiver" (para. 20). Whereas both partners in heterosexual couples often work outside the home in the paid labour force, equity in household labour has remained relatively stagnant since the mid-1990s, with wives still shouldering significantly more responsibility for domestic tasks (Parker and Wang para 11). Televisual representations that underscore the differences between women's private work and men's public work, such as those indicated above, reinforce the cultural, naturalized assumption of what men and women are "good at" and the roles that husbands and wives in heteronormative relationships ought to play in the family.

## Gay and Lesbian Televisual Representation

In the 1990s, lesbian and gay characters began to be featured more regularly in television programing, with characters on *My So-Called Life, Ellen,* and *Will & Grace* serving as main or auxiliary characters in the narratives of those series. The media activist organization GLAAD began tracking comprehensive data on LGBT representation on both broadcast and cable networks during the 2005 and 2006 season, and found that although LGBT characters were series regulars in only 2 percent of scripted broadcast programs, "unscripted reality television and cable programming ... include numerous diverse representations that better reflect the LGBT community" (para. 1). Their most recent analysis revealed that LGBT representation on broadcast television more than doubled in the last decade, reaching 4.8 percent during the 2015 and 2016 season (para. 2), including a rise in gay and lesbian series regulars on both scripted cable and streaming platforms' (e.g., Netflix, Hulu, etc.) original programs.

GLAAD's annual reports offer a snapshot of the increased visibility of LGBT individuals on television, but researchers have investigated the specific nuance with which these characters are constructed. Gay and lesbian visibility was marked by a number of representational trends, including the "coming-out" narrative (e.g., Dow 123; Harrington 207), which grapples with how characters disclose their sexuality within their narrative arcs. Despite the assumption that the coming-out process is an articulation of sexuality, and thus sex, early research suggests that gay and lesbian characters primarily exist in a sanitized space devoid of overt sexuality. Fred Fejes and Kevin Petrich, for example, contend that although "sexual innuendos and sexual activity between unmarried heterosexual couples are routine ... display or discussion of physical and sexual behavior between homosexual characters is generally off limits" (402). Lesbian characters in particular are subject to this depiction; whereas popular discourse, if not television representation, conceptualizes gay and bisexual men as hypersexual or sexually compulsive (e.g., Parsons et al. 262), Rebecca Beirne points out that as the positive representations of lesbian women increased in the late 1990s, "so did the problematic tendency to desexualize lesbian characters, coyly ignoring their relationships and intimate lives" (4). These early representations, then, leave little room to explore the intricacies of lesbian and gay intimate relationships, and, consequently, minimize their roles as partners and parents.

However, as televisual representation has progressed into the new millennium and gay and lesbian characters have occupied leading roles more frequently, series have begun to make gay and lesbian sexuality and family structures central to the diegesis. *Will & Grace*, which ran on NBC from 1998 to 2006 and returned in 2017, featured two gay male leads: the "straight-passing" Will and the "*so* stereotypical and *so* proudly promiscuous and *so* flamboyant" Jack (Snider 22, emphasis original). Although Zachary Snider argues that Will and Jack's characterizations offer little beyond the stereotypical, *Will & Grace* does highlight romantic and sexual relationships between gay men in a way previous series lacked. Indeed, at the end of the original run of the series when Will marries his partner Vince, "they are just two regular dudes in a loving marriage, without a woman necessary for their happiness" (24).

Perhaps because it was the first show with an ensemble cast of queer women (Upadhyaya) and has been heralded as "the pinnacle of lesbians on TV" (Gonzalez para. 4), a significant portion of research examining lesbian televisual representation focuses on the Showtime series *The L Word* (2004-2009). Unlike many of its queer representational counterparts, and likely because of its home on a subscription cable channel, *The L Word* readily features explicitly sexual relationships. Yet as Chambers maintains, the lesbian sexual relationships in the series must be contextualized within the framework of lesbians as "an object of heterosexual desire in popular culture and pornography" (90). In this way, Samuel Chambers argues that *The L Word* "sells" to straight male audiences, and "this move undercuts significantly any plausible chance the show might have of challenging heteronormativity" (91). Merri Lisa Johnson also finds traces of heteronormative ideology through the way *The L Word* reproduces compulsory monogamy in the relationships between its characters. She argues that the over-abundance of cheating plots in the series, while often between queer characters, does not "queer" relationships but rather fails to "detail a vision of 'long-term' that is not synonymous with stifling monogamous arrangements" (134), which falls in line with more conservative, heterosexual relationship ideals. Echoing these assertions of conservatism, Lorna Wheeler and Lara Wheeler suggest that the first season of the series presents relatively conservative sex scenes; however, they note that the following seasons explore "many different versions of lesbian sexuality, from exhibitionist to playful, from romantic to sadist"—a move they call "daringly queer" (109). Taken together, scholarly insight calls into question whether a series as ostensibly ground-breaking as *The L Word* does enough to destabilize heteronormative discourses of love and sexuality.

Researchers have also examined more contemporary television series and have analyzed the ways in which same-sex-headed families either collude with or recontextualize the traditional, heteronormative family structure. In their analysis of *Modern Family, The New Normal, Sean Saves the World,* and *House Husbands*, each of which feature gay husbands and fathers, Clare Bartholomaeus and Damien Riggs contend that "the four television programs are united by homonormativity—they are premised on the heteronormative presumption of appropriate roles for fathers and mothers, men and women, and these are applied to the gay fathers with little interrogation" (169). Others have reiterated this reading of *Modern Family* in particular. Steven Doran, for instance, concludes that Cam and Mitchell's relationship is one of homodomesticity, in which the characters fit into a "narrative of apolitical normativity" by suppressing "any aspects of gay identities or lifestyles that refuse to fit into the heteronormative fantasy of the domestic" (98-99). Although Peter Kunze argues that the writers of

*Modern Family* do spend the first season "normalizing" (i.e., making them heteronormative) Cam and Mitch to appeal to the broadest range of viewers, he points out that this does open an avenue through with to explore concerns unique to same-sex parents in later seasons.

Scholarship on the representation of the family, gendered expectations of the family, and general LGBT representation on television serves as the groundwork to understand how same-sex headed families on television navigate the intersecting cultural spaces of these areas. Perhaps unsurprisingly, televisual representation has historically depicted "family" as featuring the heteronormative relationship of husband and wife, and thus "wife" has come to exist only in relationship to the role of "husband." In part because of previous laws restricting same-sex marriage in most states, committed lesbian and gay couples on television have not been granted the labels of "husbands" or "wives" until recently, further reifying the heteronormative understanding of marriage. Yet even as the tide of representation has shifted on television towards a more inclusive family structure, a significant number of representations of same-sex couples, as well as the subsequent literature produced about those representations, focus on families with husbands who are fathers. Drawing from academic and societal definitions of the changing nature of family constitution—and following Bartholomaeus and Riggs's call "to consider if some of the issues [they] have raised [for gay fathers] also play out in terms of lesbian and bisexual mothers" (173)—I investigate how the ABC Family (now Freeform) drama *The Fosters* negotiates the contemporary landscape of "family" and wives' roles within it. Specifically, I contend that *The Fosters,* unlike many of the same-sex representations that have come before it, resists mapping heteronormative roles onto a lesbian couple, and, instead, the show articulates lesbian wifedom and motherhood as their own particular subjectivity.

## Freeform's *The Fosters*

Mediated representations, and television in particular, offer a way to explore the ways in which cultural ideologies are represented and recirculated into our social world. John Fiske suggests that television should be viewed as a "bearer/provoker of meanings and pleasures, and of culture as the generation and circulation of this variety of meanings and pleasures within society" (1). In other words, the meanings and pleasures people derive from television shape their cultural context, which necessarily influences how they see and experience the world. Jason Mittell further contends that mediated representations of identity, including the role that sexuality plays in familial structure, "help define what a culture thinks is normal for a particular group, how behaviors and traits fit into a society's shared common sense" (306). Thus, analyzing television can reveal the cyclical way members of a society influence and are influenced by their culture; in this case, *The Fosters* offers a way to explore how the intersections of sexuality, gender, and the wife's role in the family are represented in Western culture through their televisual depiction.

*The Fosters* premiered in 2013, the same year that California resumed granting marriage licenses to same-sex couples. Set in San Diego, the series centres on Stef and Lena Foster, lesbian wives raising a multiethnic family of both their biological and adopted children. The series, which recently concluded its fifth season, has received wide acclaim for its representation of LGBT themes. For instance, *Entertainment Weekly* critic Sarah Caldwell has praised the series, noting that "seeing a lesbian, biracial couple on a family TV show is a big deal ... if you look at the demographics of most TV shows, it's easy to realize how important, and deliberate, this choice was" (para. 4). Because of this representation, *The Fosters* was the 2014 GLAAD Media Award winner for Best Drama (Goldberg, 2014).

In what follows, I use the first season of *The Fosters* to explore how Stef and Lena reflect partnering and parenting vis-à-vis the changing nature of the ordinary family. I argue that *The Fosters* pushes against the historical representation of same-sex couples as simultaneously heteronormative and desexualized through its explicit focus on lesbian sexuality and the unique challenges presented to lesbian wives. Moreover, I maintain that the series' focus on lesbian wives disrupts the traditional masculine-feminine gendered expectations that guide both representations of heterosexual couples and same-sex husbands. Finally, I contend that *The Fosters* politicizes lesbian relationships by addressing the legal and cultural frameworks that same-sex couples face as they seek legitimization of their relationship. As such, *The Fosters* offers a compelling representation of lesbian wives that complicates and redefines what it means to be a wife and mother in the twenty-first century.

## Problematizing the Ordinary

From the beginning of the series, *The Fosters* is grounded as explicitly domestic. The show's title serves as a double entendre, as it references both the couple's last name and their role as foster parents, and highlights the centrality of the titular couple's relationship and the significance that parenting plays in the series. The opening credits unfold with a set of images underscoring domestic life: breakfast being made, chore charts, stacks of mail on the stairs of the home, markers of how tall the children have grown over the years on a doorframe, and family photos adorning the fridge. As the credits conclude, the show's title appears as a logo stylized with a roof drawn above *The Fosters*, again referencing that the home and those within it serve as the primary focus of the series. In this way, *The Fosters* works to reify the ordinariness of the family and Stef and Lena's relationship, which is similar to other opening sequences of both domestic situation comedies (e.g., *Roseanne*, *Modern Family*) and family dramas (e.g., *Parenthood*, *Brothers and Sisters*) that feature both heterosexual and same-sex headed families and their homes. These images of domestic life allude to the fact that *The Fosters* will be just like other series with a domestic focus.

However, early into the first episode, it becomes apparent that *The Fosters* deviates from the traditional, heteronormative family structure historically featured on television. In the initial moments of the series, viewers are introduced to Callie, a young woman leaving a juvenile delinquency program without anywhere to go. Callie's case manager calls Lena, who is certified along with Stef as a foster parent in the state of California, to take Callie in, given that she "has had problems with male authority figures as of late." Less than ten minutes into the series, viewers witness the first physical intimacy between Lena and Stef—a kiss as Stef arrives home from work—which prompts Callie to ask, "So, you're dykes?" Lena and Stef's adopted son, Jesus, quickly admonishes Callie's "dyke" designation, replying, "They prefer the term people, but yeah. They're gay." Although Callie's question is crass, it highlights the unapologetic way in which *The Fosters* approaches the representation of a lesbian couple and their family; Lena and Stef's relationship is unambiguous from the outset, and Jesus's reply works to normalize their relationship in a way that resists the sanitized, desexualized representation of other lesbian and gay television couples. In other words, his lesbian mothers are "people," and, therefore, their same-sex attraction and physical affection are part and parcel of their humanity.

Unlike Rebecca Beirne's assertion that increased lesbian representation has resulted in the desexualization of lesbian characters (4), *The Fosters* positions Lena and Stef as sexually desiring women, and makes their sexuality a key component of their healthily functioning marriage. Although explicit sex, as featured on programs such as *The L Word*, cannot be expected in a series that airs on the family-based network Freeform, Stef and Lena are often featured covered by sheets but are obviously nude in bed together. In a number of first season episodes, they engage in passionate kissing, particularly after making up after a fight, or after an emotional instance in which they express their love for one another. Moreover, they have conflicts related to the regularity of their intimacy. In "The Morning After," Lena and Stef learn that another lesbian couple who are friends of theirs are separating, and Lena tells Stef, "Jenna says they haven't had sex in over a year." When Lena questions how long it has been since they have been intimate and Stef does not immediately reply, Lena asserts, "If you have to think about it, it's been too long." Stef blames this on their busy lives and responsibilities, and Lena suggests they should have "a date night like they used to, with cocktails and dinner and other stuff," in which "other stuff" acts as an innuendo for sex. In an attempt to get their sex lives back on track, the couple humorously schedules a "sex date" in their phone calendars, and later in the episode, Stef stops at a pharmacy to buy massage oil for their rendezvous. Indeed, many of the martial conflicts regarding their sex life do seem to collude with those faced by heterosexual partners. *The Fosters*, however, is able to resist the clichéd, heteronormative representation of the wife as a sexually-desired subject coyly skirting the advances of her husband; instead, it positions both Lena and Stef as wives who are sexually pursuant at different times during the series. In other words, it works against the notion that one of the wives must occupy the sexually-desiring husband role.

It is not just the focus on equitable lesbian sex that makes the series different from the ordinary heteronormative family. The show also presents the challenges facing Stef and Lena that are unique to same-sex couples and lesbians in particular. Doran contends that representations of gay identity on television marginalize gay and lesbian characters "by seeking to erase the difference that is inherent to being gay and by suppressing anything about gay identities that might clash with heteronormative society" (99). Yet these obstacles significantly drive the narrative for Lena and Stef in *The Fosters*. In "Family Day," Lena meets with her gynecologist and asks if she is still able to conceive at her advanced age. After receiving affirmation from her doctor, Lena and Stef make the decision to attempt to have Lena carry their biological child with the assistance of a sperm donor. Although they initially desire to have an anonymous donor, Lena becomes enamoured with the idea of her handsome, smart, and cultured co-worker, Timothy, donating the sperm. Timothy initially agrees to sign a contract that Stef describes as stating "basically that we're the parents. Not you." In the season one finale, "Adoption Day," Timothy reneges on his promise, telling Lena, "I really thought I could do this, but when I actually read the contract and saw it all laid out, I couldn't get past the idea that there would be this kid in the world that came from me that I wouldn't get to love or hold or play with. I think it would just destroy me." The season ends with Lena revealing her pregnancy to Stef, and the uncertainty they will face given Timothy's refusal to sign the contract. Much like Julia Erhart points out in her analysis of the sperm donor conception narrative in the lesbian-centred film *The Kids Are Alright*, Lena and Stef experience "anxieties and vulnerabilities … whereby a donor could gain recognition and rights regarding children that he has not taken the time to raise" (91). Although this issue may be applicable to heterosexual couples as well, especially those that struggle with infertility, it is a concern for all lesbian wives who hope to have biological children. By making this a major plot point of the first season narrative, *The Fosters* disavows the heteronormative mandate of representing same-sex couples as exactly the same as their heterosexual counterparts and further problematizes the need to make same-sex wives and mothers seem ordinary. Moreover, these narrative decisions discursively separate wives from mothers; given that Lena and Stef cannot biologically conceive a child on their own, their sex life is firmly grounded in the role of intimate wives, although the decision to become mothers transcends the private sphere in that it includes a third party (i.e., Timothy).

## (De)gendering Lesbian Wives

At first glance, *The Fosters* appears to be a series that reifies the gendered division of labour within and beyond the home, particularly when Stef's and Lena's occupations are considered. Stef, a police officer, works in a masculine-dominated field, and is regularly featured while wearing her uniform. Lena, on the other hand, is a vice-principal of a charter school, a position she has gained through her "hippy-dippy ... Ph.D. in child whatever-the-hell it is," as Stef's ex-husband Mike describes in "Consequently." Indeed, the contrast between Stef's rule- and discipline-oriented position and Lena's liberal, "touchy-feely" approach to education grounds the women in a traditional dichotomy of masculinity and femininity, and thus so-called husband and wife roles. This binary is called into question, however, as the two enact their occupations. Through a series of flashbacks in "Vigil," viewers learn that Stef and Lena came to foster Jesus and his twin sister, Mariana, after their current foster family, who could no longer care for them, dropped them off at the police station. As Stef's primarily male co-workers pass by the children without a second glance, Stef's growing concern about Jesus and Mariana leads her to speak with them and offer them lollipops as consolation. Although the flashback ends there, the resolution of the situation is clear: Stef's compassion, a trait typically associated with femininity, guides the way in which she approaches her job, and this representation complicates the easy assumption that Stef would serve as the "husband" in the relationship, given her masculine-associated profession.

Similarly, Lena's authoritarian role complicates the gendered assumptions of the female-dominated education profession. Given that she is not simply a teacher but instead a vice-principal, one of her primary roles is that of disciplinarian. Because each of the children attends Anchor Beach, the charter school over which Lena presides, she is in the unique position of having to discipline their children in both private and public spaces. During the episode "Things Unsaid," Jesus takes part in a physical hazing ritual after he joins the wrestling team. After seeing his black eye, Lena confronts the wrestling coach and condemns the violent practice, much to Jesus's embarrassment. When they arrive home and Mariana addresses the tension between Lena and Jesus, Lena replies that he got a little "roughed up at practice" and she "had to have a talk with the coach." Mariana sympathizes with her brother, telling Lena, "You're not just the vice principal, you know. It's not that easy hearing people calling you 'Mean-a Lena' all the time." That the other kids at school have adopted the moniker "Mean-a Lena" is indicative of her disciplinarian reputation, yet Mariana's comment that she's "not just the vice principal" underscores Lena's dual role as the children's mother, which assumes that she will take an empathetic, or feminine, approach when navigating the complicated terrain of mother and administrator. Although Stef's and Lena's approach to parenting may seem to collapse the distinct roles of work and motherhood, this is simply because of their chosen occupations rather than an essentialized notion that women's public and private lives are indistinguishable.

Consistent with representations of heterosexual couples in domestic television programs, series featuring gay male couples have worked to gender male characters in line with prevailing norms of masculinity and femininity—positioning one partner as the provider and authoritarian and the other within a feminine domestic and emotional frame (e.g., Bartholomaeus and Riggs). *The Fosters*, conversely, problematizes the notion that all romantically involved couples must adhere to heteronormative gender roles; Lena and Stef navigate marital and parenting responsibilities in relatively gender-neutral ways and resist and challenge the notion that they should decide who will occupy the role of masculine husband and who will be the feminine wife. For instance, throughout the first season, they are a dual-income household with jobs of relatively equal status; they negotiate who will take the children to doctor appointments as well as extracurricular activities, and they hand down disciplinary action to their children in relatively equal measure. In "The Honeymoon," Stef and Lena wake up the morning after their wedding and address one another as "Mrs. Adams-Foster"—a pointed rejection of the heteronormative mandate that wives must take their husbands' last names and a nod to their equality in the relationship.

Perhaps what is most illustrative of Lena and Stef's egalitarian relationship, though, is the contrast presented through the continued presence of Stef's ex-husband, Mike, in the Fosters' lives. Although he exists on the periphery of Lena and Stef's family unit, Mike and his traditionally masculine persona still serve as a guiding force for understanding gendered representation in the series. Mike, who is also

Stef's partner on the police force, plays a relatively active role in parenting his son with her, Brandon. After Callie and her younger brother Jude come to live with the Fosters in the pilot episode, Brandon considers moving out of the full house into Mike's apartment. In "Hostile Acts," Brandon angrily laments that he was never given a choice with whom to live, and he spends the episode staying with his father. Contrasted with Stef and Lena's rule-driven house, Mike embodies the "cool dad" role; he notes that Brandon should not set the table because they will eat in front of the TV, and if he decides to move in full time, he will move the kitchen table out of the way to set up Brandon's keyboard. They watch action movies, and Brandon asks if his dad is still playing poker and "milking all those guys for beer money." In addition to his masculine interests, Mike steps in to cover the cost of Brandon's piano lessons, which cost $150 an hour per week, as he fulfils the role of financial provider typically associated with normative masculinity.

However, Mike's masculine presence in Stef and Lena's family extends beyond fathering his biological son to also include their other children. In "Quinceanara," Mike gives Stef and Lena a gift to help cover the cost of Mariana's fifteenth birthday party, echoing the financial support he gives to take care of his own son's interests. This extra-familial parenting extends to Jesus as well; as Jesus' body struggles to adjust to the new dosage of ADHD medication in "House and Home," his heart begins racing while he and Mike are playing basketball in the driveway. Rather than take medication to alleviate his symptoms, Mike suggests Jesus play "a contact sport" to release his aggression. Stef and Lena are initially reluctant, but they agree to take Mike's advice and allow Jesus to sign up for the wrestling team. These characterizations speak to a broader trend in television. As Snider contends:

> Television series that feature same-sex pairings are not necessarily even succumbing to negative heteronormative clichés; they are instead simply borrowing from the standard character, plot, and laugh-line blueprints of some of television's most successful and memorable shows, specifically with regard to their marital relationships and how their heteronormative spouses behave toward one another. (13)

In all of these instances, not only does Mike's role as a third parent deviate from the typical representation of parenting in televisual same-sex couples, his active presence in the series also makes the masculine husband-feminine wife trope that many of these representations embody unnecessary. Stef and Lena, then, are free from the gendered constraints that usually plague same-sex couples on television.

## The Politics of Love, Parenting, and Marriage

In addition to being an explicitly lesbian show through the ways in which it deals with lesbian sexuality and challenges to lesbian reproduction, *The Fosters* makes the cultural and legal hurdles faced by same-sex wives central to its narrative. In particular, the series emphasizes the struggles associated with the legitimization of same-sex couples and their families, and discursively redeems the couple through the eventual cultural and legal acceptance of their union. The questioning of Lena and Stef's relationship legitimacy comes in a number of ways throughout the series and is often grounded in heteronormative societal assumptions. For instance, when Stef is shot on the job and hospitalized in "Vigil," the nurse initially addresses Mike rather than Lena, noting, "Your wife's condition is critical." Mike corrects her, saying Stef is his ex-wife, and Lena must interject that she is Stef's domestic partner, at which point the apologetic nurse begins to speak to Lena. Similarly, in "Quinceana," Lena takes Mariana to a shop to buy a dress for her party, and the seamstress asks Mariana in Spanish if her father's tie will match her dress for the father-daughter dance. Mariana's friend Lexi replies that Mariana does not have a father but rather two mothers. Visibly taken aback by this information, the seamstress offers that Mariana can dance with a "close family friend"; Lexi replies matter-of-factly, "She's dancing with her moms. Right?" In both of these instances, normative cultural assumptions about what constitutes a marriage and family are enacted, offering overt reminders of the ways in which these assumptions affect same-sex couples' struggle for legitimacy. In other words, part of the struggle of being a wife in a same-sex marriage is contending with a heteronormative culture that not only assumes "married couple" equates to "husband and wife," but also that those husband and wife roles serve essentialized functions in the family. In this context, a woman in the hospital should have a husband, not a wife, seeking an update about her health, and a young girl should have a father, not two mothers, to dance with at her coming-of-age party. However, by centralizing these plot points, *The Fosters* resists the traditional expectations of heteronormative couples and modifies the definition of "wife" and "family" to also include lesbian partners.

The intersection of conservative religious ideology and the acceptance of non-heterosexual sexuality presents further challenges in Stef and Lena's relationship, particularly regarding how they navigate relationships with their family and friends. In "Saturday," Jesus reveals that he would like to attend a church camp with his girlfriend, Lexi, and Stef initially declines, reasoning, "Church camp? So we can subject our son to a bunch of people who don't approve of our family? Um, no." Stef shares Jesus's desire with her own father, Frank, who suggests that it may be good for him to attend, and questions why Stef had herself stopped going to church. Stef laughs and recalls a time as a teenager when Frank caught her "cuddling" with a friend on the couch. She tells him, "You never talked to me about it; you never asked me about it. All you did was send me to see a man who proceeded to lock me in a room and tell me being gay was a sin," which justifies her dissatisfaction with religion.

Later in the episode, Lena and Stef invite Lexi and her parents over for dinner to discuss the issue, and Frank makes a surprise appearance at Stef and Lena's home. After Stef tells Lexi's parents that she and Stef are reluctant to let Jesus attend the camp because they "do not want to put Jesus in any kind of situation where he might possibly hear anything negative about his family or that his mothers' relationship is wrong in the eyes of God," Lexi's parents maintain that they have misunderstood their religious ideology, and are deeply supportive of the Foster family. Frank intervenes to say, "I'm not a Catholic, but the church is not in favour of same-sex marriage." When Lexi's mom says, "Well, we are," Frank continues, "How can you do that? How can you claim to be Catholic and not follow the teachings of the church? You can't just pick and choose." Lexi's father challenges Frank's position, stating, "You sit at this table, and you call these people family, but you don't think your daughter has a right to marry Lena?" This instance addresses the growing tension between religious institutions' official positions on same-sex unions and the personal ideology of their parishioners (Masci and Lipka para 8). That many religions still only endorse and perform unions for the heteronormative coupling of husband and wife presents an obstacle for lesbians who seek legitimacy not only legally but also culturally in the minds of their conservative, religious loved ones. Indeed, the legitimacy of their desire to marry would never be called into question by their religious friends and family were they seeking to be husband and wife rather than wives.

Given the scheduling of the series' debut in relationship to California's referendum on marriage equality, Stef and Lena's wedding midway through the first season offers a timely representation of the legal legitimization of same-sex unions. Leading up to the event, the legal status of Stef and Lena's relationship is questioned a number of times. In "Consequently," Jude asks if Stef and Lena are married, and Lena replies, "Not legally, but in our hearts." Similarly, when Lena's ex-girlfriend, Gretchen, is in town for business in "Clean" and is visiting with the couple, she tells Mariana that she "likes to play the field ... but your moms make marriage look almost bearable." Stef and Lena correct her assumption about their marital status, and Stef mentions, "I think marriage is a state of mind, not a matter of state.... We're domestic partners. That's the same thing." Initially, Lena agrees with this assessment and shares, "I don't need a piece of paper and ceremony to prove our love and commitment." However, the ensuing conversation reveals that although Lena hopes to eventually get married, Stef is reluctant given her failed marriage to Mike.

In one of the series' more heteronormative representations, Stef proposes to Lena as she is recovering from her gunshot wound in "Vigil," and the couple weds in "I Do." Lena's dad becomes ordained to perform their wedding ceremony and begins the service as follows: "Now that the Supreme Court has finally seen fit to recognize that all people are entitled to equal protection under the law—" and the wedding guests erupt in applause. He then continues: "—and have the right to the same challenges and triumphs, benefits and burdens as everybody else, I'm very proud to welcome you here to the marriage of my daughter, Lena Elizabeth Adams to Stephanie Marie Foster. And we're honoured that you're here to witness this magical event, the moment when two souls declare that they have become one." Through this touching tribute to his daughter and her new wife, Lena's father underscores that their relationship as wives is no different than the heteronormative understanding of a romantic couple while also acknowledging the complex legal battle same-sex couples have waged to grant legal status and, thus, legitimacy to their relationships. The uniqueness of their marriage is reinforced at the reception, as Mariana has the DJ play rapper Macklemore's marriage equality anthem "Same Love," which she dedicates to her moms. To be a wife in a lesbian marriage, then, is to constantly struggle within and against a heteronormative cultural and legal structure that automatically assumes wives have husbands and that the legitimacy of the lesbian marriage must be consistently and explicitly advocated for.

## Conclusion

As Pamela Demory and Christopher Pullen argue, "an understanding of the Western romantic narrative tradition must be incomplete without an understanding of modern queer love" (8). As the representation of romantic and familial relationships between LGBT couples continues to increase with the diversification of the contemporary television landscape, so, too, must the examinations of the cultural ideologies forwarded by these representations. In particular, these investigations should explore in what ways same-sex couples offer similar and divergent understandings of sex, love, partnering and parenting, and the possibilities of adding LGBT couples and families to the already complex picture of the modern American family.

Lesbian wives Lena and Stef of *The Fosters* offer one such avenue to achieve this aim. Whereas heterosexual couples on television simply *are*, especially those who embody the heteronormative trope of masculine husband-feminine wife, the negotiation of gendered expectations is inherent in representations of same-sex couples. Specifically, do they fall neatly into husband and wife roles, mirroring their heterosexual counterparts? Or do they challenge the idea that same-sex couples must reflect this heteronormative mandate? *The Fosters*, which is explicitly lesbian in its focus, does not obfuscate the challenges associated with being lesbian wives but rather makes legal and cultural struggles central to its narrative. In this way, *The Fosters* challenges the notion that lesbian wives have the same experiences as heterosexual wives. Moreover, rather than relying on the masculine and feminine gendered tropes that often guide conflict in sitcoms and dramas—including those featuring same-sex relationships wherein one partner plays the gendered role of the husband and the other plays the wife—*The Fosters* represents Lena and Stef as complicated individuals who embody traits associated with both normative masculinity and femininity. Thus, the series does not essentialize marriage as needing a masculine husband and feminine wife, even in a lesbian couple. As such, it presents a discursive model of an egalitarian relationship free of limiting, prescriptive ideas about gender.

Although it was beyond the scope of this project, *The Fosters* is an exemplary text to examine how other issues of identity affect the notions of "wife" and "family." Stef and Lena, an interracial couple, have biological, adopted, and foster children; racial identity often comes to the fore, as Lena struggles with her biracial identity, and as she helps Mariana and Jesus navigate their Mexican heritage while not being raised in a Latinx home. Furthermore, Callie and Jude's status as foster children causes significant anxiety for the whole family, as the children deal with the uncertainty of their living arrangement and as Lena and Stef seek legal recourse to officially adopt them. As family structures continue to evolve and include same-sex partners and parents, mixed-race couples, and biological and non-biological children, it is imperative to explore how those changes affect understandings of wifedom and motherhood.

## Works Cited

Adams, Rebecca. "'Traditional' Families Are No Longer The Norm, According To Pew Report." *Huffington Post*, 24 Dec. 2014, www.huffingtonpost.com/2014/12/24/traditional-families-pew-report_n_6377136.html. Accessed 18 May 2019.

Bartholomaeus, Clare, and Damien W. Riggs. "Homonormativity in Representations of Gay Fathers on Television: Reproductive Citizenship, Gender and Intimacy." *We Need To Talk About Family: Essays on Neoliberalism, the Family and Popular Culture*, edited by Roberta Garrett, et al., Cambridge Scholars Publishing, 2016, pp. 157-76.

Beirne, Rebecca, editor. *Televising Queer Women: A Reader*. Palgrave MacMillan, 2008.

Butsch, Richard. "A Half Century of Class and Gender in American TV Domestic Sitcoms." *Cercles*, vol. 8, 2003, pp. 16-34.

Caldwell, Sara. "*The Fosters*." *Entertainment Weekly*, 4 June 2013, www. ew.com/article/2013/06/04/fosters/. Accessed 5 May 2019.

Demory, Pamela, and Christopher Pullen. "Introduction." *Queer Love in Film and Television*, edited by Pamela Demory and Christopher Pullen, Palgrave MacMillan, 2013, pp. 1-12.

Chambers, Samuel A. "Heteronormativity and *The L Word*: From a Politics of Representation to a Politics of Norms." *Reading* The L Word: *Outing Contemporary Television*, edited by Kim Akass and Janet McCabe, I.B. Tauris, 2006, pp. 81-98.

Doran, Steven Edward. "Housebroken: Homodomesticity and the Normalization of Queerness in *Modern Family*." *Queer Love in Film and Television*, edited by Pamela Demory and Christopher Pullen, Palgrave MacMillan, 2013, pp. 95-104.

Dow, Bonnie J. "*Ellen*, Television, and the Politics of Gay and Lesbian Visibility." *Critical Studies in Media Communication*, vol. 18, no. 2, 2001, pp. 123-40.

Erhart, Julia. "Donor Conception in Lesbian and Non-lesbian Film and Television Families." *Queer Love in Film and Television*, edited by Pamela Demory and Christopher Pullen, Palgrave MacMillan, 2013, pp. 83-94.

Fejes, Fred, and Kevin Petrich. "Invisibility, Homophobia, and Heterosexism: Lesbians, Gays and the Media." *Critical Studies in Mass Communication*, vol. 10, no. 4, 1993, pp. 396-422.

Fiske, John. *Television culture* (2nd ed.). Routledge, 2011.

Gabb, Jacqui. "Imag(in)ing the Queer Lesbian Family." *Journal of the Association for Research on Mothering*, vol. 1, no. 2, 1999, pp. 9-20.

GLADD. "Where We Are on TV Report—2005-2006 Season." *GLAAD*, 2007, www.glaad.org/publications/tvreport05. Accessed 18 May 2019.

GLADD. "Where We Are on TV Report—2016." *GLAAD*, 2017, www.glaad.org/whereweareontv16. Accessed 18 May 2019.

Goldberg, Lesley. "GLAAD Names ABC Family's 'The Fosters' Best Drama." *The Hollywood Reporter*, 14 Apr. 2014, www. hollywoodreporter.com/live-feed/glaad-names-abc-familys-fosters-best-drama-695495. Accessed 18 May 2019.

Gonzalez, Briana. "19 Lesbian and Bisexual Girl TV Shows and Movies You Should Already Be Watching." *Pride,* 30 Mar. 2015, www.pride.com/television/2015/03/30/19-lesbian-tv-shows-and-movies-you-should-already-be-watching. Accessed 18 May 2019.

Harrington, C. Lee. "Lesbian(s) on Daytime Television: The Bianca Narrative on *All My Children*." *Feminist Media Studies,* vol. 3, no. 2, 2003, pp. 207-228.

Johnson, Merri Lisa. "'L' is for 'Long-term': Compulsory Monogamy on *The L Word*." *Reading* The L Word: *Outing Contemporary Television,* edited by Kim Akass and Janet McCabe, I.B. Tauris, 2006, pp. 115-38.

Kunze, Peter C. "Family Guys: Same-Sex Parenting and Masculinity in *Modern Family*." *Queer Love in Film and Television,* edited by Pamela Demory and Christopher Pullen, Palgrave MacMillan, 2013, pp. 105-16.

Lauzen, Martha M., et al. "Constructing Gender Stereotypes Through Social Roles in Prime-Time Television." *Journal of Broadcasting & Electronic Media,* vol. 52, no. 2, 2008, pp. 200-14.

Leistyna, Pepi. "Social Class and Entertainment Television: What's So Real and New About Reality TV?" *Media/Cultural Studies: Critical Approaches,* edited by Rhonda Hammer and Douglas Kellner, Peter Lang, 2009, pp. 339-59.

Masci, David, and Michael Lipka. "Where Christian Churches, Other Religions Stand on Gay Marriage." *Pew Research Center,* 21 Dec. 2015, www.pewresearch.org/fact-tank/2015/12/21/where-christian-churches-stand-on-gay-marriage/. Accessed 18 May 2019.

Mittell, Jason. *Television and American Culture.* Oxford University Press, 2010.

Olson, Beth, and William Douglas. "The Family on Television: Evaluation of Gender Roles in Situation Comedy." *Sex Roles,* vol. 36, no. 5-6, 1997, pp. 409-27.

Paige, Peter, and Bradley Bredeweg, creators. *The Fosters.* Nuyorican Productions and Disney-ABC Domestic Television, 2013.

Parker, Kim and Wendy Wang. "Modern Parenthood." *Pew Research Center,* 13 March 2013, www.pewsocialtrends.org/2013/03/14/modern-parenthood-roles-of-moms-and-dads-converge-as-they-balance-work-and-family/. Accessed 18 May 2019.

Parsons, Jeffrey T., et al. "Hypersexual, Sexually Compulsive, or Just Highly Sexually Active? Investigating Three Distinct Groups of Gay and Bisexual Men and Their Profiles of HIV-Related Sexual Risk." *AIDS and Behavior,* vol. 20, no. 2, 2016, pp. 262-72.

Petroski, David John, and Paige P. Edley. "Stay-at-Home Fathers: Masculinity, Family, Work, and Gender Stereotypes." *The Electronic Journal of Communication,* vol. 16, no. 3-4, 2006. www.cios.org/ EJCPUBLIC/016/3/01634.HTML. Accessed 18 May 2019.

Qiu, Wei, et al. "Children's Perceptions and Definitions of Family in China, Ecuador, Turkey and the United States." *Journal of Comparative Family Studies,* vol. 44, no. 5, 2013, pp. 643-62.

Skill, Thomas, and James D. Robinson. "Four Decades of Families on Television: A Demographic Profile." *Journal of Broadcasting & Electronic Media,* vol. 38, 1994, pp. 449-64.

Snider, Zachary. "Gay It Forward: How *Will & Grace* Made Gay Male Couples Okay on Television." *Queer TV in the 21ˢt Century,* edited by Kylo-Patrick R. Hart, McFarland and Company, 2016, pp. 9-25.

Upadhyaya, Kayla Kumari. "10 Episodes of *The L Word* That Put Its Importance before Its Imperfections." *AV Club,* 8 May 2015, www. avclub.com/article/10-episodes-l-word-put-its-importance-its-imperfec-218837. Accessed 18 May 2019.

Wheeler, Lorna and Lara Raven Wheeler. "Straight-Up Sex in *The L Word.*" *Reading* The L Word: *Outing Contemporary Television,* edited by Kim Akass and Janet McCabe, I.B. Tauris, 2006, pp. 99-110.

Chapter Eleven

# More than "the Sniper's Wife": Kathy Leissner Whitman and the *Mad Men* Mystique

Jo Scott-Coe

In the early hours of 1 August 1966, before Charles Whitman climbed the tower at University of Texas (UT) at Austin to commit what was then the deadliest rampage shooting in American history, he murdered two family members, stabbing them in the privacy of their bedrooms. He murdered his mother, Margaret, a devout Catholic who was seeking divorce after twenty-five years of marital abuse and who had recently taken refuge in Austin, and his wife, Kathy, who was only twenty-three years old and had completed her degree and just finished her first year of teaching high school biology, despite four years of marital turmoil.

On a cultural scale, Whitman's brutality can be read as a flashpoint of confused and entitled white misogyny at the cusp of second-wave feminism—two years following passage of the Civil Rights Act (1964) and three years after publication of *The Feminine Mystique* (1963). Whitman's private murders of Kathy and Margaret must also be understood as attempted erasures of counter-narratives in marriage and wives' resistance in the home: a domestic prelude to the public gun massacre from the top of a landmark university tower within direct view of the Texas State Capitol dome. First under cover of darkness and then against the bright blue sky, Whitman's murders enacted a synecdoche of male domination, a performance of dominion in the face of his own powerlessness—striking the heart of his family, university, community, and country as if to say, "because I can." The connection between mass shooting and intimate-partner violence has become a recent, serious area of study and discussion (Spitzer; Mayer; Berman), but researchers have long explored the connection between men's violence and their conformity to strict, heteronormative codes of gender and sexual expression, often from a young age (Kimmel; Klein; Pascoe; Parkinson).

One impediment to seeing the realities of Kathy and Margaret can be located in something I will call, for now, the "*Mad Men* mystique"— an enduring normalization, mystification, nostalgia, or glamorization of toxic masculinity that remains largely unquestioned across social divisions, functioning as it does within the privilege of invisibility (Kimmel 5-8; Corbett 149-52). The *Mad Men* mystique influences how narratives frame exceptionality as a quality that simultaneously underscores Western male individualism while also suggesting that one man's flaws or crimes set him apart from society—at once making him deserving of understanding or sympathy as well as protecting his social influences and contexts from critique.

Jenny Diski has argued, for example, that Don Draper, the title character of AMC's series *Mad Men,* functions as a hollow figure, portrayed as a "moody, unknowable mystery," whereas, in fact, his story is "so transparent you can see the empty sky through it." The backstory reveals that Draper's character, whose real name is Dick Whitman, appropriates the name of a fellow soldier killed in war, thus attempting to valorize his old self through a narrative of patriotic sacrifice and enabling him to go AWOL. Although Draper-Whitman never kills anyone directly, his new identity depends upon the violent death of his namesake; as the series develops, we see Draper-Whitman habitually dispose of other people—particularly wives, lovers, and even his own kids—reducing them to tropes in support of his vacant quest for selfhood.

Similarly, Charles Whitman's peers, mentors, and family saw his violent acts as inexplicable in the context of his all-American good looks, Boy Scout pedigree, and external "niceness" (Lavergne 51, 70-71, 75). His own father, an open abuser of his wife and sons, "sobbed and said that he did not know what happened, that his son was just not like that" (Lavergne 242). The grand jury agreed that Whitman went "berserk ... with no warning to family or friends" (1-2). Shorthand characterizations of Whitman's status as an exceptional (rather than all-too-ordinary) villain also unwittingly reinforced the gendered nature of his public assault, as if his bullets shattered America's (or Austin's or Texas's) mythical innocence—as if an entire civilization had all been violently taken in.

Denial and exploitation are the common ground, with both the fictional Whitman and the historical one poised and framed in the narratives as "good catches," despite the reality of their despicable or violent acts. But more than that, audiences are drawn into complicity rather than critique by typical storytelling patterns that further enable these men to pass as misunderstood, sensational, made for TV, or true crime special cases. This mystique—which rejects the tedious and quotidian reality—operates to the detriment of real wives, mothers, and girlfriends whose lives in *Mad Men* as well as in historical situations are thereby relegated to the home, workplace, or sexual subplots, then conveniently discarded as saucy, dreary, pathetic, or hysterical moral compasses.

But the sixties in fact presented a powerful moment for resistance, when women writers—including Tillie Olsen, Jean Rhys, Sue Kaufman, Adrienne Rich, Nikki Giovanni, and Audre Lorde—began to claim room for lost or silent/silenced perspectives. Although neither Draper/Whitman nor Charles Whitman has erased this moment, the style of their stories has crowded our attention. Half a century later, the minimization of wives' and domestic partners' experiences across a spectrum of race and class remains a secondary result of sensational-ized coverage of public terrorism—even as violence in private spaces all-too-often precedes the public spectacle, as with the Mandalay Bay massacre in October 2017 (Sahagun), or is fused into the spectacle, as with the North Park Elementary School shooting in April 2017 (Fairley and Medina).

The surviving personal letters of Whitman's wife, Kathy Leissner—dated from before her marriage in summer 1962 through July 1966, one month before her death—trace her evolving roles and perceptions as a young fiancée and then new wife who was a working college student, military spouse, daughter, Texan, and teacher. Kathy's correspondence with her family, especially her husband, provides an intensely intimate portrait of marriage in the *Mad Men* era, document-ing the perceptions of one wife beneath the "ordinary" summaries or flashy surfaces and long before the violent ending. Kathy's correspon-dence brings her presence into view as a subject in her own life—no longer reduced, as Janis P. Stout describes (quoting de Beauvoir) as "the ally, in her silent objecthood, with 'unconsciousness and, finally, death'" (9).

The permission to read Kathy's surviving language posthumously—more than fifty years after her murder—enables us finally to see patterns as well as gaps that reveal how her narrative, like those of so many wives, "speaks of and through silence out of a tradition of being silenced" (Stout 9). Her personal letters show how Kathy in real time used her own language to resist, mitigate, and indicate silences—rhetorical manoeuvers that would be impossible to hear half a century later without the advocacy of her eldest brother, Nelson Leissner.

## Identifying the *Mad Men* Mystique: Women Inside, Outside, and Through

In 1963, Betty Friedan's *Feminine Mystique* coined the phrase "the problem that has no name" to address an unspeakable malaise among white college-educated women who found themselves adrift in a state of commercially idealized yet unsatisfying marriage and motherhood (15-32). *Mad Men* is a mirror image of Friedan's theory, rendering the trouble she identified through highly manicured and male-centred nostalgia, stylizing—even advertising—rather than critiquing the problem. The mere presence of wives, mothers, and mistresses is deemed enough to service the heterosexual character arc of a white man whose chosen name is not even his own.

But inside the history that is merely glossed by the series are real women—not all New Yorkers or Ivy League graduates, not all actresses or models or stay-at-home mothers, not plastic stereotypes of "ice-princesses" or "vixens"—whose testimony can and does witness their lived experience. Even though Kathy Leissner Whitman does match elements of the demographic profile in Friedan's thesis, and as the un-speakability of certain aspects of her struggle somewhat parallels the elusiveness of Friedan's problem, Kathy does not fit Friedan's diagnosis but instead sheds bright light on the mystique perpetuated by *Mad Men*.

From a historical point of view, one may locate or name Kathy's most immediate problem in her husband, Charles Whitman. On a broader level, Kathy's challenge was to define herself within a marriage troubled by a cycle of intimate partner abuse at a time when such topics were less available in vernacular language. In fact, the record documents how Kathy's ability to name problems within the context of her relationship evolved over time, whereas her husband's inability to hear his wife's voice and to reflect on his own inadequacies was ultimately realized not in naming but in violence—a culturally acceptable method available to men for self-expression.

Friedan's critique similarly does not apply to Kathy's mother, Frances, or her mother-in-law, Margaret—the two other significant wife models in Kathy's immediate family circle and who were both directly and indirectly victimized both by Whitman as well as his father. Like her daughter, Frances was college educated and professionally certificated as a teacher, and her degree was particularly unusual for her generation: she achieved it by the age of nineteen, prior to her marriage in 1939 (Scott-Coe, "Listening to Kathy"). Kathy's brother, Nelson, put it this way: "You have to understand, in my family, when my daddy married mother, mother was the only woman who had a college degree. None of my aunts. No one went to college" (Leissner). The 1940 census indicates that Margaret had some high school education, completing ninth grade before marrying at age seventeen and giving birth to her first child, Charles Whitman, in 1941. All three wives worked outside as well as inside the home: Kathy as a phone operator and teacher, Frances as a lifelong elementary school teacher, and Margaret as a bookkeeper for her husband's plumbing business, and then later (after her separation) as a cashier at an Austin cafeteria.

Marital and parenting roles also varied for all three women. Margaret had three children; Frances had four (including a planned "change of life" baby); and Kathy had difficulties conceiving and never became a mother. Due to a combination of factors, Kathy lived apart from her husband for nearly two of their four-year marriage. Margaret separated from and began seeking divorce from her abusive husband (Whitman's father) in early 1966, despite her lifelong identity as a devout Roman Catholic. Seven years after the shootings, in 1973, Frances divorced her own husband after he confessed to a long-time affair; she eventually remarried (Scott-Coe, "Listening to Kathy").

To differing degrees and at different times, these three wives did not always conform to the usual expectations for white and middle-class women in their specific regional and religious contexts. Although each spoke up within the chronologies of their own lived experiences, their voices have been silenced over time by simplistic narrative patterns overemphasizing traditional wifely ideals that only underscore value to their male partners: suffering, loyalty, sexual attractiveness, and maternal virtue. Similarly, in the absence of speech or written testimony, the bodies of these women were too easily reified within the social and literary traditions of patriarchy (Lerner 49-53).

Wives' resistance in the narrative of the massacre at UT Austin has long been buried by the violent public spectacle committed by the man who victimized Kathy in private but knew how to look nice to his friends. There are three layers of erasure here. Actual physical violence against women's bodies in private is itself silencing. Stories that gloss women's lives and aestheticize their deaths silence them yet again. Repeated narratives become ingrained, which makes the remnants of wives' perspectives increasingly difficult to recover. The cumulative loss becomes more significant, as silences redouble and multiply, becoming so loud as to require us to turn up the volume on crucial discoveries that might have begun with a whisper.

It is finally possible to see how Kathy attempted to resist intimate forces that she did not anticipate would finally contain and silence her as a wife. In this way, her husband's violence—a horrific strike against any woman who wanted to experience intimacy with another person while also seeking to live on her own terms—cannot and should not remain the last word.

## Artifacts and Language: A Life Prior to Marriage

It may seem impossible to consider Kathy's story and to read her words apart from the knowledge of her brutal death. Rather than denying that reality, it can be helpful to understand that Kathy was not passively occupying space prior to her murder but living a life forwards—surviving and constructing meanings through tools available to a young woman of her upbringing, education, ethnicity, and social class. The recovery of Kathy's voice situates her in contrast with the fictional wives of *Mad Men*, who are ultimately and finally subsumed into the faux redemption of Draper/Whitman's Coca-Cola dream.

Through her letters, we can now see Kathy as a married woman who has no frame of immediate reference that would lead her to anticipate or fear self-erasure, domestic abuse, or murder. It is particularly grounding to have a full picture of her early personality and family structure prior to meeting Whitman. Raised in a small rural town southwest of Houston, in Needville, Texas, Kathy grew up the eldest child and only daughter in a family of four. (Her youngest brother was not born until approximately eighteen months before her murder.) Kathy's parents were prosperous working people; her mother was an elementary school teacher, her father a rice farmer and cattle rancher. The family was active in the local Methodist Church, where Kathy sang in the choir and went on hayrides with the youth group. Whereas her father was a regular church attendee, her mother was less traditional in her practice, preferring to serve the church by assisting with bookkeeping and other behind-the-scenes community service (Leissner).

From ages ten to fifteen, Kathy maintained a scrapbook of girlhood memories—preserving photographs of friends, select notes from her parents, and short captions to herself about memorable football games, birthday parties, church camps, concerts, and, eventually, dates with boys. Her high school yearbook and senior edition of *The Blue Jay Chatter* document her participation as well as leadership in diverse activities, including the volleyball team, the band, Future Homemakers of America, the yearbook staff, the National Honor Society, the senior play, and the science club. Collections of class photographs from elementary through high school show that she was popular and enjoyed sustained, reciprocal friendships. Her senior class voted her "Senior Cutest," "Valentine Sweetheart," "Miss Needville High School," and "best personality." In the Senior Class Will, Kathy made a humorous reference to her ability to speak up, writing that she gifted a close friend "her ability to stick her foot in her mouth" (*Blue Jay Chatter* 4).

Although Kathy was economically privileged in comparison to most of her peers, her parents did not protect her from work that crossed traditional gender roles: she learned about childcare by babysitting her brothers, and she also helped her father by driving the rice truck or herding cattle. Many class activities during Kathy's high school years, including the senior banquet, were hosted at her parents' home, demonstrating a practice of sharing personal resources. When one of Kathy's childhood friends suffered the death of her mother, Kathy's family essentially adopted the girl until her father died and she moved away (Giese). By the time Kathy graduated from high school, she had a serious boyfriend who was so trusted by her family that he was allowed to drive her to enroll at UT Austin in the fall of 1961 because her parents remained home to assist neighbours with clean-up and recovery following the devastation of Hurricane Carla (Scott-Coe, "Listening to Kathy").

A portrait emerges here of a young woman who, prior to marriage, thrived when interacting with others. It is not difficult to see how Kathy and her family would represent an attractive package of resources for a young man who came from an abusive home and who had learned to see relationships as transactional opportunities. By the middle of her freshman year of college, at age eighteen, Kathy introduced Whitman to her parents, and before her sophomore year began, she married him. Thus, her primary social identities shifted from "daughter" to "wife" within just one year—a shift that quickly affected her college studies as well as her physical and emotional health. It removed her from the framework of social, economic, and emotional stability she had been able to take for granted until marriage.

Some of the most moving evidence of Kathy's social intelligence survives in her letters to Whitman around the time of their engagement, during July 1962, just before and after her nineteenth birthday. Because of the whirlwind nature of their plans, she repeats not only the word "happy" but also "shocked" in one letter to describe the reactions of her family as well as herself—in part because her parents, particularly her father, had expressed reservations about the prospect of a summer wedding date and then suddenly decided to approve. In the same letter, Kathy's anticipation of her in-laws' reaction is also gently understanding: "Precious, I sure hope your folks don't object too terribly" (10 July 1962).

But whereas Whitman's letters during this period often employ sweet talk to smooth over his anger at Kathy's father and to lay out menial requests or expectations, Kathy's writing takes time for specific and in-depth responses to exchanges she is having with her parents, extended family, and women she knows well. Most touching are her cheerful and detailed summaries of talks with her closest married or engaged friends—about weekly budgets for groceries, the cost of contraception, the planning of children, bathroom habits, frequency of sex, menstruation, and even mismatched desires for intimacy. She employs these narratives to assert, indirectly, her own preferences within the context of her private bond with Whitman: "I got so tickled at her and some of the odd things they do" (3 July); "Isn't that horrible! … He must not be very considerate" (16 July). She anticipates their union for the companionship it will provide: "Won't it be wonderful when we don't have to be lonesome. It doesn't seem very far off at all" (3 July).

These early letters demonstrate Kathy's ability to function successfully on multiple levels at one time and to be present in the moment when connecting her own priorities and knowledge. In addition to recovering from an unidentified medical operation, she was completing summer school classes at another college, acting as go-between for Whitman and her family, and coordinating wedding preparations. She depicts marriage neither as an all-encompassing solution nor an interruption of her pathway; marriage simply appears as a welcome, happy intersection of events and choices in her life. Implicit in Kathy's letters is an expectation that, as a wife, she will experience mutuality and partnership rather than Friedan's malaise or *Mad Men*'s erasure.

For one thing, she is assertive about her reproductive freedom. Kathy writes to Whitman of a disappointing visit with the local doctor (a neighbour and family friend) who refused to provide her with a prescription for oral contraceptives, despite a fixed wedding date less than one month away. This is a vivid historical reminder that prior to *Griswold v. Connecticut* (1965) or *Eisenstadt v. Baird* (1972), individual doctors and men still exercised a great deal of control and discretion over women's choices, even though the pill had become widely available to American women in 1960. Responding to the doctor's decision, Kathy asserts herself: "I told Mother I was going to some Dr. who would give me the pills. I'll tell you about the cream later. It doesn't sound bad at all" (19 July). In a subsequent letter, she references a planned early August visit to a doctor in Austin, apparently a contact of Whitman's, who would enable her to secure what she wanted (25 July).

Although Kathy was deeply attuned to other people's needs and moods, particularly Whitman's, she is still addressing situations within her own terms during this pre-marital period. When he sends a cryptic and hungover letter vaguely alluding to his "state of mind" after an apparent 4 July drinking binge, Kathy confronts Whitman head on: "Honey, what is it you want to tell me. I'm curious! I hope it's nothing bad." She repeats her concern both in the middle and at the end of the same letter: "Please write me about what's wrong. I can't wait until next Friday. Please"; and "The more I think about it, the more I hope that my honey is feeling better than he was when he wrote that letter" (6 July). This is only one of many examples where Whitman mentions anger or anxiety that he seems unable or unwilling to examine, whereas Kathy shows that her native instincts are to seek, understand, and expect a response.

A quieter but no less visible area of identity in the letters at this time regards religion. Whitman had been raised and confirmed as a Roman Catholic, attending parochial elementary and high school; equally important, he was socialized in gender-segregated groups, as an altar boy, a member of the parish Boy Scout troop and, eventually, the Marines. A mixed marriage in 1962 was no small matter, and Kathy was the first person in her family to marry a non-Protestant. Although the ceremony was planned for Kathy's hometown of Needville, it did not take place at the Methodist church of her upbringing but at St. Michael's Catholic Church. The wedding was also officiated by a visiting priest, a companion of Whitman's. On the surface, Kathy and her family appear to have made significant concessions, but these were essentially cosmetic agreements. Kathy did not convert to Whitman's faith, and there is no record that she signed the customary promise to bring up her children as Catholics. Kathy's brother also recalled that despite Whitman's desire for a Catholic ceremony, perhaps to please his devout mother, he downplayed the importance of religion to Kathy's family (Leissner).

Whatever Whitman may have said to pass as WASP-like and put his future in-laws at ease, one of his letters to Kathy less than a month before the ceremony refers to his priest friend who was supposed to arrange her hasty "instructions" in the faith (19 July), whereas his letter only a few days prior to the ceremony states that he wanted Kathy to think about whether she would attend mass with him the morning before the wedding (11 August). Interestingly, not one of Kathy's letters during this interval includes a single mention of religion, clergy, or church. However, religion is not always a subject Kathy avoided, and in letters to her family dated less than a year later, she refers comfortably to two discussions she had with a Baptist military chaplain (11 Apr. and 22 May 1963), who expressed concern about the mixed-faith nature of her marriage. A condolence letter from an Austin pastor after Kathy's murder also records her active participation in a Methodist congregation. It is reasonable to infer that Kathy was passively resistant to Catholicism, even if she did not explicitly object to the shape of her husband's practice, whatever form it took. She was refusing, as a wife, to comply with the clerical and canonical definitions of her "place."

But she was also making concessions. There are clear signs that well before her engagement was officially announced, Kathy was already adjusting her original educational pathway (from pharmacy science to science education) to facilitate her role as a married woman. In one letter, she anticipates the positive impact of this choice on Whitman: "Honey, I figured out that since I changed my major I will graduate in August before you graduate in June. I could work that long semester in the Austin school system ... Sure would make things nice and would make your senior year easier, wouldn't it?" (3 July). It is worth noticing here that she is framing an indisputable economic benefit to him in the form of a rhetorical question—inviting him to approve of an asset she would provide, as if to make it less threatening.

In context, however, it would be a sweeping oversimplification to read Kathy's affectionate planning and her change of major as first steps of willing wifely martyrdom. From the evidence available in her early experience, Kathy had no reason to expect that married life would undermine or exclude mutuality, and she was not yet conceding important aspects of her identity. Even though her marriage took place relatively quickly, it appears that, in good faith, like many young women of this generation, she saw herself making a reasonable investment in a future that would include completing her degree, working, and having children—not unlike it had been for her own mother.

## Military Life: A Double-Edged Sword

Until Kathy's epistolary records were shared, it was assumed that because Kathy graduated "on time," within four years of her enrollment at UT Austin, she had remained behind when Whitman's unsatisfactory academic performance returned him to active duty with the Marines in February 1963 (Lavergne 25). In this way, Kathy's story was shaped by positive stereotypes: because she managed to complete her degree while her husband struggled, she must have had a linear academic path.

Correspondence now reveals that Kathy withdrew from the university to join her husband for six months in North Carolina. Her exit coincided with a moment of significant marital crisis, as indicated by letters from Frances to Whitman and from Kathy to Frances in January and early February 1963—within the first six months of the marriage. Frances's letter is a remarkable personal document, blending appeals of logic with affection for her son-in-law, to help him recognize that Kathy's misery was a reasonable response to his efforts "to completely dominate" his new wife, who, as Frances writes, "*is* a young woman, not a child, as you seem to think" [...] and "a *person*, not a doormat" (emphasis in original 28 Jan. 1963). Instead of getting counselling as Frances advised, the couple left Texas. Through the letter, Kathy not only breaks the news to her parents but also provides them with her own rationale for leaving; she speaks directly to her mother in specific sections of the letter and also intercedes on her husband's behalf (see my comprehensive first-time explication of this correspondence in "But What Would *She* Say?").

Beginning here, and for the ensuing six months of her time in Jacksonville, North Carolina, there are profound layers of doublings in Kathy's letters to her family. On the one hand, Kathy acts as intercessor, communicating her withdrawal and her move as an independent choice as well as an issue of "fate" (14 Feb.). On the other hand, once the move has occurred, Kathy maintains a steady and self-affirming line of communication with her mother in the face of severely isolating factors, including the geographical change, lack of telephone, and the weekly three-day stints when Whitman leaves her in the apartment while he attends on-base trainings. Kathy frankly describes being homesick for Texas and miserable in the new setting, where her husband seems to recognize people but she knows no one:

the town is "terribly dirty, and all Marines" (9 Mar.), "nothing but a big swamp with a lot of hack shops in the middle" (30 Mar.). She also describes time passing so slowly she feels they have already been there for a year (26 Mar.).

But Kathy also reveals her instincts as a survivor and persistent actor rather than passive observer. She fills out "a dozen" job applications (19 Mar.), even though opportunities are curtailed both inside and outside the home. Whitman's efforts to maintain economic control are not subtle, as when Kathy tells her mother how Whitman would allow her to keep 20 percent of her own earnings—only sentences before describing his "phobia" about her returning home (19 Mar.). After one job interview, she writes that it did not work out because of "too many experiences of married women getting pregnant and quitting. I guess you can't blame them but boy it sure would have been nice!"—a direct reference to open discrimination by employers against wives at the time (2 Apr.). When she finally secured a job "typing statements and contracts" at Liberal Credit ("the biggest pawnshop in town"), Kathy is glad to have a job even though the hours are extreme: noon to 10:00 p.m., five days a week, which means even less time with her husband (15 and 29 Apr.). The following month she tells her mother why she is leaving this position and taking a new job at the phone company: Liberal Credit "had a very poor business policy of firing any girl who gave notice. I had heard this from several girls in the office" (16 May). Kathy here mixes her own motivations of self-preservation with her judgment about unfair treatment of women co-workers.

Kathy describes her circumstances with self-deprecating humour, avoiding blaming her husband whenever possible, thus conforming somewhat to a traditional wifely role. But she also simultaneously conceals and reveals problems; she recounts Whitman's odd behaviour as if normal, yet she records rather than hides his actions from herself or her mother. One night, Whitman returned from judo lessons, directed her to change clothes, and then showed her "all the new holds he had learned that day" using a mattress in the kitchen (2 Apr.). This is the only written reference in the entire archive where Kathy makes to Whitman physically laying hands on her—in context, a reference both jarring and normalizing. Kathy also waits more than a month to reveal that a car accident occurred during their move to Jacksonville. She raises the subject because they are in a cumulative financial "bind" due to the burden of car expenses: "I may have to borrow some money from you, if I can, to get some clothes until my first paycheck. I don't have anything for warm weather" (11 Apr.). Here, her delay in reporting and her direct request for help function simultaneously to save her husband's face and to raise a flag about self-care and economic stress.

With some degree of exasperation, Kathy's mother offers support however she can, even insisting that she pay for phone calls, to which Kathy reiterates a non-sequitur that sounds like a defensive script supplied by her husband: "We cannot afford a phone just now" (13 Mar.). Yet as late as May, phone installation had not occurred, suggesting that whatever financial reasons might have existed at first, isolation and control may have been Whitman's underlying motive. Kathy recounts to her mother a lengthy description of how she was awakened by the military police one night and escorted to a phone booth to call her husband at the base, where she had to pick him up to prepare for a battalion alert due to trouble escalating in Haiti: "I almost killed myself getting to the base and I was a nervous wreck when I did get there. I imagined everything in the world that could have happened to you + Daddy + the boys" (10 May). The story illustrates the heightened worry, even terror, Kathy experienced as a spouse—like other military wives—simultaneously responding to orders yet excluded from official information. Also buried in plain sight is the reality that her stress and anxiety would have been significantly reduced if a phone in the apartment enabled Whitman to reach her directly.

During this period, occasional scapegoats or proxies emerge in the letters as mechanisms for Kathy to declare clear negative feelings about toxic influences she recognizes: the husbands of women raising children in her apartment complex: "he is a real *!* and not worth a plug nickel!" (8 Apr.); the Haitian dictator, Duvalier: "causing a lot of trouble" (10 May); and her demanding in-laws: "I'd give anything if I didn't have to talk to them. I know it's going to be one big argument. I have to hold my tongue" (20 June).

Kathy is also understandably preoccupied with immediate activities that bring a sense of personal order: cleaning wax buildup off the floor, hand making curtains and clothes, babysitting neighbours' children, attempting new recipes, and colouring her hair. She renders one of her more menial labours—ironing Whitman's underwear at the Wash-ateria for a Friday inspection—with a subtle awareness of the absurdity: "A couple of ladies looked at me like I was an idiot, but I kept on starching" (25 Mar.). Shared pleasures on the couple's weekends together are modest, such as seeing the movies *Giant* and *To Kill a Mockingbird*. In addition to being gone on manoeuvres, Whitman reports to her parents that he may get a job as a bouncer in a club six nights a week (31 Mar.). Referring to their overlapping schedules, Whitman admits to her mother, "Kathy and I hardly see each other" (25 Apr.).

As the couple gets closer to deciding whether (and how) Kathy will return home, elision occurs between "I" and "we," between singular and plural identities. Writing of the unresolved question about whether Whitman will eventually be reinstated at the university, Kathy speaks as if transcribing an agreed-upon speech: "If they put us back in school, we still have to serve 4 years as an officer" (15 Apr.). More concrete attempts to manipulate his wife's decisions occur when Whitman initiates side-conversations with Kathy's mother. For example, he finishes a letter Kathy had started before leaving for work, trying to draw her mother into a plan to convince Kathy to get pregnant (25 May). On another occasion, nearly two weeks later, after learning that her husband called her parents while she is at work, Kathy records a mental note to herself and her mother: "I didn't know Charlie was going to call you the other day" (3 June).

Whitman's interdictions read as attempts to undercut his wife's confidence and choices by testing the bond between Kathy and her family, especially her mother. Raising questions about whether Kathy can handle moving back to Texas, living alone, and resuming classes, Whitman finishes another letter Kathy started as follows: "I know she can do it scholastically, but I don't know if she is fully aware of the difficulties she will have. Would you and Daddy please write us a sober letter as soon as possible mentioning all the stumbling blocks you can think of and giving us your opinion on the deal" (10 June). From Frances's point of view, such manly posturing must have been déjà-vu all over again, reprising the very problems she had articulated to her son-in-law only a few months earlier in January 1963. Whitman remained clearly oblivious to the stumbling blocks his wife had already confronted and managed since marrying him. Furthermore, Kathy had been writing to her mother about wanting to return home as early as 19 or 25 March, with increasing clarity about exactly how to manage the details of her return, in letters dated 18 and 25 May and 10 June.

Frances remains a diplomatic and steady ally in her newly married daughter's instincts to resume her education. We can also infer that she resisted Whitman's effort to enlist her into a conspiracy about rushing Kathy into pregnancy when he responds, "Mother, about our secret, you are right, but I imagine that I am soft headed sometimes. I imagine we'll just have to wait until we get out of the corp [sic]" (3 June). Early on, Kathy repeatedly writes to her mother about feeling surrounded by pregnant women and mothers raising children alone. Frances demonstrates empathy rather than pressure: "Have you met anyone you can talk to? The apartment sounds like a madhouse with all those children" (Mar. n.d.). Kathy herself openly shares her mixed feelings when she experiences a pregnancy scare: "Cross your fingers," she writes, followed by "that's all we need right now!" (1 Mar.). When she sees a doctor and learns that she is "definitely not pregnant," she reports, "that husband of mine is disappointed and I'm relieved!" (3 Mar.).

In an interesting way, the Marine Corps itself provided an imprimatur for Kathy's separation from her husband: because Whitman would be sent to Cuba, leaving her alone in Jacksonville anyway, it was easier for a military wife to justify the benefits of returning to Texas and resuming her studies. Additional pressure to stay behind came not from Kathy's mother or father but from her in-laws. As she writes to Frances, "the Whitmans spent 45 minutes trying to talk us out of doing this. Their whole point was that they didn't think our marriage would hold up to being apart so much. That is really the least of our worries because we know it can be done. I'm anxious to start back to school" (1 July). Regardless of how Whitman had sought to shake her confidence, Kathy knew her capabilities, her desires, and her true allies.

## Separated and Thriving—A Wife Alone

In July 1963, Kathy returned to Texas and then re-enrolled at UT for the fall semester. From this point until December 1964, she lived apart from Whitman except for short visits during periods of authorized military leave. Her letters during this window show the insecurities one may expect to find in writings to a husband who had been controlling and abusive, but, significantly, they also document that Kathy was deeply insightful when it came to naming problems in their relationship. From the safety of distance and time, she was beginning to trust herself and regain her individual bearings. An intense close reading of Kathy's language patterns in letters written to Whitman between 11 July 1963 and 24 June 1964 reveals growing confidence and a desire to establish new rules for her marriage.

In the earliest weeks of their separation (starting summer 1963), Kathy misses her husband terribly and is most vulnerable his angry moods. Shortly following their first anniversary, she apologizes in a long letter for complaining about not hearing from him and also pledges not to smoke on campus or to "nag" him about his gambling: "I'm so sorry if I made you mad at me." In the same letter, her efforts to build him up are heart wrenching: "Honey, please stop cutting yourself down in your letters. I think you're the best person in the world and I don't like to hear you calling yourself those awful names" (27 Aug. 1963). Whitman's anger and expressions of self-loathing appear to trigger hyper-responsibility in Kathy as a wife—a powerful illustration of the bind faced by any "angel in the house" when her role as the moral centre turns against herself, reserving forgiveness and assurance for her partner (doing his military or husbandly "duty") and accepting blame, however inappropriate, for herself.

Ironically, by November, Whitman was arrested and court martialed not only for only gambling but for loan sharking, keeping an unauthorized firearm, and threatening another serviceman. Kathy's spousal good judgment was thus, coincidentally, validated by the ultimate masculine authority structure that held her husband accountable for even more infractions than she knew. Her correspondence now gives us a vivid sense of the context within which Kathy received this news. In late October, during a busy time of her semester ("just watch Charlie be home right when I have a crop of exams!" she wrote to her parents 1 Oct. 1963), Whitman had a ten-day leave period to visit her in Texas. After his departure, and one day before her husband was arrested, Kathy wrote a letter to her parents about the stress of preparation for upcoming exams and paper due dates in her zoology, geology, and botany classes: "I really feel like I'm drowning." She also reported results on a Bible pop test: 90 percent. She added that she was looking forward to the "welcome relief" of

Thanksgiving, remarking that her husband had not called and that she had trouble sleeping (30-31 Oct. and 1 Nov. 1963).

At exactly this time, Whitman was arrested at Camp Lejeune and confined to the brig for two weeks, and silence becomes a way for Kathy to communicate resistance. In his *Memoranda* notebook, Whitman refers to a gap in communication after his wife learns the news: "I haven't heard from Kathy since she found out where I am" (7 Nov. 1963). The next day, he references a letter from Kathy (one not available in the private archive), wherein "she seems very disgusted with me" (8 Nov. 1963). Photos document that rather than enjoying a relaxed holiday, Kathy took time away from classes to attend Whitman's court martial in North Carolina the week of 25 November. What follows is a pronounced lull in Kathy's correspondence through most of November 1963 and into January 1964, although one surviving message from her to Whitman in a Christmas card is both assuring and future focused: "No matter what happens I'm still terribly proud and glad that I am your wife ... Sweetheart, please think of me always and all the things we have to live for" (n.d. Dec. 1963). She also tells her parents exactly how she feels about addressing Christmas cards according to the list Whitman had sent her: "certainly no fun but a welcome break from studying" (12 Dec. 1963).

As Kathy's letters to Whitman pick up again in February 1964, her writing demonstrates insistent, if gentle, insights about how she wants their marriage to be different. Although notes of insecurity and self-doubt remain, Kathy seems grounded in a healthier reality, returning to her pre-marriage framework of confidence: she is taking major-related classes, making new friends, and reconnecting with old ones, and having regular contact with her parents, brothers, and cousins. She spends time in many letters assuring Whitman of her devotion and boosting his confidence ("you are the most attractive and appealing man I've ever seen" 21-23 Feb. 1964), yet she also reflects on how their emotional connection can be improved (23-24 Feb., 6 May, 13-14 June, 27 June). She often uses examples from campus life and pop culture as a springboard (or rhetorical shield) for her assertions about marriage and intimacy. Some of her most pointed insights come through the specific moments she recounts from her marriage and family life course, taught by male sociology professor Dr. Henry Bowman:

[He] was talking today about women being taught to protect and defend themselves against men from the time they are born, because of the advances and things men try to force upon them throughout life. This constant defensive attitude assumed by women often causes women to be unyielding and frigid in marriage. Therefore, when you think about it, men actually create the very thing they deplore in marriage. Pretty good hypothesis, huh! I sure do enjoy this course. I want you to take it. Every day, I'm more convinced that we are as perfect as can be. (20-21 Feb. 1963)

It is important to point out that prior to the establishment of women's studies, women's history, or gender studies as college disciplines, marriage and family life courses facilitated discussions about sexuality and gender roles for men and women, both married and single. Kathy's unguarded delight in this class as well as her appeal to external knowledge and male authority about behaviour patterns of men" and women" in social context—alongside her desire for Whitman to join her in learning—do not contradict her final sentence about their perfection as a couple. In her own way, Kathy seems to be signaling her belief that a healthy connection can allow room for new understanding between marriage partners—a true resistance, even refutation, of the mystique described by Friedan and mirrored by *Mad Men*, a mutual vaccination against poisonous gender codes. If Whitman had been able to truly hear Kathy, it would not only have saved her life, her mother-in-law's, and those of his public victims—it might have transformed his own.

## Reunion, Resistance, and Shadows

When Whitman was discharged from the Marines and returned to Austin in December 1964, he had lost his scholarship and his status as an officer in training. He had trouble keeping jobs, worked late hours studying, and struggled with heavy course loads. His most secure social privileges were the invisible ones he had not needed to earn (whiteness, maleness, and good looks). By contrast, Kathy secured her college degree and a teaching credential, also landing a full-time job as a biology instructor at Sidney Lanier High School. Between 1965 and

1966, she was the main economic provider in her household and supported her husband so he could finish school, exactly as she had proposed prior to her marriage.

This period of reunion and marital transition did not go smoothly. One married friend, John Morgan, reported talk of divorce between the couple during summer 1965. Kathy's brother, Nelson, went on the record for the first time in 2016 to share his memory of Kathy's visit home not long before her murder and the shootings. Nelson overhead Kathy admitting to their parents that she "loved" Whitman but that he "[could] be violent" and that she "wished she'd never met him" (qtd. in Scott-Coe, "Listening to Kathy"). As a wife, Kathy was trying to figure out how to resist and survive.

In the months leading up to that verbal articulation, her surviving letters to her mother and family are fewer and more muted in style. She is thrilled to have a new baby brother. She documents the accomplishment of concluding her studies, anticipates teaching students, and shares pride in her performance: "those are the best grades I've ever made" (22 Jan.). But she also misses her family intensely, experiencing a renewed and deep "homesickness" (22 Jan 1965). She repeatedly longs for more family visits: "I sure wish Austin were about 100 miles closer to home!" (24-25 Feb. 1965), suggesting that her mobility was inhibited upon her husband's return. Whitman resumes his pattern of triangulation and interdiction, as evidenced in the archive by interrupted letters, phone calls, and plans for possible visits. Kathy admits to feeling lonely upon adjusting to his return: "I feel like I am keeping house for a ghost" (11 Feb. 1965). She also expresses hope of pregnancy if certain plans work out—including an update of how the GI Bill will impact the couple (28 Jan. 1965, 16-18 Feb. 1966).

But while Kathy often brushes away her mother's inquiries about marriage trouble in letters ("doing just fine ... both making a big effort ... enough on that" [27-28 Sept. 1965]), she worries in detail about trouble in other areas of her life. The couple's new pet dog, Scocie, seems especially vulnerable to injuries (hit by a car, kicked by a little boy, restricted to certain parts of the house, found temporarily paralyzed and whining). In literary terms, the dog becomes an objective correlative for the anxiety and abuse Kathy had trouble openly articulating even to herself. She is blunt about her father-in-law when her husband goes on a hunting trip: "I just hope Charlie gets home safe and sound. I don't trust Mr. Whitman with a gun" (14 Nov. 1965). When her mother-in-law ("Mother Whitman") declares her intent to remain in Austin and seek relief from the violence she had suffered throughout her own marriage, Kathy writes the following: "All reports say Mr. Whitman has lost 30 lbs. and is about to crack. She doesn't seem to care. It's not unusual that she doesn't have one ounce of feeling for him after all she's been through. She likes her job real well" (26 Apr. 1966).

Although Kathy sounds supportive of her mother-in-law's pursuit of divorce, it may have felt like an extreme solution unavailable or premature for herself—at age twenty-three, despite her employability, family support, and economic security, she might have worried about being viewed as "damaged goods" Even when verbalizing fear to her parents in 1966, Kathy likely rationalized that her own circumstances were not yet severe enough to merit the option of divorce. She prioritized Whitman's wellbeing during this period, encouraging him to see a counsellor in March 1966 to deal with family stress (and his father's stalking phone calls). Kathy was accustomed to being on the receiving end of Whitman's manipulations, temper, and physical threats. The counsellor's only surviving record documents Whitman's admission of at least two physical assaults against Kathy prior to killing her and further indicates his perceptions of Kathy's fear (Heatly 1). A former roommate recalled after the massacre how Kathy "dreaded an accidental pregnancy," whereas a landlady reported that Kathy was afraid to turn over one of Whitman's guns "for safekeeping" because she was afraid of a beating (Lavergne 44).

Whitman's final words demonstrate, in the most awful way, how deeply he had absorbed a gendered and sexualized view of marital control. In a letter received by Kathy's parents the day of Kathy's burial, Whitman matter-of-factly informed his in-laws that he had killed their daughter following what he called a last sexual "interlude," adding that "she has always been a fine lover." He also referred coldly to how Kathy fought for her life despite his best intentions to kill her "as painlessly as possible," commenting, "She was a very strong girl" (qtd. in Scott-Coe, "Invisible Women, Fairy Tale Death"). This artifact captures how easily Whitman fell back upon normalizing, self-romanticizing language for his most intimately horrific, "mad" acts, and it provides an ugly and telling glimpse of the dehumanizing attitudes and treatment that Kathy confronted from her wedding day to her last night alive.

Personal strength and resistance alone were not enough to save Kathy's life, or her mother-in-law's, as the stories of many wives can teach us if we inquire and if we listen. To leave Whitman and start over, with no assurance that she could prevent a degrading or violent backlash, would have been a terrifying prospect for Kathy. Yet the unavoidable reality was that every aspect of her existence, her forward direction, her abilities and continued successes already demonstrated how Kathy was pulling steadily away from Whitman's orbit—a reality that would have deeply threatened any man whose sense of entitlement far outstripped his actual achievement. It should not necessarily surprise us that the violent habits of the father became manifest in public through the knife and bullets of the son.

## Conclusion

Whitman's private and public crimes enacted violence simultaneously intimate and depersonalized, literally a show of force functioning as a personal and cultural signal (or advertisement) for male domination in the face of women's resistance. We continue to avoid confronting this signal and instead choose nostalgia and mythology over curiosity and reflection. Like binge-watching the hyper-manicured *Mad Men*—or staring into the latest media coverage of men doing sensationally "mad" acts—we fail to inquire about what was silenced or crowded off camera, offstage, and out of the history books. *Mad Men* reinforces only a pastiche of sixties knowledge, a polished version that reinforces the lone "ad man" norms, just as coverage of mass shootings generally elides understandings beyond the "lone gunman" legend. Repetitive fixation on public spectacle divorces and isolates us from hushed contexts that contain powerful and potentially transformative meanings, often authored by women who dared to transcend, however quietly, the gendered social order.

In "Silences," a talk first delivered at Radcliffe in 1962, Tillie Olsen describes the cultural realms that undercut women's voices in history: "Women are traditionally trained to put others' needs first, to feel these needs as their own" (35). Even in the absence of primary artifacts or documents, we can help locate what's missing by posing different questions. Cynthia Enloe writes the following: "Violence against women almost everywhere has been a topic kept out of the public arena or only sporadically and very selectively allowed into it in the form of 'scandal.' This, in turn, has not only delayed for generations public officials tackling such abuse, but also entrenched the silencing of those women who have been the targets of that violence" (73). More than half a century later, we still have plenty of reasons to ask why women's successes, achievements, and independence may be perceived as more scandalous or provocative than the violence performed against them behind closed doors.

In the stories of Kathy, Margaret, and Frances, we can find nuanced portraits of survival and resistance as vital foreground rather than simple prelude or footnote to the violence of men. Kathy's newly discovered language provides a dark parable about how wives and intimate partners may not so easily or openly adopt desired new roles without systemic support, including legal and social policy reforms, as well as more sophisticated cultural understandings of links between gender and brutality.

A profound and senseless violence continues in the quiet suppression of wives' lost narratives and the denial or dismissal of their very real authority. There is a different knowledge available to us if we reach deeper and find meaning where madness both manifests and masks itself in ordinary behaviour and in ordinary lives. We must admit the ways we participate in, and perpetuate, this suppression while we are entertained—whether by gunfire or glossy tumblers of scotch—rather than really listening to what women in daily jeopardy may have to say about the mystique of marriage. Perhaps this subject is only mysterious when we refuse to recognize wives, and the complex layers of their resistance, in three dimensions.

## Works Cited

Berman, Mark. "The Persistent Crime that Connects Mass Shooters and Terror Subjects: Domestic Violence." *The Washington Post*, 15 Aug. 2017, www.washingtonpost.com/news/post-nation/wp/2017/08/15/the-persistent-crime-that-connects-mass-shooters-and-terror-suspects-domestic-violence/?utm_term=.2d3c57614af7. Accessed 26 May 2019.

Corbett, Ken. *A Murder over a Girl: Justice, Gender, and Junior High.* Henry Holt, 2016.

Diski, Jenny. "Mad Men's Too-Visible Man: Don Draper, Non-Enigma." *The Harper's Blog,* 12 Apr. 2013. harpers.org/blog/2013/04/mad-mens-too-visible-man/. Accessed 26 May 2019.

Enloe, Cynthia. "Whom Do You Take Seriously?" *The Curious Feminist: Searching for Women in a New Age of Empire,* University of California Press, 2004. pp. 69-82.

Fairley Rainey, Rebecca and Jennifer Medina. "San Bernardino School Shooting Leaves 3 Dead, Including Student." *The New York Times* 10 Apr. 2017. www.nytimes.com/2017/04/10/us/san-bernardino-school-shooting.html?_r=0. Accessed 26 May 2019.

Friedan, Betty. *The Feminine Mystique.* 1963. Laurel/Dell, 1983.

Giese, Bette. Personal interview. 15 Dec. 2015.

Heatly, Maurice D. *Appointment Report of Charles J. Whitman.* 29 Mar. 1966. pp. 1-2.

Kimmel, Michael S. *The Gendered Society.* Oxford University Press, 2000.

Klein, Jessie. *The Bully Society: School Shootings and the Crisis of Bullying in America's Schools.* New York University Press, 2012.

Lavergne, Gary. *A Sniper in the Tower: The Charles Whitman Murders.* University of North Texas Press, 1997.

Laurence, Patricia. "Women's Silence as a Ritual of Truth." *Listening to Silences: New Essays in Feminist Criticism,* edited by Elain Hedges and Shelley Fisher Fishkin, Oxford University Press, 1994, pp. 156-67.

Leissner Whitman, Kathleen, and Frances Leissner. *Select Letters 1962-1966.* Private archive of Nelson Leissner.

Leissner, Nelson. Personal interview. 27 Oct. 2015.

Lerner, Gerda. *The Creation of Patriarchy.* Oxford University Press, 1986.

Mayer, Jane. "The Link between Domestic Violence and Mass Shootings." *The New Yorker* 16 June 2017, www.newyorker.com/news/news-desk/the-link-between-domestic-violence-and-mass-shootings-james-hodgkinson-steve-scalise. Accessed 26 May 2019.

Morgan, John. Statement regarding Charles Joseph Whitman for Texas Department of Public Safety. 2 August 1966. Austin Police Department. Austin History Center. p. 1.

Needville High School. *The Blue Jay,* 1961.

Needville High School. *The Blue Jay Chatter,* Spring 1961.

Olsen, Tillie. *Silences.* Laurel/Seymour Lawrence Edition, 1983.

Parkinson, Debra. "Intimate Partner Sexual Violence Perpetrators and Entitlement." *Perpetrators of Intimate Partner Sexual Violence: A Multidisciplinary Approach to Prevention, Recognition, and Intervention,* edited by Louise McOrmond-Plummer et al., Routledge, 2017. p. 44-54.

Pascoe, CJ. *Dude, You're A Fag: Masculinity and Sexuality in High School.* University of California Press, 2007.

Revesz, Rachael. "There's a Terrifying Link Between Mass Murder and Domestic Violence that Nobody Is Talking About." *The Independent,* 10 Oct. 2017, www.independent.co.uk/voices/stephen-paddock-las-vegas-domestic-violence-fantasy-boston-bomber-orlando-shooting-a7993186.html. Accessed 26 May 2019.

Scott-Coe, Jo. "But What Would *She* Say? Reframing 'Domestic Terror' in the UT Austin Shooting." *Pacific Coast Philology*: Special Edition on Archives, Libraries, and Properties, vol. 52, no. 2, 2017, pp. 165-67.

Scott-Coe, Jo. "Invisible Women, Fairy Tale Death: How Stories of Public Murder Minimize Terror at Home." *American Studies Journal,* vol. 62, 2017 www.asjournal.org/62-2017/invisible-women-fairy-tale-death-stories-public-murder-minimize-terror-home/. Accessed 26 May 2019.

Scott-Coe, Jo. "Listening to Kathy." *Catapult.co* 30 Mar. 2016, catapult.co/stories/listening-to-kathy. Accessed 26 May. 2019.

Sahagun, Louis. "At His Local Starbucks, Las Vegas Shooter Remembered for Berating His Girlfriend." *The Los Angeles Times,* 3 Oct. 2017, www.latimes.com/nation/la-las-vegas-shooting-live-updates-at-his-local-starbucks-vegas-shooter-1507060195-htmlstory.html. Accessed 26 May 2019.

Special Report of the Grand Jury, 147th Judicial District Court of Travis County, Texas. 5 August 1966, pp. 1-2.

Spitzer, Robert. "The Relationship Between Domestic Violence and Mass Shootings." *Interview. All Things Considered. National Public Radio*, 7 Oct. 2017, www.npr.org/2017/10/07/556405489/the-relationship-between-domestic-violence-and-mass-shootings. Accessed 26 May 2019.

Stout, Janis P. *Strategies of Reticence: Silence and Meaning in the Works of Jane Austen, Willa Cather, Katherine Anne Porter, and Joan Didion.* University Press of Virginia, 1990.

Whitman, Charles. *Daily Record of CJ Whitman.* Austin History Center, Feb. through Mar. 1964.

Whitman, Charles. *Memoranda Notebook.* Austin History Center, Nov. 1963.

Whitman, Charles. *Select Letters 1962-1965.* Private archive of Nelson Leissner.

## Chapter Twelve

# Aspects of Wifehood

Elisavietta Ritchie

### Sorting Laundry

Folding clothes,
I think of folding you
into my life.

Our kingsized sheets
like table cloths
for the banquets of giants,

pillow cases, despite so many
washings seams still
holding our dreams.

Towels patterned orange and green,
flowered pink and lavender,
gaudy, bought on sale,

reserved, we said, for the beach,
refusing, even after years,
to bleach into respectability.

So many shirts and skirts and pants
recycling week after week, head over heels
recapitulating themselves.

All those wrinkles
to be smoothed, or else
ignored, they're in style.

Myriad uncoupled socks
which went paired into the foam
like those creatures in the ark.

And what's shrunk
is tough to discard
even for Goodwill.

In pockets, surprises:
forgotten matches,
lost screws clinking on enamel;
paper clips, whatever they held
between shiny jaws, now
dissolved or clogging the drain;

wellwashed dollars, legal tender
for all debts public and private,
intact despite agitation;

and, gleaming in the maelstrom,
one bright dime,
broken necklace of good gold

you brought from Kuwait,
the strangely tailored shirt
left by a former lover...

If you were to leave me,
if I were to fold
only my own clothes,

the convexes and concaves
of my blouses, panties, stockings, bras
turned upon themselves,
a mountain of unsorted wash
could not fill
the empty side of the bed.

# Elegy for the Other Woman

May her plane explode
with just one fatality.
But, should it not,
may the other woman spew
persistent dysentery from
your first night ever after.
May the other woman vomit
African bees and Argentine wasps
May cobras uncoil from her loins.
May she be eaten not
by something dramatic like lions,
but by a warthog.
I do not wish the other woman
to fall down a well
for fear of spoiling the water,
nor die on the highway because
she might obstruct traffic.
Rather: something easy, and cheap,
like clap from some other bloke.
Should she nevertheless survive
all these critical possibilities,
may she quietly die of boredom with you.

## Clearning the Path

My husband gave up shovelling snow
at fortyfive because, he claimed,
that's when heart attacks begin.

Since it snowed regardless I,
mere forty, took the shovel, dug.
Now fifty, still it falls on me

to clean the walk. He's gone on
to warmer climes and younger loves
who will, I guess, keep shovelling for him.

In other seasons here, I sweep
plum petals or magnolia cones
to clear the way for heartier loves.


## One Wedding Night

He blinks to note the old
woman parked in his bed, all

wrinkles and bellies, breasts
not as full as they seemed.

*Which* psychological drive, she
wonders, pushed her to sleep

with this grandfather figure,
and what if, in the midst
of things, his heart fails?
What would the rescue squad—

those husky bucks—speculate?
Not the usual bimbo here

who makes an old man's pump
seize up when he tries—

He turns down, she turns
off, the unkind light.

In silence they strive
to ignore imperfections,

remember the rules, or
at least work around them,

holding each other
lightly as Luna moths.


## This Sunday Morning, Proust's Madeleine
### *"Married Sex Gets Better in the Golden Years"*
### *New York Times* 24 February 2015

Fud-ge Swirl gelato in our second cup ...
And I am swirled back more than one decade
to other Sunday mornings late in bed,
*The New York Times* and coffee with ice cream
till this dissolved in heat, and we in bliss.

But you're eighty-three, apparatus dead,
not good for much... *My* memories don't fade.
Not quite so old, my every nerve tuned up
glows incandescent with ignited dreams ...
Sundays now don't even rate a kiss.

# Notes on Contributors

**Rebecca Jaremko Bromwich** is a Canadian lawyer who practices as a Crown Attorney. She is also a law professor who teaches criminal law and conflict resolution, a mother to four children, and a wife.

**Ariadne A. Gonzalez** is an assistant professor in organizational communication at Texas A&M International University. Her research centres on issues of difference and focuses on immigrant and transnational workers' work-life experiences, border crossing experiences, and the implications of "dirty work" and how these relate to Latinx and immigrant workers' occupational identity. She obtained a Ph.D. in organizational communication from Texas A&M University—College Station.

**Lynn O'Brien Hallstein** (PhD Ohio State University) is an associate professor of rhetoric at the College of General Studies and an affiliated faculty of the Women's, Gender, and Sexuality Studies Program at Boston University. She is the author of *Bikini-Ready Moms: Celebrity Profiles, Motherhood, and the Body*, which won the Organization for the Study of Communication, Language, and Gender's 2016 Outstanding Book Award, and *White Feminists and Contemporary Maternity: Purging Matrophobia*. She co-edited *Academic Motherhood in a Post-Second Wave Context: Challenges, Strategies, and Possibilities* with Andrea O'Reilly and *Contemporary Maternity in an Era of Choice: Explorations into Discourses of Reproduction* with Sara Hayden, which won the Organization for the Study of Communication, Language, and Gender's 2011 Outstanding Book Award for an Edited Volume. She has been published in variety of feminist and communication journals.

**Holly Willson Holladay** is an assistant professor in the Department of Media, Journalism and Film at Missouri State University. Her research focuses on the relationship between media texts, media audiences, and negotiations of identity (e.g., gender, class, race, and sexuality). Her work has previously been published in *Television & New Media*, *Southern Communication Journal*, *The International Journal of Cultural Studies*, *Participations: International Journal of Audience Research*, and a number of edited collections.

**Jo Scott-Coe** is author of two books: *MASS: A Sniper, a Father, and a Priest* (Pelekinesis) and *Teacher at Point Blank* (Aunt Lute). Her writing has appeared widely, in publications including *Salon, Catapult, The Los Angeles Times, Tahoma Literary Review, Pacific Coast Philology, American Studies Journal, Talking Writing, River Teeth, Ninth Letter,* and many others. She is associate professor and assistant chair of English and media studies at Riverside City College, where she was named the fifty-seventh distinguished faculty lecturer in part for her research on the epistolary history of Kathy Leissner Whitman. She is currently at work on a new book.

**Suzanne Kamata** is an associate professor of English at Naruto University of Education in Tokushima, Japan, where she has lived for the past thirty years. She has published twelve books, including many which concern foreign wives in Japan, such as *The Broken Bridge: Fiction from Expatriates in Literary Japan* (Stone Bridge Press, 1997), *Losing Kei* (Leapfrog Press, 2008), *Call Me Okaasan: Adventures in Multicultural Mothering* (Wyatt-Mackenzie Publishing, 2009), *The Beautiful One Has Come: Stories* (Wyatt-Mackenzie Publishing, 2011), and *Squeaky Wheels: Travels with My Daughter by Train, Plane, Metro, Tuk-tuk and Wheelchair* (Wyatt-Mackenzie Publishing, 2019).

**Leanne Letourneau** is a doctoral student in the Humanities Inter-disciplinary PhD program at Concordia University. Her PhD research focuses on integrating educational studies, policy studies, and geography of sexualities to create a pilot design for a queer education program at the secondary level. Using an anti-oppressive and intersectional framework, her research will assist educators, students, and policymakers in critically questioning how we conceive of difference, particularly regarding gender and sexual diversity.

**Hinda Mandell** is associate professor in the School of Communication at RIT in New York, and is a co-editor of *Nasty Women and Bad Hombres: Gender and Race in the 2016 US Presidential Election* (University of Rochester Press, 2018); the author of *Sex Scandals, Gender and Power in Contemporary American Politics* (Praeger, 2017) and co-editor of *Scandal in a Digital Age* (Palgrave Macmillan, 2016). Her essays ranging from politics to parentings have appeared in the *Los Angeles Times*, *Chicago Tribune*, *USA Today*, *Boston Herald*, *Palm Beach Post*, *Politico*, and in academic journals, including *Women's Studies in Communication*, *Visual Communication Quarterly*, and *Explorations in Media Ecology*.

**Jane Marcellus** is author of *Business Girls and Two-Job Wives: Emerging Media Stereotypes of Employed Women* (Hampton Press, 2011) and a co-author of *Mad Men and Working Women: Feminist Perspectives on Historical Power, Resistance, and Otherness* (Peter Lang, 2014). She is a professor at Middle Tennessee State University. She can be found online at janemarcellus.com and on Twitter @janemarcellus.

**Natalie McKnight** is a professor of humanities and dean of the College of General Studies at Boston University. She has published numerous books and articles on Victorian fiction, including *Fathers in Victorian Fiction*, *Suffering Mothers in Mid-Victorian Novels*, and *Idiots, Madmen, and Other Prisoners in Dickens*. She is president of the International Dickens Society and co-editor of *Dickens Studies Annual*.

**Robyn Alexandria Pepin** is a PhD Candidate in law and legal Studies at Carleton University, Ottawa, Ontario. Her dissertation research focuses on Ontario's anti-bullying framework and its potential impact on Indigenous students who move off reserve to attend high school in northern Ontario. She is also the Senior Editorial Assistant for the Canadian Journal of Law and Society/ Revue Canadienne Droit et Société and a Research Associate with EPID@Work (Enhancing the Prevention of Injury and Disability @ Work) Research Institute at Lakehead University, Thunder Bay, Ontario. The research discussed in this chapter was completed during her M.Ed. with a specialization in women's studies at Lakehead University. Thank you to Dr. Lori Chambers for providing valuable feedback on this chapter and to the Social Sciences and Humanities Research Council and Canadian Federation of University Women's Canadian Home Economics Association Fellowship for personal funding.

**Elisavietta Ritchie**'s poems, stories, articles, photography, and translations from Russian, French and Indonesian, are widely published. *Tightening the Circle over Eel Country* won the Great Lakes Colleges Association's "New Writer's Award for Best First Book of Poetry 1975-1976." Subsequently three full collections of short fiction have been published, and some 20 collections of poetry. The most recent fiction collection is The *Scotch Runner,* and the newest collection of poetry is: *Lunatic Moons: Insomnia Cantatas* has Ritchie's poems paired with paintings of cats by Suzanne Shelden. For more information see www. elisaviettaritchie.com

**Beverley Smith** is a longtime activist for the rights of mothers and wives in relation to unpaid labour and emotional labour. She is a retired school teacher and mother to four children, one of whom is her co-author in this anthology, Rebecca Bromwich. Married for fifty years, she is also a wife.

**Ester Botta Somparé** is an Italian anthropologist, who has been living and teaching in Guinea for more than ten years. She currently directs the Masters of Social Science and Development Program at the Kofi Annan University. Her research interests include concerns related to the the sociology and ethnology of education in Guinea, pastoralism, and mobility.

**Shalene Valenzuela** was born in Santa Barbara, CA. She received a BA in art practice at the University of California at Berkeley and an MFA in ceramics from California College of Arts and Crafts. She has participated in artist residencies at the Clay Studio of Missoula, the Archie Bray Foundation, the Watershed Center for the Ceramic Arts, and the LH Project. She has taught at the Flathead Valley Community College, the University of Montana, the Oregon College of Art and Craft, the Clay Studio of Missoula, the Missoula Art Museum, the Richmond Art Center, the ASUC Studios at UC Berkeley, and CCA Extended Education. Her work has been featured in several group and solo exhibitions nationally and is included in numerous private collections. She was the recipient of the Jessie Wilber and Frances Senska Individual Artist's Innovation Award from the Montana Arts Council in 2013, and is currently the executive director at the Clay Studio of Missoula. To learn more about Shalene's art, see www. shalene.com